THE BLUEWATER HANDBOOK

A GUIDE TO CRUISING SEAMANSHIP

BY STEPHEN AND LINDA DASHEW

ILLUSTRATED BY STEPHEN L. DAVIS
INTRODUCTION BY JOHN ROUSMANIERE

BEOWULF PUBLISHING GROUP
OJAI, CALIFORNIA

Also by Stephen and Linda Dashew

"The Circumnavigators' Handbook"
Published By W.W. Norton & Co.

Design and Layout
Anne McAuliffe

Beowulf Publishing Group
550 Del Oro Road, Ojai, California, USA

Photographs not otherwise credited were taken by the authors.

Manufactured by Hadden Craftsmen, Inc.

Typesetting By
Continental Typographics

Typesetting and Paste Up By
Marketing Resources

Distributed in the United States by
Hearst Marine Books, an Affiliate of William Morrow and
Co., Inc.
105 Madison Avenue, New York, NY 10016.

DEDICATION

This book is dedicated to
Stanley A. Dashew, more
familiarly known to our
family as "Daddy's Daddy".
He has passed his love of
sailing and the sea along to
us, supported our every
project with enthusiasm
and praise, been there to
encourage us when our
own enthusiasm wavered,
and contributed his fine
photography to our book
projects. In short, he's
always there when we
need him. Thanks "Daddy's
Daddy". We dedicate this
book to you, with love.

CONTENTS

Introduction 1

Preface 5

BEFORE LEAVING

1   Preparing the Boat 13

    Securing Against and Removing Water 15

      Preventing Deck Leaks 15

      Storm Shutters 16

      Pumping Systems 16

      Cockpit Drains 19

    Safety Systems 19

      Preparing for a Knockdown 20

      Inspecting Your Rig 21

      Visibility at Sea 21

      Safety Gear 21

      Safety Harnesses 22

      The Liferaft 23

      Collision Patches 23

    Storm Canvas 27

      The Trysail 27

      Cutter Rigged Storm Canvas 28

      Storm Canvas for Sloops 28

      Sizing and Construction of Storm Sails . . . 32

2   Upgrading Basic Boathandling Skills 35

    Maneuvering Under Sail 37

      Sailing in the Anchor 38

      Getting Out of Irons 41

      Using Sails to Steer 42

      Sailing Off an Anchor 43

      Using the Stern Anchor as a Brake 46

  Maneuvering Under Power 47

      How Different Hulls and Props Work . . . 48

      Using Engine Torque to Circle 49

      Minimum Maneuvering Speeds 50

      Cross Wind Dangers 50

      Getting Off a Lee Berth 51

      Dodging and Emergency Turning Techniques . 52

UNDER WAY

3 Sailhandling in Rough Weather 55

  Changing Headsails 58

      Working the Foredeck 58

      Keeping Headsails Aboard 58

      Headsail Take Down Systems 59

      Getting Headsails Off in a Blow 60

      Setting Headsails in Heavy Weather 60

  Reefing the Main 61

      Safety Lines 61

      Slab Reefing-Two Approaches 63

  Special Precautions 65

      Running in Heavy Air 65

      Tripping Reefs 65

      Gybing 65

  Furling Systems 66

      Luff Groove vs. Hank on Systems 66

The Zip Stop Systems 68

Twin Headstays 73

   Side by Side or Fore and Aft Twins? . . . 76

   Rigging Twin Headstays 78

4 Being Comfortable at Sea 81

   To Windward 84

   Off the Wind 85

5 Ensuring Safety at Sea 89

   Working on Deck 90

    The Use of Safety Harnesses 92

    Rigging a Jackstay 93

    Moving About 95

    Safety Factors 97

   Going Aloft 99

    The Right Gear 100

    Lifting Systems 102

    Working Aloft 104

    Handling the Deck Winch 105

6 Clearing the Decks 107

   Don't Compromise Your Stability! . . . 109

7 Sailing Shorthanded 113

   General Considerations 114

   Crew Size 116

   Communicating with Hand Signals . . . 117

    Daytime Signals 118

    Night Signals 119

   How to Handle Spinnaker Poles 121

    Getting the Pole on the Mast 121

    Rigging the Pole 122

Gybing 122

Vertical Mast Stowage 124

Do you Need a Storm Pole? 124

8 Standing Watch 125

Watch Systems 128

Long Passages 128

Short Passages 129

Avoiding Collision 129

Identify the Other Vessel's Heading . . . 132

How to Read Running Lights 133

Using Radar 134

Emergency Maneuvering 136

Visibility at Night 137

Preparation for Running at Night 137

Techniques for Seeing Further 138

Working With Moonlight 138

The Affect of Rain Squalls 140

Your Range of Vision 140

Staying Alert 143

9 Responding to the Inner Sense 149

10 Towing Dinghies 155

Dink Design 156

Guidelines for Towing 158

11 Coping With Rigging Failure 161

Spares to Carry Aboard 164

Using Replaceable Terminals 165

Cable Clamps 166

Fast Reaction Can Save Your Spar 166

IN HEAVY WEATHER

12 Understanding Heavy Weather 169

    What is Heavy Weather? 171

        Weather Systems 171

        The Importance of Wave Shape 172

        Bottom Contour and Currents 172

    Is Your Boat Ready for Heavy Weather? . . . 173

        Psychological Considerations 174

        Staying Comfortable 176

        Dealing with Sea Sickness 176

        Working in the Galley 176

    Preparing for an Imminent Blow 177

    Sea Room 178

        How Much Searoom is Enough? 180

        Using Harbors of Refuge 181

13 Employing Storm Tactics 183

    Beating 184

        Reducing Windage 184

        A Clean Bottom is a Safe Bottom 186

        Special Sails 186

        Using the Right Sail Combination . . . 187

    Heaving-To 188

        Navigational Considerations 190

        Techniques 190

        In Heavy Weather 191

    Lying Ahull 191

    Forereaching 192

        Balancing the Rig 192

Helming 194

The Risks Involved 196

Running Off 196

What to Expect From Your Boat 197

What Causes a Broach? 199

Dealing with a Knockdown 201

Maintaining the Right Speed 202

Steering Techniques 204

Slowing Down 205

14 Avoiding Heavy Weather 207

Local Systems 208

Weather Patterns and Systems 210

Sources of Weather Information 212

General Tactics 214

Reducing Your Risks 214

Revolving Storms 216

15 Assessing the Seaworthiness of Modern Racing Yachts . 219

UPON ARRIVING

16 Entering Strange Harbors at Night 223

Weighing the Alternatives in an Emergency . 227

17 Anchoring 229

Different Strategies for Different Situations . . 231

The Key Factors 231

Which Anchor do you Use? 232

What is the Right Size of Anchor? . . . 233

How to Tell Bottom Conditions 234

The Right Amount of Scope 234

Anchoring in Coral 235

Dealing with a Foul Bottom 240

Setting the Anchor Under Power 242

Anchoring in Traffic 244

Two Hooks are Sometimes Better than One . 244

Stern Anchors 246

Handling the Anchor from your Dinghy . 246

The Bahamian Moor 248

Reducing Loads 250

Shock Absorbers 250

Lowering Your Attachment Point 251

Riding Sails 253

Retrieving the Anchor 256

In Strong Winds 256

Clearing a Foul 258

Anchor Bouys 258

Exposed Anchorages 259

Special Precautions Required 261

When to Put to Sea 262

Be Wary of Crowded Anchorages 263

The Dangers 263

Getting to Sea in a Hurry 267

Mooring Mediterranean Style 268

Anchor Selection 272

Picking the Right Spot 272

Tactics 274

Lines to Shore 275

18 Accounting for Tides 279

        Tying Up - Special Considerations 282
        Anchoring - Allowing Extra Scope 283
19 Navigating Through Coral 285
        The Right Sun Angle 287
        Affects of Weather 288
        Special Considerations 289
20 Crossing a Harbor Bar 293
        Current 295
        Tidal State 296
        Sea Conditions 296
        How Will Your Boat React? 296
        Timing Your Crossing 298
        Emergency Considerations 299
        Steering Techniques 300
21 Getting the Dinghy Through Surf and Ashore . . 301
        The Right Dink 303
        Timing Your Ride In 304
        Types of Beach Surf 304
        Small Boat Handling in the Surf Line 306
        Powered Inflatables 308
22 Leaving the Boat Unattended 311
        Pumps 312
        Anchoring - Special Requirements 313
        Double Checking 313
23 Preparing for a Hurricane 315
        Where to Shelter? 318
        Using Mangrove Swamps 320
        Tying Up 320

Anchoring Out 320

Special Gear to Carry 321

24 Salvaging a Mistake 323

Legal Considerations 323

Rigging a Towing Bridle 326

Dealing With Leaks 327

How to Tow 330

Steering Without a Rudder 333

Drifting Ashore 334

Emergency Anchoring 336

Getting Afloat Again 336

Kedging Off 337

Design Characteristics to Consider 338

Emergency Gear 339

Deciding on a Plan of Action 344

Using the Tide 345

The Importance of Timing 345

25 Choosing the Right Yacht 347

Safety Factors 352

Evaluating the Risks You Face 352

Special Reenforcements 355

Sea Trials 358

Epilogue 361

Acknowledgements 364

The 50-foot ketch *Intermezzo*, anchored in Robinson's Cove, Moorea,
French Polynesia.

INTRODUCTION

This is the ideal book for anybody who hopes to go cruising but is a little intimidated by the challenges and risks of the adventure. I don't know of any couple better qualified than Steve and Linda Dashew to describe how to go about surviving and enjoying voyaging in a small yacht. The kind of people who thrive on independence, challenges, and careful preparation, Steve and Linda are ideal role models, as well as teachers, for people attracted to cruising in the new generation of lively, seaworthy boats. They started out by reconditioning an old ocean racer, an orphan of outdated racing rules, which they sailed from California to Florida—the long way. They dipped in and out of Pacific coral atolls and battled Indian Ocean gales along the way, learning from their mistakes and developing the good habits that are the basis of sound seamanship. They then earned every sailor's envy by building and equipping a new "dream" boat, light in weight and modern in appearance but as sturdy as she is fast, on which they finished their circumnavigation.

When they first headed offshore with their two young daughters in *Intermezzo,* the Dashews were sufficiently smart and mature to admit that they had a lot to learn. But they were by no means novice sailors. In particular, years of dinghy and catamaran racing had honed a meticulous respect for detail. I saw this one day almost ten years ago as I watched Steve rig an outhaul on one of his 30-knot racing catamarans. Instead of simply guessing at what was needed and charging ahead, as most people would do, he paused for a moment to calculate the forces on the mainsail, which he factored against the line's breaking strength to determine exactly how many parts there should be in the tackle. He did all this work in his head as he stood there, seemingly in meditation, with the line in his hand. I was impressed. Not surprisingly, the same assiduous attention to detail permeates *The Bluewater Handbook* and its distinguished predecessor, *The Circumnavigators' Handbook*.

Perhaps technical mastery came easy to Steve because he is an engineer, but his strength as a seaman is his unwillingness to depend entirely on technology and mathematical guidelines. He learned long ago on cruises aboard his father's big schooner, *Constellation*, that seamanship is a human art and not a science, and this book is as much about the philosophy of good seamanship as it is about specific skills and equipment. "There can never be a pat formula for action or reaction in any given situation," the Dashews write almost in the first words of the text. While that rule of thumb may discourage some beginners looking for easy cookbook solutions to all their sailing problems, wiser words have rarely been written about boathandling.

I know no book about cruising in which the words "caution," "common sense," and "alertness" appear as frequently as they do in this one. Referring time and again to their own experiences—most of them pleasant, some not so—the Dashews not only describe what equipment to carry and how to use it, but also ask the important seamanship questions that sometimes have no ready answers but must be constantly kept in mind by the cautious cruising sailor. In one of their most important chapters, they write of an "inner sense," a trained intuition that all good seamen have for boats. Acquiring that intuition takes experience; doing the right thing when it alerts you that something is wrong takes knowledge and skill. An important first step toward both developing that inner sense and mastering those seamanship skills is to read this excellent book.

Conservative and practical as the Dashews are, sailing on *Intermezzo II* is anything but a hair-shirt operation. As you'll see in these pages, Linda and Steve have found ways to make cruising comfortable and pleasurable as well as fast and safe. They enjoy varied meals and even carry a popcorn popper to provide predawn munchies when they're hove-to off an unfamiliar harbor. Rather than being hermits, they love company and often leave the boat for extended sightseeing trips ashore. And during years of onboard living, their daughters, Elyse and Sarah have grown into bright, delightful, healthy girls. The Dashews' writing has the same easy companionability as their style of life. "Come aboard," they say. "Sail with us. Here's how to do it. See, it's not that difficult; all it takes is some experience and common sense and caution. You can do it, too."

And you can.

John Rousmaniere
Author, *The Annapolis Book of Seamanship, Fastnet, Force 10,* and many other books about the sea

Intermezzo II, the authors' 62-foot cutter, reaching off the island of Tortola in the British Virgin Islands.

PREFACE

One of the things we have always enjoyed about cruising and racing is the constantly changing mix of wind, waves, boats, and crew. No two situations are ever exactly alike, and the learning experience never stops. There is always a new combination of seagoing skills to be used on the next wave.

A procedure that works one time on a moderate-displacement 40-footer may be totally out of place on a smaller, heavier sailboat. Boathandling that would get a 30-foot sloop out of a tight squeeze may be impractical on a 50-foot schooner. Yet from each situation you can garner new data on which to base your next approach to the sea.

Seamanship is derived from this ever-changing pattern of characteristics. As such, there can never be a pat formula for action or reaction in any given situation, and it is not the purpose of this book to put forward ironclad rules of seamanship. But experience has taught us certain fundamentals on which to base our approach to the sea, and it is some of these that we endeavor here to pass on to you. We will highlight important aspects of the ancient art of seafaring that seem for the most part to be left for the school of experience to teach. *You must be careful, however, to interpret our experience in light of the characteristics of your personal boat, the sea state, the weather, and your own individual skills.* If there is a cornerstone of our philosophy it is common sense, coupled with an alertness to the current environment and to the one that may be brewing.

That we have certain prejudices is undeniable. You will want to know how we came to hold them in order to assess our ideas and how they apply to your own boat and type of sailing. Cruising and racing have been a way of life in our family for many years. I started sailing with my father on heavy-displacement traditional vessels; John Alden designs loomed large in my

childhood. The 76-foot *Constellation*, perhaps the archetype of
the successful staysail schooner, took me as a youngster on a
20,000-mile cruise. In the fifties the 60-foot ketch *Chiriqui*,
another Alden design, gave me my first taste of ocean racing. As a
teen and young adult, I raced high-performance dinghies. Trying to hold up the bow of a Thistle on a breezy run teaches you
about downwind helmsmanship rapidly-or at least about

Beowulf V, in which the authors held the world record for speed under
sail at 35.58 miles per hour measured over an 800-meter course.

righting a swamped planing dinghy. Next came a stint with high-speed multihulls. The competition wasn't as keen as it was in the dinghy fleet, but I loved the speed. In the late fifties and early sixties I was frequently sailing the only catamaran about, something that is hard to imagine in this day and age. As my quest for speed heightened, I began to design and build my own cats, which were, in their day, the fastest sailboats in the world.

Family life came along in the mid-sixties. I was so flustered the first time I took Linda, my bride-to-be, sailing that we led the entire multihull fleet around the windward mark, *in reverse.* I eventually recovered, and with Linda riding the trapeze and pulling strings, the two of us, with occasional crew, won a number of national and world championships.

After our two daughters were born, longer-term cruising desires found us back with the "leadmines." A lovely 50-foot fiberglass ketch, designed by Bill Tripp, *Intermezzo*, became our home for a number of years while we sailed in a westerly direction.

Intermezzo was a heavily built, pre-OPEC ocean racer. Her long overhangs, lofty rig, and minimum-wetted-surface hull were those of a vintage Cruising Club of America racer/cruiser. Because of her small diesel and folding prop, we learned to take care not to get ourselves into places that we couldn't sail out of.

In the process of cruising from California westward across the Pacific I found myself in the yacht design and construction business, building Deerfoot class yachts for other sailors with a cruising philosophy similar to Linda's and mine. These vessels tend to be strongly built, long, moderately beamed, easily driven, and very quick. They also tend to be sailed primarily by husband-and-wife crews. The tactics you would employ in stormy conditions in these designs would not be appropriate in heavier, slower yachts, although the same rules about watchkeeping, weather, or exposed anchorages apply to all cruising yachts.

After sailing *Intermezzo* across the Pacific, Indian, and Atlantic oceans, we had the opportunity to put our own ideas to work in another boat and had the pleasure of watching our new home being built from scratch. *Intermezzo II,* even though she was different in many ways from any of our previous yachts, never-

Steve Dashew at the helm of *Intermezzo II* during a severe gale off
Cape Hatteras.   Sean Holland photo

theless represented our own ultimate bluewater cruiser. At 62 feet she would be considered by many to be a handful for Linda and me to sail on our own, yet she was easier to handle in every respect than her smaller namesake. Her strong aluminum construction and powerful hull shape at first led me to ease off on some of the cruising maxims that had become ingrained through previous experience. But as the miles slipped under our new keel I came back to the same, conservative brand of seamanship I had been taught as a youngster and had relearned with my own commands.

Intermezzo II took us across the South Atlantic a second time and via a circuitous route back to California, from whence we had started oñ *Intermezzo* some six years previously.

Two aspects of our cruising need to be highlighted. We sailed *without insurance*, and if we had to leave either of our *Intermezzos* stranded, it would have been a grievous financial blow to our future plans. Second, except for one brief period, we sailed *without crew*. Linda and I felt we could cope easily enough at sea, and thus we and our daughters could enjoy the privacy of having the boat to ourselves in port, too.

At sea our duties were divided. I looked after the ship and navigation while Linda kept up with the considerable demands of our two youngsters, maintenance, and the galley. In heavy weather we worked together on sailhandling but normally that was solely my bailiwick.

Cruising closer to home, on both the east and west coasts of the United States, has reminded us that conservative seamanship is not something that begins with bluewater voyaging. The elements can be just as challenging on Long Island Sound or off Catalina Island as they are off Cape Hatteras or the bottom of Africa. You may use your boat less often than a bluewater voyager does, but your approach to the sea must be the same. This book came about in part because of two major yachting tragedies in the Northern Hemisphere winter of 1982-83. Some 18 yachts were washed ashore by an "unusual" storm at Cabo San Lucas, on the southernmost tip of Mexico's Baja peninsula, and then 30 more were blown ashore in another "unseasonal" blow off Papeete, Tahiti. In both cases elementary rules of seamanship

and common sense were flaunted. Many of the cruisers caught in these storms who were interviewed afterwards stated that they had felt uneasy about their tactics, but since everyone else in the anchorage seemed to be doing the same thing they thought they would be all right.

In the Tahiti disaster, although an excellent hurricane hole existed a little more than a day's sail away, most cruisers stayed in Papeete harbor, hoping the storm would pass as storms there usually did, without damage. At Cabo San Lucas, boats were anchored on top of each other very close to the beach. A storm blew up, a breaking sea developed, and soon the beach was awash with broken dreams. There was plenty of warning to get out to sea and safety, but most chose to ride the storm out with a lee shore at their backs anchored in heavy traffic.

We passed through Cabo San Lucas on our way north two months after the disaster. Life in this sleepy Mexican village was back to normal. The beach, a major tourist attraction, had been cleared of wreckage, and there, in the same tight corner, 40 more yachts were anchored just off the beach.

Throughout this book you will find disaster photos and a few stories that will set your nerves on edge. We don't wish to scare our readers, but we feel it best to be realistic about the consequences of relaxing your vigil at the wrong time. At the same time we feel cruising is the safest lifestyle and one of the most relaxing ways to spend your time that has yet been invented. The actual incidence of disaster for cruisers in general is low. For those that practice a conservative brand of eyes-open sailing, risks will be held to an absolute minimum.

The one thing we have learned from our years at sea is that there is no single answer. But by calling on our own experiences and on those of other cruisers, by factoring in the handling characteristics of the vessel we are on and the sea, current, and wind conditions, we know we will find an approach to our environment that will see us home safely.

We hope this book will help you to do the same.

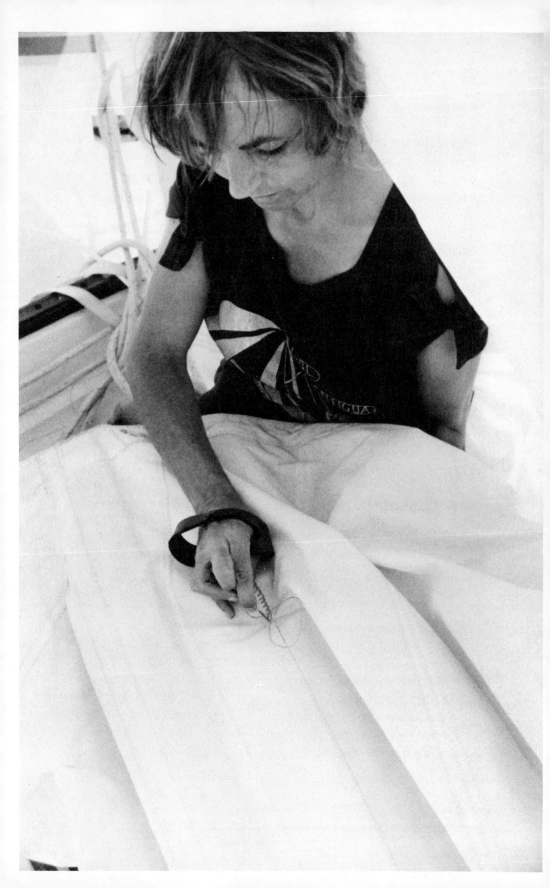

PREPARING THE BOAT

Some folks feel that the level of preparation they need to go sailing varies according to the type of cruising *they* plan. While this proposition sounds reasonable on its face it falls down in operation. You can never be 100 percent sure of the wind and sea conditions that you are going to encounter. What starts out as a pleasant afternoon sail on a lake can turn into a survival contest if a summer squall line suddenly appears. Obviously the farther offshore your plans take you, the greater the level of readiness you need. But to conservative sailors, that line between onshore and offshore grows thinner the greater their experience.

Defensive seamanship goes hand in hand with defensive preparation. In the end we all hope the details that are attended to in advance go unused. But to deal with the sea on an equal basis you must have the cards stacked in your favor.

Most production cruising boats built today have adequate structural integrity to take the modest amount of punishment that the occasional weekend sail deals them. If conditions are not too severe, these boats may even take some measure of heavy weather in stride. It is in certain areas of detailing, however, that production boats often fall short of the requirements for serious cruising. With a few simple tools and basic do-it-yourself skills, though, the seaworthiness of your boat can be substantially upgraded.

SECURING AGAINST AND REMOVING WATER

You should begin with an inspection of areas that potentially could permit water to get belowdecks. Cockpit lockers should have good seals and be fitted with positive latches that are kept fastened while you are at sea. Every ventilator box, engine air-intake, and through-deck aperture must have a cap to seal it off. If your boat has a dorade box, be sure it has an inside cap, too, in case the deck box is lost.

Plugs or caps should also be available for each anchor pipe. Deck hatches should have tight-fitting storm covers to protect their gaskets from direct wave hits. Sliding hatches and washboards should have inside locks to prevent their opening if motion becomes severe or you experience an accidental knockdown. A simple barrel bolt will usually do the job.

Side windows and ports can be vulnerable in heavy going, and you should have storm shutters available for each one. Try them out in good weather, and make sure they are easy to use when conditions get rough. Many experienced voyagers mount permanent heavy, clear plastic storm shutters on their boat's windows and ports.

Companionway hatches are notorious sources of leaks in wet weather. Even a precisely fit slide, when directly hit with a breaking sea, will emit showers below. A 1-inch-by-4-inch piece

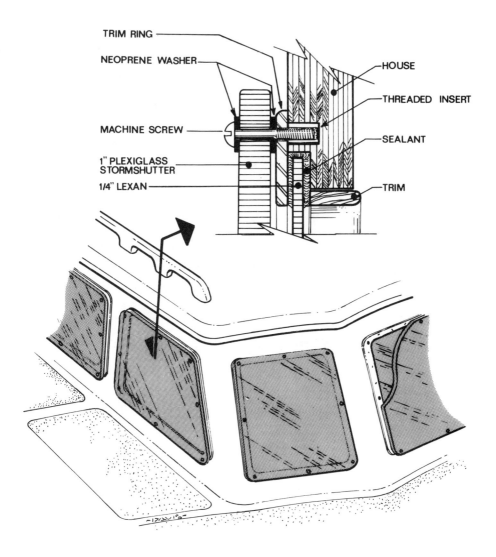

Many experienced cruisers fit permanent storm shutters. Doing so avoids the problem of deciding when to dig them out during heavy weather.

We had 1-inch thick Plexiglas doghouse windows installed aboard
Intermezzo prior to leaving New Zealand for the Indian Ocean.

of teak fastened vertically to the cabintop just outboard of the hatch slide will deflect any seas that come aboard, keeping you much drier below.

Despite all precautions, in heavy weather some water inevitably finds its way below. In order to insure efficient removal of this water, you must have clean bilges. Although your bilge sump itself may appear clean, motion at sea can dislodge accumulated dirt, which can then clog your pumps. All pumps should have strainers, and both pump and strainer should be easily accessible for maintenance. Some installations will benefit from a strum box, a cagelike strainer built around the pump. And remember to keep the limber holes clear. If you install through them a chain fastened directly to the hull at one end and tied down at the other end with shockcord, the chain can be pulled back and forth through the holes to free dirt easily and quickly.

You should locate a large-capacity hand pump where it is easy to use in rough going. Many cruisers prefer to carry two pumps, one on deck close to the helmsman and a second below. Carry spare diaphragms and valves for your pumps, and know how to replace them. The main engine water pump, if fitted with a T-junction and a simple valve on the incoming water side, will also act as an excellent emergency pump. Better yet, consider fitting an engine-driven pump especially for emergency use. Units that can pump up to 80 gallons per minute are available, and in a pinch one could save your boat. Electric pumps—submersible, impeller-driven, or diaphragm type—are handy for normal pumping, but you should not rely upon them for emergencies. You might also consider rigging a bilge-level alarm from a float switch and a buzzer to give you early warning of any problem.

Inventory all your through-hull fittings, and have soft wood pegs of the proper size made up for each one. Hang each peg with a lanyard in a convenient spot near the hole it fits. Be sure each valve is in good operating order. The main engine and generator exhaust pipe should be fitted with shut-off valves for use in following seas. Since through-hulls that are above the waterline at rest may be submerged when the boat is heeled, each pump or exhaust line (including those for the heads) should have an antisiphon loop.

Because a sea can inundate your cockpit, the cockpit drains must be capable of emptying the water within 1 minute. While most of the water from a filling wave will be rolled out, the drains will have to do the work of emptying the footwell below sea level. On many modern boats with high freeboard, you can install large drains that lead aft from the cockpit straight through the transom. An average production 35-footer should have at least two drains, each at least 2 inches in diameter. Drains that can be run through the transom should be 3-inchers.

SAFETY SYSTEMS

Heavy weather is as much a state of mind as a condition of wind and wave. If your boat is well secured inside, you can shrug off an occasional knockdown. But if a knockdown means spilled lockers, broken jars, or maybe a gash from a flying object, it becomes much more serious.

Visualize being flat in the water. Then look at every object and piece of gear stored below to see if it will stay put if you are suddenly heeled. Lockers with hidden finger latches are the biggest problem. The contents of windward ones especially may be hurled at the latch, usually opening it in the process. You should either install lockable hidden latches or replace them with external latches. There are covers made for finger latches that protect them to some degree from the objects inside the lockers. Perhaps you can tie the locker doors closed with short lengths of rope. How about your reefer tops, stove covers, and floorboards? A simple "door button" can keep these potentially lethal flying objects in place. The batteries and stoves must also be held securely in place, even if the boat rolls over.

If there is storage behind or underneath settees and bunks, tie a ¼-inch light line to eyestraps tucked behind the cushions to restrain all but the very heaviest loads.

Having the interior well secured enables you to push harder in some conditions than might otherwise be possible. On a well-built cruising boat with an interior that stays put, the occasional

Photo courtesy of Barient, Inc.

Winches should be stripped, cleaned, and lubricated at least twice a year to avoid this sort of a mess!

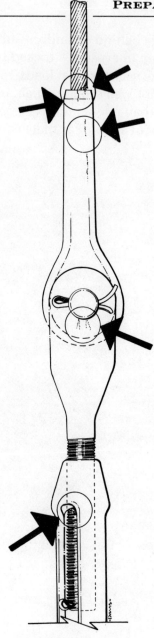

Turnbuckles and swages should be carefully checked on a periodic basis. Signs of fatigue or overstressing can usually be seen before failure occurs. Check the threads and swages for cracking. Clevis pin holes should be inspected for elongation as well as for cracks.

knockdown is not going to be that serious. But if gear is flying across the cabin, your evaluation of the conditions will change rapidly. As conditions deteriorate and the risk from severe knockdowns becomes more acute, the safety of your crew will be enhanced if you have taken these precautions.

Belowdecks, you should be able to move from handhold to handhold on either tack. Have a look at the companionway ladder and cabin sole. Will they provide good traction when they are wet and the boat is heeled? Bunks should be fitted with substantial leeboards or weather cloths. If you're at the opposite side of the bunk and are thrown against the board or cloth, will it hold?

Your visibility to others at sea, especially to shipping, is important. Running lights at the rail level should be supplemented with a masthead tricolor. A masthead strobe, to be used only in emergencies, is also good to have. Understand that the new Rules of the Road prohibit the use of a strobe for any situation other than distress, but as a last resort in collision avoidance such a use would be tolerated by the U.S. Coast Guard, even if it is not technically legal. In international waters, any use of the strobe other than distress is also illegal. Your radar reflector should be mounted as high as possible. If it is the common three-plate, collapsible kind, be sure it is installed in the rain-catch position to be most effective.

Your personal safety gear should really be the same whether you are sailing in Long Island Sound or off Cape Horn: the best. Start with the man-overboard pole. Go for the full-height ocean-racing version. A strobe, horseshoe ring, and good-sized sea anchor should be part of the package. We like to connect our components with long floating lines, so the sea anchor deploys to windward and the flag downwind, with the buoy and light in the center. The whole package then presents a long target for the swimmer.

Your man-overboard system must be easy to launch. Since that means it will be out in the open, the floating line and fabrics used on the horseshoe buoy will deteriorate in sunlight and should be replaced annually if you sail year round. Consider also carrying aboard a personal strobe light and whistle for each crewmember.

Safety harnesses should be easily accessible. At sea they're worn with a short tether when you're steering and a longer one when you're working on deck. Before you go to sea, check the action of the safety hook to make sure it is smooth. A drop of oil before each passage keeps it working freely. A jackstay is the best place to attach the harness on deck. A ³⁄₁₆-inch 1 × 19 plastic-coated wire attached at the side of each coaming and run

The safety wire through the turning blocks at the base of the maxi-boat *Kialoa III*'s mast will help prevent possible injury to the crew should the block explode. It is a good idea aboard cruisers as well.

around your staysail stay gives you complete access to the boat without your having to change hook-ups as you move about. There should be attachment points near the companionway hatch and the helmsman's position as well.

Liferaft size and type will vary with your sailing environment. At the top of my list for survivability is the double-bottom ballast-chamber style developed and patented by Jim Givens, which gives you both thermal insulation from cold water and rollover protection. If you're sailing far offshore, you will want a supplemental survival kit for the raft, along with extra fresh water and a solar still for desalinization. It is a good idea to carry an emergency position-indicating radiobeacon (EPIRB) with a fresh battery in the raft as well as inside your boat. Remember that liferafts deteriorate in storage if they get wet inside their cannisters. Check yours once a year, and renew perishables packed inside it.

Try out your emergency steering system in port. Most systems will benefit from the addition of relieving tackles. Experiment to find the best reduction ratios and attachment points.

A collision patch to stem temporarily the flow of water through a hole under the waterline should be ready to use at all times. It is commonly made of sailcloth or vinyl and is generally best shaped in a circle, with long lines attached to grommets evenly spaced around its edge. Try it out in port, and work out a deployment plan with your crew.

Before departure, you will want to have a look aloft. Spare headsail halyards and a halyard messenger line are a must in case a halyard is lost. Check over your headboard slides, and see that the sail track where the head reaches when the sail is reefed is well secured. You should check all your sails for stitching wear and chafe. Chafe patches on the main and working headsails where they rub on the spreaders will save sail-mending time later on. A simple lacing of 3/16-inch line through the foredeck lifelines will also help keep dropped sails aboard.

Each time we prepare for a passage we refer to a checklist. We start by running all electrical and mechanical gear to be sure they are in order. We make sure our various running, binnacle, and deck lights work. The rig is checked aloft for cracked or

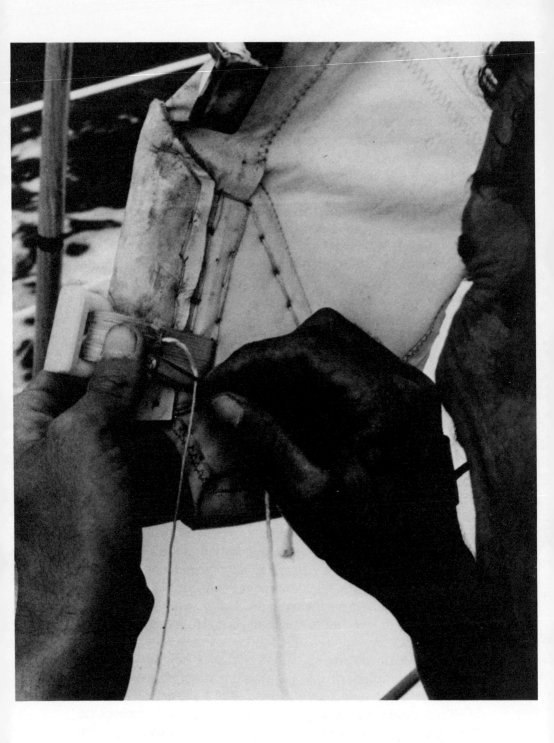

Headboard slides are prone to chafe and wear. Check the stitching and bindings for chafe. If in doubt, renew them.

Vicki Carkhuff photo

strained tangs or swages. We also look for rough edges that need silicone or taping to prevent sail snags. On deck the lifelines are checked at their swages. We work all the seacocks to be sure they are free, and we give the emergency pumps a throw. Flashlight and portable strobe light batteries are renewed. We inventory our charts, and we verify that we are carrying an up-to-date Light List, Pilot, and Nautical Almanac. We check the engine oil and water and batteries. Each hatch and port gasket is inspected for tears that might become leaks. And if the watertight integrity of our hull or fittings is at all suspect, everything that might get soggy in lockers goes into plastic bags.

Topside we also prepare double lashings for all deck gear, leaving extra sections of lashing line at various handy points around the deck. If our dinghy is on davits and we are heading offshore, we swing it aboard. We double-check the emergency rigging gear and make sure that we have cable clamps, a piece of 1×19 wire to match the longest shroud, cable cutters, and a Norseman-type mechanical terminal fitting aboard. We also like to have a pair of spare steering cables aboard. The working cables and steering chain themselves are checked for cracks or meat hooks. Our navigation timepieces are rated against an accurate time tick and verified over several days. The barometer setting is also double-checked. We make sure a mask, snorkel, and a pair of swim fins are handy in the cockpit in case one of us has to make a quick trip over the side.

We have learned the hard way that before heading out to sea we must dog our hatches and fit storm covers. Once outside, if conditions are moderate, we remove the covers and open hatches. On the way out, we take a bearing or two to be sure the compass deviation table is still accurate.

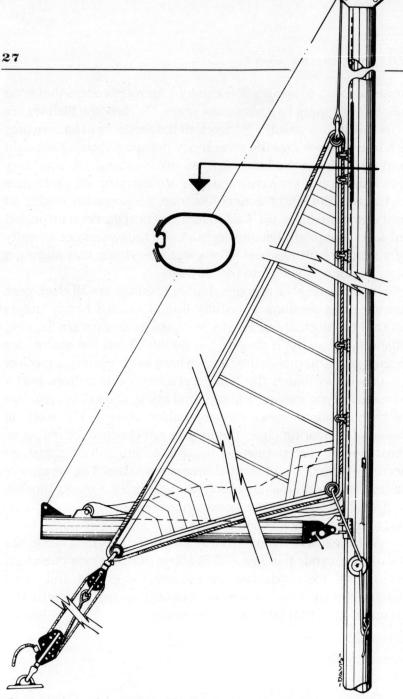

The storm trysail works best if it has its own track on the mast. The sheets should be attached to the clew when the trysail is in storage. Remember to reinforce the sail track where the headboard pulls. You should also reinforce the track where the mainsail loads the mast when that sail is reefed.

STORM CANVAS

The question of what type of storm canvas to carry takes a little more analysis. For offshore work we feel that nothing but the best will do. When you come right down to it, the space it consumes and its cost are such a small percentage of all that goes into the boat that even coastal cruisers are better off with a proper inventory of heavy-weather sails.

When you talk with experienced offshore sailors you find that their storm canvas rarely sees action. In all our miles of sailing we have never been down to our very smallest sails, yet I would never go offshore without them, nor would many other experienced seamen, as the following story illustrates.

The port watch of *Samantha* looks uneasily over the stern quarter across the Tasman Sea. For the past 2 hours the lowering sky has signaled the arrival of a frontal system. The skipper rolls out of the sack at the deck crew's call. He taps the barometer, grunts, and then rubs his eyes. "All right, mates," he calls, "looks like we're in for a bloody northeaster."

The crew methodically begins preparations. *Samantha*, enroute from Fiji to New Zealand, was stripped down for "battle stations" even before she poked her nose into the trade winds three days ago. Heavy gear was stowed below. The dink, outboard, and sailboard were all stuffed into the forepeak and lazaret, and the dorades were removed and capped as the 42-foot sloop moved south into cooler air.

Although *Samantha* is moving easily now with #2 genoa and

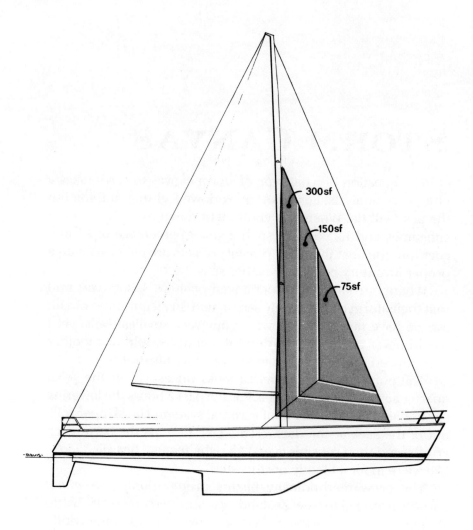

With a properly proportioned cutter rig, storm canvas can be carried inboard on the staysail stay. The progression shown is for *Intermezzo II*.

full main in the Force 4 southwester, the crew realizes that when the windshift that accompanies the front hits there will be little time to change sails.

The storm jib is hanked onto the intermediate forestay. The storm trysail is removed from its bag at the base of the mast and flaked out on deck. First the headboard is checked, and then each sail slide is examined for wear and each lashing for chafe. Two lashings need repair but rather than resew them now, the crew uses light parachute cord over the sewn lashings as a temporary fix.

Next the crew run the seams, the leech, and the corners. They pay particular attention to where the panels overlap along the leech, because these spots are the most vulnerable. Once their inspection is complete, they double-gasket the trysail, lead the sheets to the rail, and turn their attention to checking the storm jib already hanked on the inner forestay.

The first drops of cool rain begin to fall. To the west flashes of lightning play amongst the clouds. The wind drops, and the sails slat. *Samantha* rolls drunkenly in the confused cross swell. A bit of breeze from the northwest fills in and then gives way to a southwest puff. The breeze backs, comes in from the northeast at 10 knots, and then dies again. Suddenly the rain begins in earnest. The crew scrambles to drop the genoa. As the rain beats down, ever harder, they strip off the large headsail and dump it into the forward cabin, replace the storm cover over the hatch, and hoist the storm jib. The 40-square-foot sail looks like a diaper in the foretriangle.

The 35-knot wind arrives with a crack of thunder. Within 15 minutes it is blowing a steady Force 10, 50 knots and more. The crew struggles to get the main down and gasketed. Double lashings are applied, and the boom is dropped onto the coachroof and then secured.

The storm trysail is next. Although the tiny sail is only 20 feet on the hoist and 10 feet on the foot, it takes the crew 20 minutes to set. The job would have been easier had it been done in advance, but then *Samantha* would have been shorn of adequate sail in the confused seaway before the front hit.

Samantha and her crew are now rolling along at hull speed

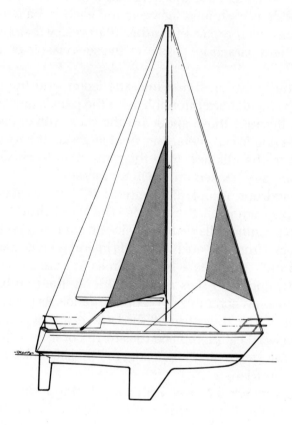

A sloop will want to balance her rig with storm trysail and storm jib. When it is blowing too hard for both, the trysail will give way to the storm jib, but having the storm jib at the end of the bow will make tacking difficult.

with less than 15 percent of the normal sailplan set. Since the center of effort is low, she heels little. The rig is easy to handle and adjust, and the crew is comfortable, if a bit exhausted. If the front doesn't worsen, they can carry this rig through the night. By morning the stormline will have passed and the breeze lightened.

Having a sufficient inventory of properly prepared storm sails is essential. We like to carry more than just a trysail and a single storm jib. Two or even three jib sizes are better, not only because storms themselves vary but also because conditions vary so during any one storm, requiring different amounts of canvas to adjust boatspeed and angle as the wind and sea mature or drop off. *Storm sail inventory is no place to compromise.*

Aboard our first *Intermezzo* we carried a 100-square-foot storm staysail constructed of 11-ounce Dacron and a 60-square-foot hurricane jib built from 7½-ounce material. Rather than carry a storm trysail, we put a third, trysail-sized deep reef into the Dacron main and heavily reinforced the head. I now feel this decision was a mistake. It meant that in ultimate conditions we would be calling on a sail we used every day. If the sail had failed, the result could have been disaster.

Because *Intermezzo II* was a cutter, we could rely on both a heavy staysail and two sizes of storm jibs. With the cutter configuration we felt safe without a trysail since the rig was designed to sail with only a staysail while going upwind in a heavy blow. A sloop rig, on the other hand, would need a trysail to balance the storm jib, particularly if you needed to claw off a lee shore.

Some sailmakers tend to underbuild storm sails. The sails are so small, the reasoning goes, that the total loads, regardless of the wind strength, are light. What this approach ignores is the misuse to which storm canvas is frequently subjected.

In storm conditions it is all too easy for the sail to chafe against shrouds, slat back and forth as you run, or flog madly if a sheet fails or a tack goes less than perfectly. Flogging in a real blow will make short work of all but the strongest sails.

As a result, we preferred to build our storm sails from material usually two weights above that of our heaviest regular cruising sails. In addition, we had all the sides of the sail run with two tapes rather than the usual one. The clew, head, and tack had extra reinforcing as well as webbing in case the rings should begin to pull out. The headsail hanks were a size or two larger than normal, and those at the head and tack were closely spaced.

Storm trysails must have tremendously strong heads. The slides at the headboards should also be oversized and closely spaced. When the sail is set, it will be far below the masthead, and there will be no halyard support to hold the head against the mast. The total load of the sheet, trying to pull the head away from the mast, will be taken by the headboard and the slides attaching it to the track.

This all means that the track must also be extra strong. If the spar is aluminum, it is a good idea to weld doubler plates to the back of the track where the headboard falls to prevent the track from opening up under load. Wooden spars will require extra reinforcing with hardwood inserts and extra fasteners.

Storm sails should always be stowed with their sheets attached (the logbook should note where the sheets lead). Once a year the sails should be removed, inspected for decay or damage, and hoisted to refamiliarize the crew with how they lead.

We found it good practice to attach halyard pennants to our storm sails. These wire extensions allow the halyard to lead to its normal position on the winch, reducing the load on rope-to-wire splices. We also set our storm jibs on tack pennants, so the sail flies off the deck a bit. When you sail in really large seas, it is necessary to raise headsails off the deck anyway, so they won't be blanketed in the troughs.

Handling storm headsails when running has its own set of problems. If the sail is set unboomed, it will slat back and forth, eventually damaging the sail. Yet most whisker or spinnaker poles are too large to wrestle with in storm conditions.

The answer may be a modified "jockey" pole or reaching strut. If it is set up with a closed-end fitting to hold the sheet, instead of the usual open end used for the spinnaker guy, it makes an ideal storm jib whisker pole.

Finally, the staying system of the boat's spars must be

considered. The rigging plan or the way the mast is tuned may make it difficult for the spar to stay straight when the mainsail loads are not applied at the masthead. Deeply reefing a main or setting a trysail puts aft and side bending loads into the middle panels where support is sometimes lacking. If you have not had occasion to find out how your spar reacts with storm canvas set, find a rigger or sparmaker to advise you.

No sailing yacht should put to sea, even for a short cruise, without a proper inventory of storm canvas. These sails are small, consume little stowage space, and are not expensive. They will probably stay stowed except for their annual mainte-nance check. But what a comfort it is to know that come what may, you have the equipment to deal with the conditions.

Larry Pardey photo

UPGRADING
BASIC
BOATHANDLING
SKILLS

When most sailors contemplate maneuvering their yachts in tight spots they hit the starter button on the auxiliary. The result of this approach is a lack of familiarity with handling their yacht in tight quarters under sail, which in and of itself can lead to disaster. On the other hand, you must be familiar with the handling characteristics of your yacht under power, a situation in which many vessels are at their worst. Needless to say, the way towards proficiency is practice—under sail and power and in a variety of light- medium- and heavy-air conditions.

Never depend upon an engine! This beautiful 55-foot ketch, an able sailor, powered into the harbor of Malta during a gale, when she could have easily sailed her anchor in. A sheet found its way around the prop, and before sails could be raised she was on the rocks.

MANEUVERING UNDER SAIL

The sailing Linda and I did before we got serious about cruising was without the benefit of an engine. For years we sailed in and out of all sorts of nooks and crannies, never really thinking about how we were disadvantaged. Of course, when the wind was light and we sat around waiting for the next zephyr we were frustrated, but using an engine to get from here to there was never really part of the picture.

Then we acquired *Intermezzo* and her trusty Isuzu diesel. At the turn of a key we could go when the wind wouldn't blow, we could power dead to windward, we could anchor in tight corners we would never have considered when we knew we had to sail out. Quickly we slipped into the role of auxiliary sailors. Whenever sailing required more than a small effort, on would go the engine.

One Saturday, several months after this transformation, we were approaching Emerald Bay on California's Catalina Island. It's a quiet anchorage nestled against the barren landscape and has with clear water, an islet, and invariably lots of moored boats.

"Let's sail the hook in," I suggested to Linda.

"With all these boats here?" She looked aghast. That we had sailed in and out of much tighter spots for years she seemed to have forgotten. But I was up for a bit of showing off.

We decided to use the same basic procedures we had used on our engineless boats. In the light air, with the main anchor at the ready, we would slowly make our way downwind. I would signal to Linda to let the hook go, and our forward momentum would be used to set the anchor. We readied our large, high-tensile Danforth, which we knew would bite immediately in the hard sand bottom of Emerald Bay. We worked our way upwind, dropped the main and furled the working jib, and used our small mizzen to power us downwind. *Intermezzo*'s speed dropped to 2 knots, just enough for steerage and momentum to round up, get the roller-furling jib set, and beat out if a problem occurred.

"Let go!" I yelled forward.

With a splash the anchor was down, the rattle of running chain resounding throughout the bay. At the 200-foot mark, Linda dogged the winch. A moment later, before the chain snubbed tight, I put *Intermezzo*'s helm hard over. Quickly I tossed the stern hook over and sheeted home the mizzen. She rounded up quickly and within seconds we were lying docilely, head to wind.

Linda put the windlass to work centering us between the two anchors. In a few minutes the operation was over, and we went about coiling lines, getting the dinghy ready, covering sails. No one in the anchorage had even noticed! So much for showing off.

Despite the lack of audience appreciation, Linda and I realized we had just rediscovered a very satisfying aspect of cruising: maneuvering under sail. Until then we hadn't much thought about it one way or another. When our boats had no engine, there was no choice. With the diesel aboard *Intermezzo*, we found we always took the easy route. After our Emerald Bay rediscovery, whenever possible we sailed on and off the hook and regarded *Intermezzo* as engineless when it came to picking anchorages.

We ultimately decided that in most of our cruising the engine's primary importance lay in making hot water, producing electricity, and keeping the refrigerator cold. Whether the prop turned was secondary. By practicing with *Intermezzo* under sail in tight quarters and having the right headsails up, we learned we could take her almost anywhere under sail we would care to go under power.

When we did use the engine it was always with the assumption that something would go wrong. Halyards were left

With *Intermezzo*'s
ketch rig we would
use the mizzen to
help turn her into
the wind when
sailing the hook in.
By sailing in a
continuous circle
after dropping the
anchor we could
keep the chain
from scratching
the topsides as it
payed out. The
stern anchor was
dropped as we
headed into the
wind. After
winching our-
selves between the
two anchors we
tightened both
rodes to make sure
the hooks were
well set.

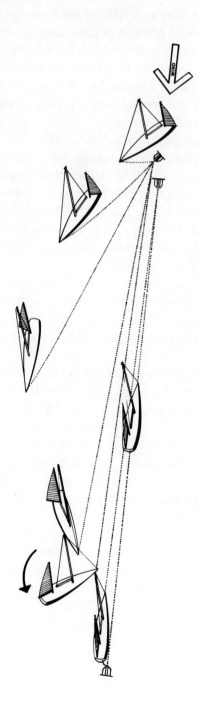

attached to furled sails, with sheets flaked at the ready in case we should have to sail out of somewhere our engine had taken us.

Our maneuvering successfully in tight quarters depended on a number of factors. First, we had to have an easy-to-handle rig. Large, overlapping genoas were left in the sail locker. Our intermediate forestay would need to be removable so we could tack the headsail quickly, with ease. Both bow and stern anchors, rodes, and chains were easy to operate and ready to go at a moment's notice. Finally, we were thoroughly familiar with *Intermezzo*'s quirks because we practiced.

To meet the first criterion we cut an old heavy #1 genoa down to a lapper. The clew came back only as far as the cap shrouds, so there was little sheet to be trimmed when we tacked. This meant I could handle the sheets by myself. To meet the second, we obtained a Highfield release lever for the intermediate forestay so it could be removed to allow the jib to sweep straight across the foredeck.

We had our first real-life test of this rig entering Cabo San Lucas at tip of Baja in Mexico. The pressure plate between the engine and transmission went out (although we didn't know that was the problem at the time), and the prop wouldn't turn.

The air was typically light, and we were using the greater part of our wardrobe to keep *Intermezzo* moving. As we approached Cabo we doused the drifter and hoisted the working jib. The forestay was released and pulled back out of the way against the mast, and we proceeded to short-tack *Intermezzo* through the 100-foot-wide harbor entrance. To help her tack and gather way more quickly in the light conditions we would hold the jib for a few seconds after her head came through the wind. This allowed the wind to blow the bow off. At the same time we let the traveler down to leeward so the main didn't begin to draw on the new tack too early, eliminating its tendency to force the bow back into the wind and place us in irons. (Backing the jib and easing the main when tacking also works well in heavy air when the sea is running.) Once inside, we headed up, let the hook down, and settled back on our chain. We didn't have the luxury of sailing the anchor into a good set, but we knew the

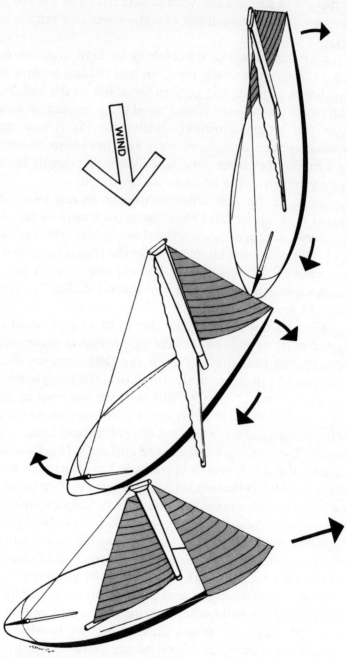

Backing the jib to windward and easing the mainsail will push the bow to leeward and get you started on the new tack quickly. As you are drifting back, reverse the rudder (with the trailing edge of the rudder to windward) so the stern goes to windward while the bow falls off.

holding was fine and the harbor protected.

By this time Linda and I were familiar with the basic characteristics of *Intermezzo* under sail. We had learned how far she would carry forward after rounding up into the wind. If we wanted to break way quickly, we would leave a main or jib up after coming head-to-wind. In light air the mainsail could be pushed to windward as a brake (a common technique in dinghy sailing).

We also understood how to trim the jib, main, and mizzen for turning ourselves into or away from the wind. If we wanted to head off quickly, we would let the mainsheet way out and sheet the jib to push the bow around. Heading up required just the opposite moves: the main came in and the jib went out. The mizzen worked as an auxiliary rudder. Backing it pushed the stern to the opposite side, while sheeting amidships would bring us nicely head-to-wind. From our earlier experience in catamarans, we knew that if we were in irons while the jib was blowing the head off, we would make sternway. So the rudder would have to be turned opposite the bow. Thus, if we were blowing the head off to starboard, the helm would be put to port while we were going backwards. That would tend to swing the stern to port opposite the bow, helping the head blow off so we would start sailing more quickly.

We try to avoid entering a lee shore harbor or anchorage under sail. If we miss a tack, I don't want to have to worry about going up on the beach. To be on the safe side we always have the main anchor off the bow roller and hanging down, ready to go in an instant. The stern anchor is ready to go as well.

Fortunately most anchorages are open enough to sail into and out of easily. If we can't sail out handily, we think twice about going in; even with the engine working well, an anchor line could foul the prop, or the engine itself could suddenly quit. I want to be able to sail out if necessary.

Sailing an anchor out takes a bit of practice. On a large boat, the procedure is as dependent upon the windlass as the vessel herself. With a fast-operating, efficient windlass, you can shorten up on the rode, set sail, break out the anchor, and then quickly pull the hook as the head is falling off. Being able to get

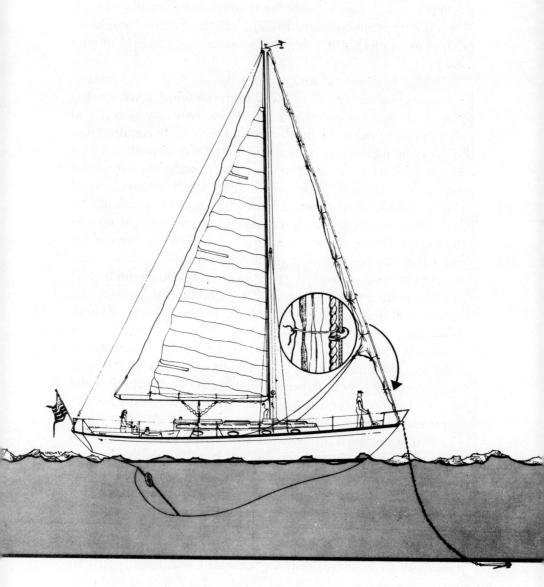

In a strong breeze it may be better to reef the main and hoist the jib in stops.

the anchor aboard quickly after you break it free reduces drag substantially and makes the all-important first tack much easier.

When you must beat out of the anchorage, pay particular attention to the distance to leeward available for falling off and then accelerating. As the anchor comes up, the jib should be backed to push the head around and the main should be eased. It will take some seconds before the boat has enough way on to allow the sails to be trimmed properly and then complete a tack successfully. Before you drop the anchor on the way in, consider how much room various wind directions will leave you to make that first tack and get out. If actually getting the anchor up could delay you long enough to dangerously compromise your maneuvering room, you may have to slip it. Be prepared to buoy the end of the rode.

Sailing out in moderate air is one thing, but what should you do when it really starts to blow? We like to hoist the main reefed flat and sheeted hard amidships. If our headsail is not roller-furling, it is hoisted in stops. Then, as the anchor comes clear, the headsail is broken out and backed to start us moving. In heavy air roller-furling makes things easier. Hoisting the jib un-furled and unstopped isn't feasible in a strong breeze because of luffing. It also tends to blow the bow back and forth.

When you're working under sail in close to land, try to anticipate headers and lifts; they can be a great help. There are other aspects to consider when you sail in commercial harbors. Big ships, for example, create wind vacuums close by their topsides, especially on hot, light-air days when the heat of the ship will force the wind up and off the water. Large buildings alter wind patterns. You can gain advance notice of these phenomena by watching wind action on the water.

The choice of sails also has to be carefully considered. In major harbors it is probably more dangerous to be undercanvassed than overpowered. You can always luff a bit to depower the rig temporarily. But if you're caught with insuffi-cient sail, failing to make a tack can become a major danger. Experience has taught us that one level of sail area below what we consider optimum is enough to keep us moving in the lulls.

A sigh of relief from all aboard signals our arrival between the stone breakwaters of East London on the southern coast of South Africa. After a hard beat in a southwesterly gale we now have only to find *Intermezzo* a berth for the night.

East London is a commercial port situated on the outfall of a small river. Each side of the ½-mile-long harbor is lined with docks, warehouses, and shipping, all snugly laid out between the hills of the river valley. There is a 2-knot ebbing current as we work our way through the breakwater.

I go forward to free up our big Danforth anchor (in the alluvial mud of the harbor the CQR would take too long to set). I remove the safety lashing and kick the anchor over the bow roller.

Linda also unties the Viking aluminum stern hook, flakes the chain out, and spreads its 100 feet of line down the deck. *Intermezzo* still carries her double-reefed main and storm staysail, as I expect any moment to have the full force of the gale descend upon us.

The running backstays are both tightened up. That will eliminate one operation when tacking. The momentary chafe on the leeward side of the main is not a concern. Elyse is detailed to the leeward runner. If we must bear away quickly she will cast it off so the main can be eased out.

"Helm's alee!" I call out of habit as our nose comes up alongside the first freighter. Normally I would stay at least 100 feet away, but the harbor is so narrow we need all the room we can get on each tack. A momentary shift luffs the staysail just after we pass the eye of the wind. Then the breeze settles back. The staysail is sheeted home, and the main traveler is cranked back to windward. At 4 knots we glide forward. Five more times we repeat the procedure. The lulls and luffs alongside the ships are ever changing, but *Intermezzo* has enough momentum to carry her through.

Linda goes to the bow as we gain the top of the harbor where the river narrows and the channel is further restricted by a few moorings placed for local yachts. To starboard we see two of our friends from Durban, who have sought shelter from the same gale. We are invited to lie alongside them.

Because of the swift ebb tide, I feel it best to go up current,

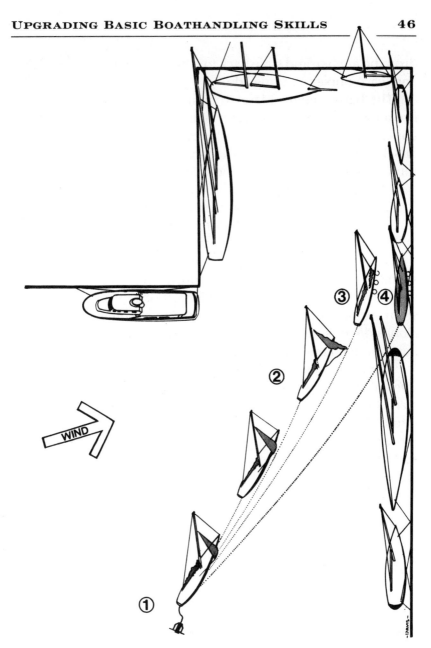

A stern anchor can be used as a brake when sailing into a tight dock. In this situation a Danforth-type anchor usually works the best as it is the fastest biting of the various types of anchors. If you have room to windward, it is better to sail upwind, drop the anchor off the bow, and then drift down to the dock.

drop the anchor, and slide back to where we can toss them a line and warp ourselves alongside.

The harbor control launch comes by and asks if we would like a tow. The rough character of its topsides and the youthful appearance of the operator indicates we are probably be better off left to our own devices. "No thanks," I reply, "but if you could retrieve our anchor after we have tied up, it would be great."

"Aye, we'll be happy to bring it back," they answer.

On port tack we ease the mainsheet to slow our way. Fifty yards upstream of our friends, *Intermezzo*'s speed drops to that of the current. Linda lets the Danforth go.

Quickly the mizzen is hoisted and backed to port. The stern swings towards shore as we drift downriver on the ebb. When we're even with the other boats, Linda snubs the rode. I toss our stern spring the remaining 20 feet, and in a moment we are safe alongside. In spite of the dirty, industrial surroundings no port has ever been more welcome.

Using anchors to assist in docking is a time-honored procedure. If you're in unfamiliar surroundings, both the bow and stern hooks should be ready to go. On other occasions sailing into a dock we have used the stern hook as a brake. To do so, though, you need to gauge the water depth accurately, allow sufficient scope for the hook to bite immediately, and have enough rode for error. It's better to be early in tossing the anchor than late.

Maneuvering under Power

There comes a time, however, when using the engine is the fastest, safest, and most expedient means of getting from one spot to another or of working your way into some really tight spot. When it comes to motoring, no two sailboats are alike, but while the exact techniques applicable to your boat may be superfluous on another, there are some common basics to operating any sailboat under power.

First you need to assess the boat and its quirks. Sailboats with large engines, efficient propellers, spade rudders, cutaway or fin keels, and low-windage rigs and hulls have the most going for them. But as engine power or propeller performance is reduced, so is the ability to use brute force to accomplish your desires, and the requirements for finesse increase.

The type of propeller a sailboat has and the boat's hull shape and the rudder design are particularly critical in determining how a sailboat backs down. Vessels with long waterlines, directionally stable hulls, and spade or skeg-mounted rudders are the easiest to maneuver in reverse, while those with long overhanging ends, full keels, and attached rudders are the hardest. And woe betide the sailor who has to master reversing a vessel with an offset prop.

Once you know how a boat's design characteristics will affect her performance under power, conduct several brief experiments to determine exactly how she will handle under different conditions.

The first data you want to acquire is the direction the boat's propeller torques, or walks, in forward and in reverse. A counterclockwise-rotating prop will torque the stern to port in forward gear and to starboard in reverse. Clockwise-rotating props have just the opposite effect. To keep things straight aboard our boats, I have always taped a small arrow to the side of the cockpit to remind me which way the boat starts off with the engine in reverse.

Prop torque, which is often cursed, especially in reverse, can be used to advantage. Consider turning in the tightest possible radius. Here torque is invaluable. Assume you are dead in the water, with a counterclockwise-spinning prop. The turn should be made in the opposite direction of the stern movement in reverse. Since the torque here will kick the stern to starboard, you want to turn the bow to port. By putting the helm hard over to

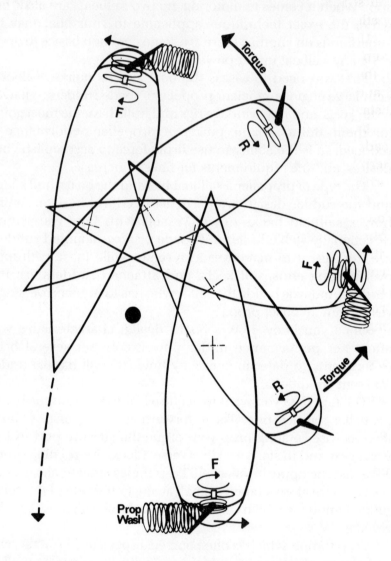

Most yachts can be rotated by using engine torque in reverse and opposing prop wash on the rudder. After determining which direction your stern "walks" in reverse turn your rudder so it will rotate the hull in the same direction when you are going ahead. If your wheel is hard to turn lock to lock, or if space is especially tight, the rudder may be left in this position while the engine is shifted from forward to reverse.

port and then giving alternate bursts of power ahead and astern, you should be able to rotate most vessels in less than three boatlengths.

Using this technique in a tight area involves forethought. Even on a windless day, the boat will have a tendency to "walk" in the direction of her stern torque. If there is an obstruction in that direction, you will want to start your turn a compensating distance away.

In any breeze you want to position the boat so the turn is made with the wind blowing the bow off. Torque will "hold" the stern against the wind. It is usually impossible to get the bow to turn upwind against any sort of breeze.

One of the major considerations in maneuvering under power is how quickly you can stop your forward way. To find the bottom line, try running ahead at various speeds or rpm's. Then, with different amounts of reverse, note how many boatlengths it takes to come to a full stop. If your boat has a folding prop, the distance may be considerable, but a good-sized three-bladed prop or reversing-pitch prop can stop most vessels in five to ten lengths.

Your ability to stop controls how fast you can maneuver in forward gear. Since the faster you go in forward, the better steering control you have, within reason, you usually use as much forward speed as possible.

It is also necessary to know the minimum forward and reverse speeds you need to maintain steerage. Wind strength affects this minimum, so keep notes. The stronger the wind, the more boatspeed you need to maintain steerageway.

In some situations wind can be used to advantage. For example, if you can back into the wind, your head will be held downhill, which tends to keep the stern moving in a straight line. Conversely, powering astern downwind is extremely difficult.

In a crosswind you must take care not to be blown onto a lee dock or moorage. Maintain enough distance from the leeward obstruction to allow for side slip as well as the stern's or bow's swinging out when you turn. On the other hand, the wind can be used to keep you clear if a windward berth is available.

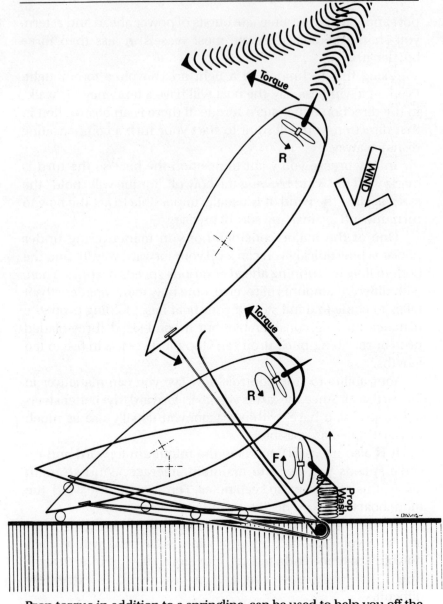

Prop torque in addition to a springline, can be used to help you off the dock when you are stuck on a leeward berth. Turn the rudder so the prop wash is directed against the dock. This, along with the angular pull of the spring line will force the stern out. If your stern torque is in the opposite direction, you will be able to back off the dock against a moderate amount of beam wind.

When you dock under power, consider not only your entrance but also your egress. While a leeward crosswind berth is the easiest to enter, it is the most difficult to leave. The first consideration, again, is prop torque. Try to tie up so that when you leave your stern torque will take you *away* from the dock. When you are ready to leave, tie a bow springline well forward, with as great an angle to the dock as is possible, and put the helm so the bow will turn towards the dock when the engine is in forward gear.

The prop wash will now be directed towards the dock by the rudder, which forces the stern out, while the bow spring also helps force the stern out. When equilibrium is reached and you can gain no additional angle, reverse helm and engine. If there is room, the wind isn't too strong, and there is enough reverse side torque, you will be carried clear. Remember that the minute you remove forward pressure from the springline the stern will begin to drift towards the dock. By practicing where you have a clear exit you will know what can be expected when the situation is a bit more tense.

You can use reverse torque to advantage coming into a dock, too, of course. If you are heading in with the bow at an angle, reverse torque can pull the stern alongside the dock, making springlines initially unnecessary.

Almost all sailboats pivot forward of their midships point. As a result, the stern tends to swing out and away from the bow when the boat is turning. Visualize the bow staying put and the stern rotating about it in sharp turns. This characteristic means that you must always make sure there is room away from the direction you are turning for the stern to swing.

This same characteristic can be used to advantage if you want to dodge something close by. For example, you may suddenly see a mooring alongside to starboard. By immediately turning to starboard, towards the mooring, you will in effect swing the stern away from it. The same principle holds in keeping the prop clear of someone who has fallen off the foredeck. Always turn towards but not directly at him or her to swing the prop out of the way.

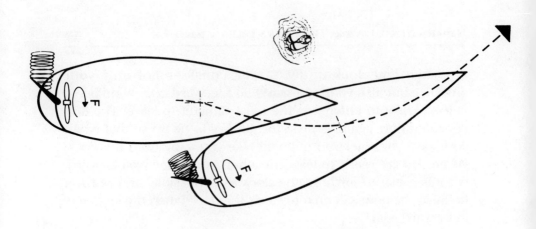

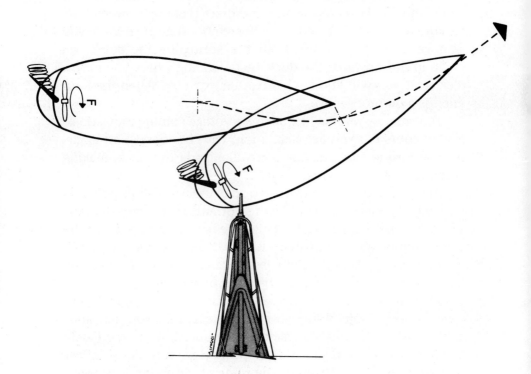

When you turn the bow in one direction, remember that the stern swings *out* in the opposite direction. Thus, if you turn the hull in towards an obstruction, the stern will swing away from it. But remember that the opposite is true as well.

Intermezzo II was the most docile vessel going astern I have ever had the pleasure of handling. Her reversing blade prop had a minimum amount of torque to be overcome. The large spade rudder, hung at the very end of the boat, took a bite quickly so that once we obtained a knot or so of speed she could be steered at will in reverse. On other boats it has been necessary for us to assume as much as a 90-degree compensating angle before starting to back down, and if conditions weren't right, we have had to give up.

Before we leave the subject of maneuvering under power let us say once again that relying on an engine to take you some-where that would be dangerous if the engine should fail is an invitation to disaster. Before engaging the prop, get in the habit of checking that all your lines are aboard. Keep the filters clean and the V-belts in good condition. Make sure the engine has plenty of coolant. And leave your halyards attached, just in case.

Here is another example of what can happen when you depend upon an engine. Note the anchor line wrapped around the propeller.   Larry Pardey photo

Stanley Dashew photo

SAILHANDLING IN ROUGH WEATHER

In moderate weather changing a headsail is generally a straightforward proposition. But as the breeze starts to pick up, what have been routine sailhandling chores become more exciting. The foredeck crew gets a chance to break fingernails, feel a dollop or two of salt water down the back, and wrestle with a wet, thrashing sail that threatens to tear itself into large chunks and pitch crewmen overboard—assuming, of course, you are trying for the fastest possible sail change. That's why the experienced heavy-hitters in the racing fraternity are called the afterguard. They leave the pointy end to the young lions. After all, racing is supposed to be fun, right?

But when you cruise shorthanded, it's usually the skipper making the sail changes. The boatspeed-to-comfort ratios are a little different from those on the racing boats, and a few minutes of lost speed are not nearly as important as keeping seawater from dripping down the back of your neck. You are both afterguard *and* foredeck crew.

Since I am a firm advocate of staying as dry as possible, and since Linda's fingernails break easily, we have, over the years, developed some straightforward sail-changing exercises to minimize the risks to which we are exposed when wrestling with wet sails and rough seas at the same time.

Intermezzo II on a hard-driving reach in the Gulf Stream. The headsails had a short foot, making them easy to douse in heavy going. Note the high lifelines around the foredeck.

CHANGING HEADSAILS

Changing sail creates several sets of problems. First, you have to be able to work securely on the foredeck. This means wearing an efficient safety harness. Handholds have to be sturdy and convenient. The bow pulpit must be strongly made and through-bolted. Handrails installed over dorade vents will protect the vents from entangling sheets as well as provide a place to brace your knees. The deck itself should be as uncluttered as possible so that you can step quickly without worrying about jamming a foot under a piece of gear.

Next, you need a means of keeping a headsail aboard immediately after it is dropped on deck. If the bow is pitching, the wind is howling, or seas are coming aboard, the headsail will want to blow or wash overboard. The better you are set up to contain it on deck, the less hands will be needed forward, and the sooner you'll be done with your work. A third lifeline, just above the deck level, and ⅛-inch line laced between the top and middle and middle and bottom wires will *temporarily* contain a wet sail. The more lacing, the better the sail containment.

When it's really blowing hard, the headsail may not want to come down on its own. It drops a few feet when the halyard is released, and then a gust may start it climbing the headstay again. When heading offshore in areas where bad weather is a possibility, we've made it a habit to attach takedown lines directly to the halyards or sail heads; we simply run a piece of ¼-inch line from the head through a block at the stem and then back aft to the mast. One person can pull the sail down using this takedown line and stay drier while standing aft, too.

If you have been beating, the headsail sheet should be eased only enough to allow the sail to drop. By keeping the sheet relatively snug, the clew will be held close to the boat, or inboard, depending on how the sheets are led.

If you are like me and want to stay dry, you will think about

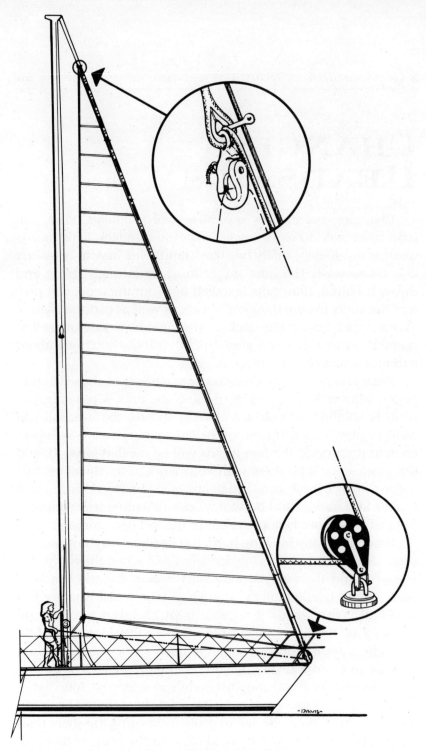

A takedown line from the head of the jib led through a block at the stem leading back towards the halyard winch makes the job of pulling down a jib easier in heavy weather (and drier, too!).

heading downwind when you change your headsails and a sea is running. Sailing almost square to the wind, the eased mainsail will nicely blanket the headsail. By waiting until the headsail is just backed (backing can be facilitated by sailing slightly by the lee—but watch out for accidental gybes)—that is, blowing through the foretriangle to windward—and then letting the halyard go, you will probably end up with a neat pile of sailcloth on the foredeck.

The necessity of using these procedures will vary with the size and weight of your headsails and how hard the wind is blowing. The heavier the sailcloth, the smaller the size, and the lighter the wind, the easier it is to get the sail down on deck. Heavier sails are easier to keep from blowing overboard, but lighter sails stow more easily.

Bareheaded now, you have to think about reversing the process. Bringing a new jib on deck isn't that big a deal on most boats. But once the sail is out of the bag, you must be careful that the wind doesn't blow it over the side. We tie on the sheets before unbagging the sail and then attach the tack to the stem right away. That way the jib is partially under control.

If, in spite of your best efforts, a sail does get over the side and you can't seem to get it back aboard, you can try one of these tactics. By heading higher and thereby getting the bow to pitch, you may get a really sharp buck to throw the sail completely back aboard, or at least allow you to get more of it back with brute force. The other approach is to tack or gybe. This maneuver will bring the sail to windward, keep the sail out of the bow wave, and make it easier to get back aboard. While you are wrestling with this problem, bear in mind that whatever happens, you do not want the jibsheet or sail to get caught in the rudder or wrap around the prop.

When you are setting a headsail in heavy air, speed is very important. The objective should be to get the sail drawing as quickly as possible. The sooner you stop it from flogging, the safer the foredeck crew will be and the less likely the sail will be damaged. For this reason some people set storm sails in stops. They use rubber bands or rotten twine, usually two or three wraps at 1- to 2-foot centers, to secure the sail until it is hoisted and ready for sheeting.

REEFING THE MAIN

Reefing the main is no fun when it is blowing, either. And while the mainsail doesn't have the same tendency to climb that headsails do, if you are off the wind, the sail will blow against the spreaders and be difficult to get down. To make life easier and save the effort of pulling down the luff, we rig a line from one side of the mast up through the reefing tack and back down to a small winch. It serves as a long cunningham and enables us to winch the main down under adverse conditions.

In order to reef quickly and to minimize wear and tear on the mainsail leech, mark the reefing lines and halyard for the proper reefing positions. When it is blowing hard we ease the halyard and take in on the clew reef line at the same time. This helps keep the leech under control. After the clew reef line is secure and the halyard is cleated, we work down the luff and tighten it. If we expect to be reefed for a short period, I frequently will not bother tying in the reef cringles but pull the mainsail over the boom to windward and simply let wind pressure hold it in position. You must be sure, however, that there are no rough spots on the boom to chafe the sail. If a sea is running the sail should be tied up; otherwise a large amount of water may collect in the mainsail folds, overstressing the leech.

When you are snugged down for a long pull, it is a good idea to tie a safety line through the clew and then ease the actual reefing line to reduce the chances of its chafing through (something it is prone to do).

If conditions deteriorate to where you need to set a storm trysail, you will probably already be shortened down. It may be necessary to use a takedown line from the head of the main to get the last part of the mainsail down to the gooseneck. Once the sail is lowered and stopped down securely, tie off the boom or drop it onto its gallows or the cabintop, so it is less likely to cause problems should you be severely knocked down. The trysail should already be on its own track, bagged at the base of

When it is really blowing try running off (sea room permitting) and blanketing the headsail in the lee of the main before letting it go. Note that for this maneuver to be effective you must be heading dead down wind.

WIND

There are a number of ways to make slab reefing easier. Conventional reefing hooks (A) are the cleanest in terms of boat speed,but require the sail to be dropped out of its track. We prefer to use a continuous line through the reef tacks and leave the slides stacked up in the track (B). This system also makes it possible to winch the main down when running in heavy airs. Always tie a safety line(C)through the clew if you will be reefed for a long period, and make sure that normal clew outhaul (D) is free from chafe.

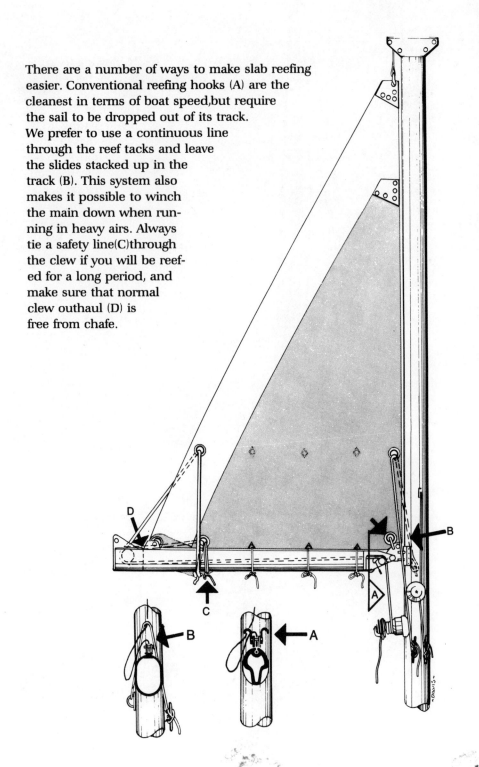

the mast, and with sheets attached with amidships and rail leads, the latter for use when you are sailing free.

You have the same problems setting the trysail that you do setting a headsail. You want to prevent flogging as much as possible. If you have premarked your sheets, the lee one can be sheeted home before the sail is set.

Every once in a while a cruiser gets caught with a spinnaker or drifter up in a building breeze. The size of the sail and the fact that it is free flying makes it difficult to get back aboard.

Once again the key is running off, easing the main, and blanketing the sail. To help matters, we move the sheet lead well forward and trim the leech down tight, so that it is touching the main. As long as you are steering straight downwind, the spinnaker will collapse behind the main. Release the tack or guy while keeping the sheet tight. Then the halyard should be eased as fast as possible without letting the sail go overboard. Speed is essential, since you don't want a gust to pull the sail out of the vacuum behind the mainsail.

One general rule holds, regardless of which sail you are changing: always have lots of ties handy. I make a habit of festooning our lifelines with 6-foot pieces of webbing and ¼-inch line. At times hundreds seem to be available, and at others, they seem to be all in use. You must have a good inventory in advance. Hanks and halyard shackles must be free and easy to operate, too.

We have saved discussion of changing headsails that have boltropes instead of hanks for last. Boltropes are difficult, potentially dangerous, and unseamanlike especially when you are sailing shorthanded. Several people are needed to pull down the sail, prevent it from tearing as it leaves the feeder, and keep it from going overboard. There is a big difference between changing a sail in light airs or at anchor and doing so when it is blowing 30 or more knots with the deck pitching. If your headsails have boltropes, I suggest practice sessions in temperate conditions offshore to develop techniques and coordination suitable for your craft.

SPECIAL PRECAUTIONS

When you start heading downwind in a large sea, observe a few special precautions with the main boom. If you are sailing anywhere near square, rig a preventer from the bow to the end, or nearly the end, of the boom to prevent an accidental gybe. At the same time, move the boom vang load outboard on the boom. If you are leading the vang directly down to the caprail, move the vang out so it comes to the rail at a 45-degree angle. Doing so reduces loading, and should you accidently roll the boom into a big sea, you may save the boom from breaking. If you are sailing with a hydraulic vang, be sure that the pressure relief valves are properly set and working.

It is also a good idea to have a "tripping reef" sewn into the main, especially if your boat has low freeboard and you tend to drag your boom in the ocean on occasion. This is a single reef point, sewn a few feet above the clew and used in the same manner as a flattening reef. It raises the boom so that it will stay clear of the water in all but the worst conditions.

Gybing when it is blowing also requires special procedures. Look for lulls that coincide with when you are going the fastest *down* a wave. Both the lull and the accelerated boatspeed reduce apparent wind and loading. From here on, the procedure is the same as in a normal gybe except that you want to begin easing the sheet out before the boom slams across the last few feet to reduce shock loading. Be careful to maintain the boom vang tension. If you don't, the boom will tend to rise up, freeing the leech. This is known for some unhappy reason as a "Chinese gybe." The result, frequently, is that the top batten gets caught between the cap shroud and mast. When the boom swings across, the batten stays put, until it breaks or the leech tears. Since easing the sheet quickly is part of this approach, pay particular attention to having the sheet neatly flaked down and ready to run.

FURLING SYSTEMS

Having now gone through the routine of handling sails in the traditional manner, we would be remiss if we didn't discuss the suitability of both main and jib roller-furling systems for the well-found cruising boat. Many sailmakers and marine hardware manufacturers claim their sails and systems can be used for roller-style reefing in heavy weather, as well as for simple furling. The sail shape, they say, works whether used as a storm jib or run out to a 150 percent genoa. Advertisements show boats moving along with the headsail rolled down to heavy-weather size. But examine these pictures closely. Note how hard it is blowing. Those ad photos aren't shot in more than 15 knots of wind!

If someone came up with a system that really worked for headsail reefing, regardless of conditions, I would be the first to recommend using it. But at present the problems inherent with the roller approach and the exigencies of sail construction and design make it impossible to get a sail that's flat and structurally sound when it is *partially* rolled. If you do depend upon roller-furling for everyday sailing, because of its handling ease, be sure you have a secondary system ready for heavy weather. Although many of the large yachts I design and build are rigged with headsail roller-furling, I always fit them with conventional staysail stays so that a storm staysail or storm jib can be *hanked* on.

A second problem that must be considered on a vessel intended for conservative cruising is changing headsails, short-handed, at sea. Since most roller-furling systems utilize a luff extrusion with boltrope attachment, there are no jib hanks to control the sail as you work with it on the foredeck. This deficiency can be dealt with in nice weather and with an adequate-sized crew. But offshore, in a seaway, with perhaps two people at most to work the foredeck, it is asking for trouble.

One way around the problem is offered by the Mariner Company. Its roller-furling system allows you to *hank* on your headsails. We used it during our circumnavigation with no more than the usual maintenance. We had wondered about long-term chafe of the jib hanks on the rolled sail, but in many thousands of miles it never proved to be a problem.

Over the years we have also looked longingly at new types of mainsail furling and reefing systems. How nice it would be to be able to pull away from the dock, yank on a line or push a button, and have the main drawing, presto!

With each new system I examined, I would ask myself the same question: What would happen if we were caught un-expectedly in a northerly gale off Cape Hatteras or by a severe line squall on Long Island Sound? Could we be assured that the system would reef or furl as flawlessly and effortlessly as our trusty conventional mainsail, which has slab reefing led to the cockpit? The answer has always been no.

The problem with most mainsail roller-furling systems is their inefficiency when used under normal conditions, the extra weight aloft, and the difficulty in furling or reefing when heading downwind in heavy going: the boat must be headed into the wind if the sail is to be furled or reefed. If seas are running large and breaking, it may not be possible to head up safely.

The criteria we set on our two *Intermezzo*s for a conser-vative, suitable mainsail-handling system have always been: the ability to reef under any condition, regardless of apparent wind direction or velocity; a flat sail when reefed, with a low center of effort; an efficient sail shape when the sail is not furled or reefed; and a system that cannot fail despite misuse by the crew. Is there such a system that offers a convenient means of furling? Read on.

My first exposure to the ultimate mainsail-furling system came from North Sail's guru, Dick Deaver. Dick had stopped by *Intermezzo II* to say hello after one of the 1982 Southern Ocean Racing Conference races. Dick described the system briefly and asked my reaction. "Another new-fangled furling gadget that might work for bay boats but not offshore ones," I said with some disdain.

A few weeks later a sloop with the mainsail furled vertically behind the mast pulled into a nearby dock. I wandered over to

This boat has been fitted with a Zipstop mainsail with a 3.5 percent roach and vertical battens.

Aulbey Bates photo

greet the new arrival. The mainsail had been built with a hollow, double luff to which was attached a substantial full-length zipper. It fastened to the mast with external slides, as did our main. As the boat sailed in, the main had looked and set like a conventional battenless mainsail, complete with slab reefing. This system, which was the one Dick Deaver had described, seemed to combine the performance of a normal main with the reliability of a proven reefing system.

With the tack of the loose-footed mainsail eased, the Zipstop head slider is pulled down from the masthead, gathering the sailcloth into a bundle behind the mast.

The owner proceeded to demonstrate. To furl, he released the outhaul on the loose-footed mainsail and pulled down a set of lines attached to a "hood." The hood was in fact a clever conical closure device that compressed the sail into the open pocket of the double-luff as the hood was pulled down, zipping the pocket formed by the double luff over the sail. It was very neat. If the system failed, the main, because it was set up normally, could be lowered and furled on the boom in a conventional manner.

From Dick Deaver I got the name of the inventor, builder, and chief honcho of the Zip Stop system, Bill Stevenson. I called Bill at his St. Michaels, Maryland, shop to find out more.

"The key to the system," Bill explained, "is the slider extrusion and its zipper." He uses a special nylon formulated in France and molded in the United States into a continuous zipper slider. This slider captures several feet of zipper along the edges of the hood with enormous strength. The self-lubricating qualities of the French nylon help the zip system minimize friction and pull smoothly. "Because of the zipper engineering and most of the load's being taken by the patented hood, the zipper is very long lived," Bill explained. The double luff is made of special ultraviolet-resistant fabric to protect the sail and the zipper tape when the sail is furled.

Another reason for the system's appeal is cost. To retrofit an existing mainsail with a luff length of 40 feet with Zip Stop could cost less than $1,000 in 1984. A new mainsail of that length with Zip Stop would run $1,800 to $2,200; and remember—the sailcover is built in.

Installing the main is easy enough. An outhaul has to be rigged to the end of the boom to take the full sheeting load of the sail. On bigger boats, say those over 35 feet, Bill recommends a double purchase. Two blocks have to be mounted under the boom for the hood control lines, and you are then ready to hoist the new main on your old track.

How does it work in the flesh? To find out I met with Bill on my Dad's 68-foot cutter, *Deerfoot*. She is primarily sailed by my Dad and one crew, and her very size demands some form of furling assistance. She was originally built with behind-the-mast

The sail is forced into a pocket formed by the two sides of the mainsail luff.

When reefed, a Zipstop main sets the same way a conventional slab-reefing main does, a big advantage in sail shape, center of effort, and reliability compared to behind, or in the mast roller furling systems.

Aulbey Bates photo

roller-furling (with a backup Swedish main hanked on for off-shore work).

As *Deerfoot* headed out the channel in the light northwesterly, the hood was pulled towards the masthead. With the outhaul sheeted home, the sail began to draw. It set beautifully. The boat accelerated smoothly in the puffs and no longer showed the tendency to heel she had with the old furling system. When the yankee was sheeted in, we were chugging to windward at 8.5 knots, a full knot better than with the old main.

Bill pointed out a patented wrinkle in his slab reefing system I hadn't noticed. Arranged below the reefing clew are vertically spaced grommets through which the reefing lines are drawn. As a reef is pulled into the sail, the cloth is bundled up in venetian-blind fashion. That cleans up the sail and reduces cringle tying time.

The breeze started to make up as the afternoon wore on. When *Deerfoot* became slightly overpressed with 24 knots apparent, it was time to reef the 700-square-foot mainsail. The halyard was eased and the clew reefing line winched home. The tack was then pulled down and tied off at the gooseneck and the halyard retightened. The operation took one person less than 3 minutes. The main was very flat and had excellent shape. But then, that is what you would expect from a slab-reefed mainsail.

Running back downwind we shook out the reef and let *Deerfoot* stretch her legs. The breeze was down to 12 knots as we reentered the harbor. Rounding up into the wind, we were ready for the ultimate test. The clew was eased off, and as the main began to luff, Bill went forward and downhauled his hood. The main disappeared into its luff pocket behind the mast.

The only potential flaws I could find in the system deal with the zipper's longevity and the ability to stow the sail in a strong breeze. The first question is strictly economic. Considering the easy installation and relatively low capital investment, the cost of replacing a zipper every few years seems acceptable. Bill expects two years' service in the tropics where the main is left hoisted year round. In higher latitudes where the sail is generally removed and stowed in the winter, life expectancy is much longer. As for the second question, if the system failed, the main would simply have to be stowed on the boom with sail ties. And therein lies the ultimate beauty of the system: if something does go wrong or if it's too windy to zip, you revert to conventional furling.

If you detect a note of enthusiasm for this furling system you are correct. Zip Stop is the first *seamanlike*, easy-to-use approach to a mainsail-furling system I have seen.

Regardless of the type of furling systems you use, be realistic about what they will and will not do for you. If your sailing waters are protected and wind strengths consistent and moderate, some of the heavily advertised systems may work out. But if you are heading offshore, be very careful about roller sailhandling gear and your dependence upon it in heavy going.

Twin Headstays

Another approach to sailhandling in the forward triangle is the use of twin headstays. Once considered only in the context of bluewater passagemaking, today they are finding their way aboard craft with more varied purposes. You need not have a trip to Tahiti in mind to make good use of this form of rigging. The versatility and ease of sailhandling they bring in the trades are even more valuable in variable winds closer to home. With a properly set up twin headstay system, you can have two weights and sizes of sails ready to go. If you're on a light beat with a large genoa and the wind comes up, changing down to a comfortable #3 can be accomplished quickly and easily, even when you're shorthanded.

Side-by-side twin headstays originally evolved for use in the trades. Two identical jibs, one poled out to each side, helped self-steering and eliminating gybe-related risks to the mainsail. There were disadvantages to the practice, though. The main often had to be set with a deep reef to reduce the rhythmic rolling induced by the poled jibs. Our own experience in various trade-wind belts taught us that stable, never-changing wind doesn't exist, which meant we were always trying to alter sail trim, and with jibs on poles that option is limited.

Intermezzo had twin fore-and-aft headstays. Reaching in the Torres Strait, between Australia and Papua New Guinea, we were using the #3 jib on the afterstay. The light #1 reaching jib is rolled up on the outer stay.

Charlie Hast photo

Intermezzo's reaching jib is being used to windward, while a drifter is free of the stay and to leeward. In heavier going the reacher would be dropped in favor of the smaller #3 shown rolled up on the inner stay.

And now the advent of powerful self-steering devices has eliminated the main reason for twin downwind headsails. At the same time, however, rig size in proportion to boat size has grown, making sail changing more difficult for shorthanded crews.

With twin headstays you can have two headsails, of different sizes, hanked on and ready to go, which means that the time you spend forward, whether you're changing up or down, is reduced sharply.

If you have roller-furling, twin headstays make all the more sense. With twins you can have two sizes of genoa or jib rolled up and ready to go at a moment's notice.

Once you have decided to go the twin-stay route, you have to decide whether you want fore-and-aft or side-by-side twins. There are advantages and disadvantages to each.

Fore-and-aft twins can be set up tighter, so offer better sail shape and control. They may require running backstays where the afterstay comes into the mast (if it comes in more than a foot or so below the forward headstay, it will cause eccentric loading). The outer headsail may have to be rolled before you can tack or gybe (there usually is not enough space between the two stays to allow clean sailhandling). This problem isn't as great as it seems, because in upwind sailing, you set the smaller, heavier sail, which is always on the afterstay and can be tacked conventionally.

Side-by-side headstays don't have the tacking and gybing problem. They can be used by all your headsails, and in some cases, especially with hank-on headsails, offer easier handling.

There are two main disadvantages to side-by-side headstays. The first is in controlling sag. The static backstay tension you wind into your rig at the dock is divided between both stays, which means that either one or the other will sag more than if all that backstay tension went into a single stay. As the winds pick up, sag results in a fuller jib—precisely what you don't want at that point. The headsails can be hollowed out more than usual to compensate for the extra sag, but then in light airs when the stay is tight, the sails will be too flat.

The second problem comes with chafe. If your headsail is set on the weather stay and you're sailing a bit free, the luff on the sail will rub across the leeward stay, which is hard on the seam stitching. The cure is to have a long vertical chafe patch put onto the luff of your headsail.

A third less severe problem is that hanks can interlock or jump from one stay to another; it is considered a fairly common

The Deerfoot 69 *Wakaroa* uses closely spaced fore-and-aft twins. The separation between the two stays is about the minimum to have any hope of clearing the outer headsail on a tack, although the normal procedure for this type of rig is to roll the outer headsail before gybing and use the inner headsail when beating.

occurrence on boats where the stays are set close together or there's considerable headstay sag. Tom Blackwell did away with conventional hanks on his third circumnavigation with the 56-foot *Islander*, preferring instead to shackle his headsails to their respective stays.

Aboard *Intermezzo II* we experimented with keeping one of the two headstays substantially tighter than the other. The theory was that we would carry the upwind headsail on the tight stay. Since it would have most of the backstay tension on it, we could get a flat sail. The loose stay would be used when we were reaching or sailing off the wind. The disadvantage was that we lost the ability always to carry sail on the leeward stay to reduce chafe. It seemed to work out, but we were totally dependent on our chafe patch to protect the luff seam stitching.

Even though I don't like twin-poled headsails, there are some excellent results to be obtained with one sail on the pole to windward and a second sheeted free when sailing off the wind. Up through moderate conditions a yankee can be carried as close to the wind as 85 degrees apparent. At the same time it seems to feed the leeward headsail, usually a light genoa, with clean air. Running off, when you would expect the leeward sail to be blanketed by the main, the poled-out sail seems to circulate wind to leeward, keeping the genoa filled down to 160 degrees apparent.

Within the bounds of one pole and two sails, which are probably sitting in your sail locker, you can carry your basic downwind sailplan from a beam reach to a shy run without removing poles or changing sheet leads.

The mainsail, fully hoisted, also benefits. It is no longer just a steadying sail but can contribute to the performance of your vessel. As long as you have spreader chafe patches, stainless rigging, and a good vang to the rail, the main won't have chafe problems.

There are several things to remember when rigging twins. First, be careful of eccentric loads in the mast. You may need running backstays. Next, take care with how the loads are distributed into your tangs at the deck. Again, eccentric loads must be watched. If you are planning long passages, you should apply vertical chafe patches to your headsails. And finally, if the mast is substantially tapered or a minimum size, check with your mast maker to see if the rig will stand the eccentric loads the twin headstays may put on it.

Do twin headstays have a place in your cruising plans? If you do even occasional passages or sail in an area with very changeable conditions, I would say yes. Based on our experience, I would go with the fore-and-aft system on yachts 35 to 50 feet long or where roller furling is utilized. When boat size gets large enough that you want to be able to carry and easily tack two different sizes of headsails *without* roller-furling, consider side-by-side twins. However, in order for side-by-side stays to be effective, the boat must be able to take high static loading on the backstay.

Sailhandling in heavy weather is probably the most onerous chore aboard. But with a little preplanning, the right techniques, and some takedown lines, it can be accomplished with a minimum of discomfort and trouble.

Shown are the working ends of side-by-side roller stays.

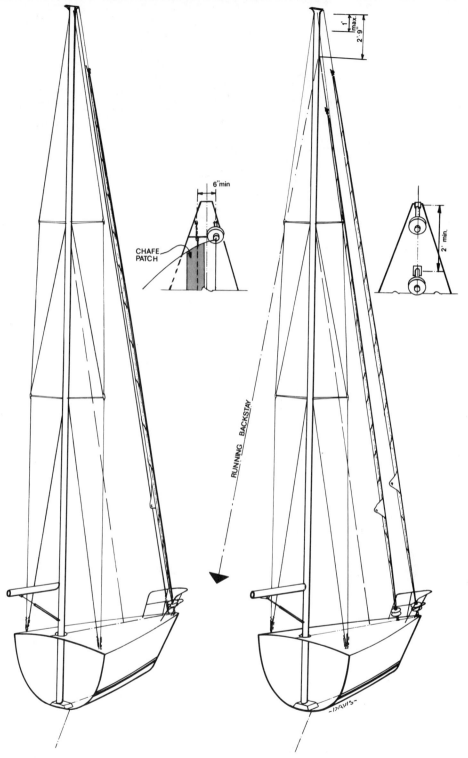

There are many ways to rig twin headstays. Shown are two approaches—side-by-side and fore-and-aft—with ideal minimum dimensional tolerances. Note the running backstays with the fore-and-aft twins. The need for runners will be determined by the vertical spread between stays at the masthead and the strength of your mast.

BEING COMFORTABLE AT SEA

It is dark and squally as *Intermezzo II* blasts her way north towards New England. The east-northeast wind and Gulf Stream seas set the tempo as her powerful hull moves along at just under 10 knots. She and I are in our element: a hard-driving reach. But below the crew is rebelling.

It's a familiar scenario on many cruising yachts. Excited to be away from the dock, the skipper revels in a strong breeze. The distaff side of the crew, on the other hand, prefers a more peaceful passage.

Mournfully I look at the steam gauge swinging between 9.5 and 10.2 knots. Today is the first good sail we have had in months. But Linda doesn't care that our 62-foot express is comparatively stable, seakindly, and comfortable. "If we were out here in the old *Intermezzo*," I say, "not only would we not be going anywhere, we would be getting creamed."

Masculine seagoing logic fails. Linda refuses to bite the apple. Behind those steely hazel eyes, I see a vision of a house and garden on stable land. It is time for action. With a sigh I put a reef in the main.

There are a number of things you can do to make your boat easier to handle and more comfortable downwind;first is a tripping reef (TR), which raises the boom so it won't drag in the water if you are heeled suddenly by a gust or wave. Preventers (P) on the main boom and spinnaker pole should lead to the bow,through a block,and back to the stern,where they can be handled from the cockpit.

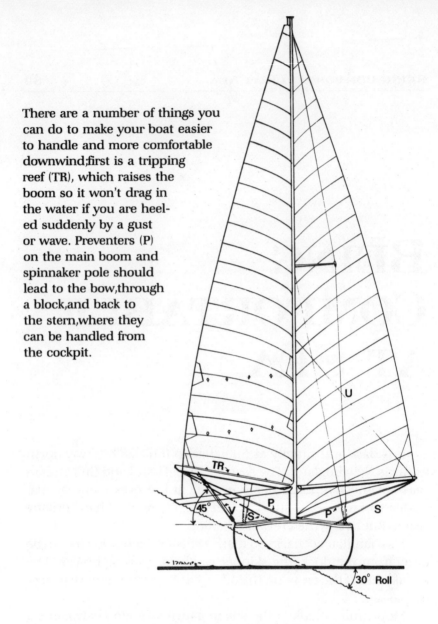

"There, there," she says solicitously. "That isn't so bad, is it?"

Intermezzo II is sailing comfortably on her feet and her speed has dropped only 0.3 knot. I am forced to agree.

This example illustrates a lesson in seagoing comfort we have learned over and over. There is an optimum balance between speed and comfort for any given occasion. Into this equation must be factored the vessel's sailing characteristics, the wind, and sea conditions. There are no hard and fast rules, but some of our experiences may help in your own experiments to achieve greater seagoing comfort at only a modest cost in distance made good to windward.

Going to windward you have two basic approaches to improving comfort. Reducing sail, and thus the angle of heel, is often the most successful. If the seas are up, slowing boatspeed will reduce pounding. Another approach is to vary your angle of attack to the seas. The further off the wind you sail, the more you reduce pounding, and the more upright the boat sails, allowing a greater spread of sail and turn of speed for a given level of comfort.

It is two days later as *Intermezzo II* approaches Cape Hatteras. The wind has gone to the north and is gusting into the forties, and we are slamming forward under deeply reefed main and heavy staysail. The steep seas opposing the Gulf Stream are now making this passage an endurance contest for all aboard.

The wind is coming to us courtesy of a stationary high-pressure system. Continual changes in velocity make it impossible to adjust the sail we are carrying to suit conditions perfectly. To make the best of the norther, we adopt the tactic of pinching up in the heaviest puffs and largest sets of seas and then falling off to a better sailing angle in the lulls or when the seas moderate.

We often found that this technique, sailing a little too close to the wind, worked well when we were temporarily overpowered or made uncomfortable by the seas. On the other hand, in very short, steep seas, falling off and reducing speed by shortening sail can be the more comfortable solution. And if you have time and sea room, it may be better simply to heave-to for a while, giving the weather a chance to abate before you continue.

Off the wind the situation is more interesting. Discomfort arises from a number of factors not at work on the upwind course. Athwartship rolling is the worst. Next is careening about on the faces of the waves as they sweep underneath the hull. The appropriate remedies will depend on the type of vessel, her self-steering abilities, the stability of wind direction and velocity, and sea conditions.

The most important ingredient in the equation is self-steering, especially at surfing speeds. On modern yachts with fin

The jibsheet(S)should lead as far
aft as possible or at the widest
angle to reduce loads on the
pole.The boomvang (V) is
best led from the rail outboard at a 45-degree
angle to a new bale
on the boom. This re-
duces boom loads,
and the safety
factors are im-
proved should
the boom dig
into a swell.

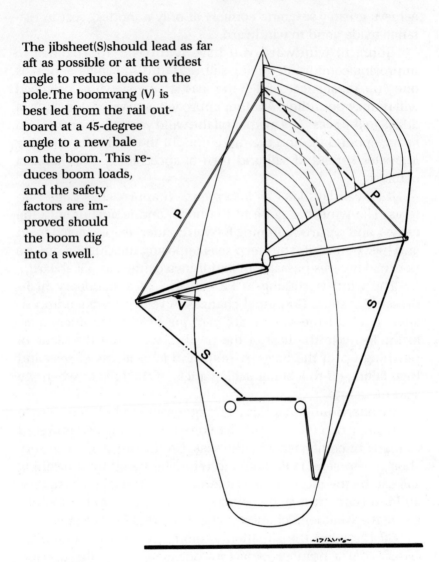

keels and spade rudders and powerful self-steering systems,
you may be able to *add* sail to reduce motion. While this may
sound like a paradox, it is manifestly true. Adding sail and speed
frequently helps combat rolling. Dynamic stability is conferred
by the increased speed, and the boat's steering gear can better

cope with the waves. The same principle that keeps a gyroscope spinning in place helps keep you stable.

It is 0600, and Linda has just informed me it's my watch. With a groan, I pry myself from the saloon cushion. We have been reaching towards Panama for the past two days in strong southeasterly winds. The Force 5 to Force 6 breeze has us at speed, and we have put 443 miles behind us in the last 48 hours.

But now the wind has shifted to the east, maybe even a little north of east. Our speed is still good, but *Intermezzo II*'s motion has increased as the wind pressure on the sails has eased. There is a chance to carry the yankee on the spinnaker pole. I decide to experiment. The slack jibsheet is lead through the end of the pole, and the pole is hoisted into position and secured. I run off square, allowing the big yankee to collapse in the lee of the mainsail. Quickly I haul it through the forward triangle and with a last effort sheet it home. I adjust the autopilot back to 210 degrees, and we are once again flying, only this time minus a lot of motion.

By winging out the yankee I have accomplished two things: first, the sail is drawing more efficiently, giving us better boat-speed. Second, its new position reduces the boat's tendency to yaw up to windward as the seas rush under our stern.

Later that afternoon, Panama is only 24 hours away at our present rate of speed. We are all looking forward to transiting the canal. The wind begins to drop a bit and continues to back until it is nearly square off the stern. *Intermezzo II* is clearly unhappy, and she swings back and forth on the leftover seas, a most un-comfortable way to travel.

The solution to the problem lies once again in sail area. With the yankee still poled out to windward, we hoist the single-luff (cruising) spinnaker to leeward. The main is still reefed from our earlier reaching, so the spinnaker fills well, and our speed jumps a full 1.5 knots. More important, our motion settles down. Even Linda comments favorably, despite our now averaging better than 11.5 knots!

Older designs, those yachts with heavier displacement and keel-hung rudders, may not be able to handle the steering loads that come with the high downwind speed and surfing. On these

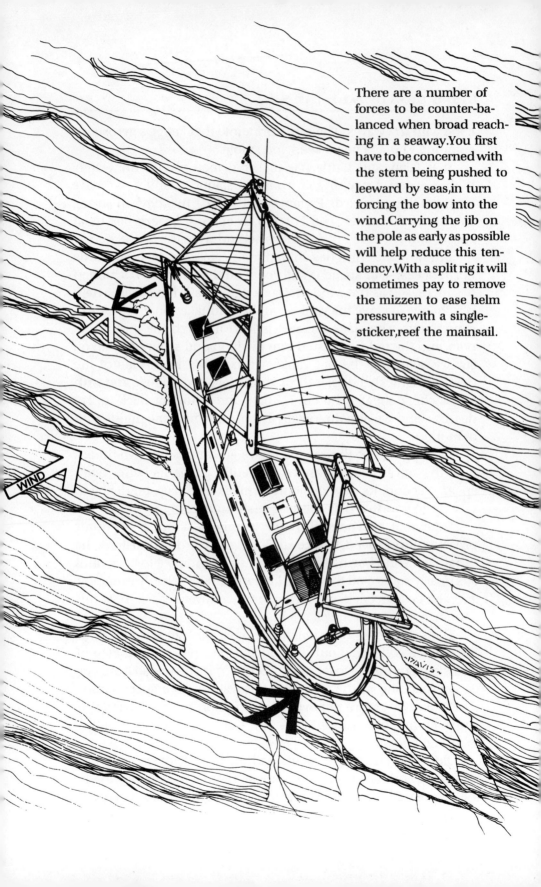

There are a number of forces to be counter-balanced when broad reaching in a seaway. You first have to be concerned with the stern being pushed to leeward by seas, in turn forcing the bow into the wind. Carrying the jib on the pole as early as possible will help reduce this tendency. With a split rig it will sometimes pay to remove the mizzen to ease helm pressure; with a single-sticker, reef the mainsail.

WIND

boats, carrying a staysail or sheeting a reefed main close to the centerline will reduce rolling.

You should avoid running absolutely square if possible. Tacking downwind, the alternative, allows the apparent wind to come forward and build, which in turn reduces motion. Sometimes as little as 10 degrees up from a dead run will do the trick. And as a bonus, most yachts actually move faster by enough to more than compensate for the increased distance being traveled.

As the seas and wind go more on the quarter, the self-steering system starts to work harder. At the point where it no longer adequately controls the vessel, the quartering seas or wind puffs will start rounding the boat up. The boat heels, the sails luff violently, and the crew may even have to assist the self-steering to get back on course. Here you have two choices. You can pick a course slightly more to leeward. (Even if your direct course is higher you may want to fall off, hoping for a freeing windshift later on. Or take a last short hitch closer on the wind to compensate.) This change in angle may be just enough to keep the wind or wave faces from overpowering the steering. If the boat still tends to round up, you will have to reduce sail. Try reducing the mizzen or mainsail area before changing down the headsails. It helps steering to keep the center of effort forward in the rig. Our own experience is that on long downwind passages, sail and course angle combinations have to be varied frequently in response to the changing wind and sea conditions.

Increasing or decreasing sail area to meet changing wind and sea conditions could well be all you'll need to do to keep your boat comfortable at sea. Being flexible in your sailing angle if you have the sea room may make matters even better; slight changes in course can make life aboard much more pleasant. (Don't be surprised if course changes need to be made frequently.) And finally, be willing to experiment. The potential combinations of wind, sea, and course are endless. There is almost always a better way.

ENSURING SAFETY AT SEA

I always assumed that if either Linda or I went for an unexpected swim while underway, it would be next to impossible for the other to get the boat turned around in time to find the one overboard. Having to singlehand because the other was seriously injured wasn't a pleasant prospect either. As a result, we developed a conservative approach to working safely on board.

WORKING ON DECK

The first risk to eliminate was becoming separated from the boat, which meant wearing a safety harness. Then, even if someone did fall overboard, he or she was still with the boat via the harness tether.

The words safety harness usually conjure up visions of sailing in gale-force winds against monster sea waves. But I feel that you are most vulnerable on a deck in calm conditions. It is then when your guard is down. You don't expect the errant wave or

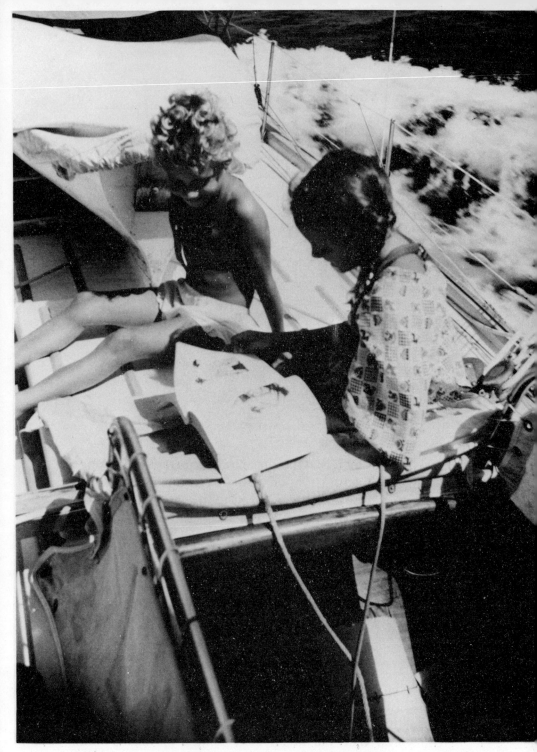

Elyse and Sarah had 20-foot tethers on their harnesses aboard *Intermezzo*, which allowed them to go from the main saloon to the cockpit while still attached. At sea they always wore their harnesses if they were going into the cockpit.

unexpected lurch that could send you swimming instantly.

For that reason it has always been our rule to wear harnesses *whenever* we leave the cockpit if under way. No, it is not always necessary, but by getting used to the harness and having it on, is second nature to use this gear if an emergency erupts. At night, we hook up our harnesses before we leave the companionway. Linda and I each rest better knowing the other is securely tethered to the boat.

The safety harness itself has come a long way. Strongly made units are now available at most marine chandleries. I like a harness with heavy-duty webbing, at least 2 inches in width, triple-stitched to D-rings. For attachment we use a caribener (a mountaineering-type hook), which is easy to operate and has a mechanical interlock; if you are thrown to the end of the tether the strain can be enormous. For cold weather we have safety harnesses sewn directly onto our flotation jackets.

Tethers should be made from $\frac{7}{16}$-inch three-strand nylon. We each have two: a long one for use on deck, which when hooked back on itself (when not in use) reaches to 12 inches off the deck, and a short one (about 3 feet long) for use when we are seated or at the wheel.

There are definite rules about where you hook safety harnesses. We found that padeyes or weldments at the companionway hatch were handy for coming on deck in rough weather. Another attachment point should be close by the helmsman so he or she can use the short tether. When working on deck we hook onto a jackstay of $\frac{3}{16}$-inch plastic-coated stainless steel wire. The jackstay is attached near the cockpit and then runs forward to the inner headstay and back aft again on the other side. The decks should be kept clear for a straight shot from cockpit to bow in order for the safety harness to run on this wire smoothly. Then, once you hook onto the jackstay, you can work anywhere on deck without ever having to unhook. And if you do find it necessary to unhook, always attach the second tether securely before releasing the first.

Avoid using lifelines and stanchions as attachment points. They are notoriously unreliable under load. Standing rigging should be used only as a last resort.

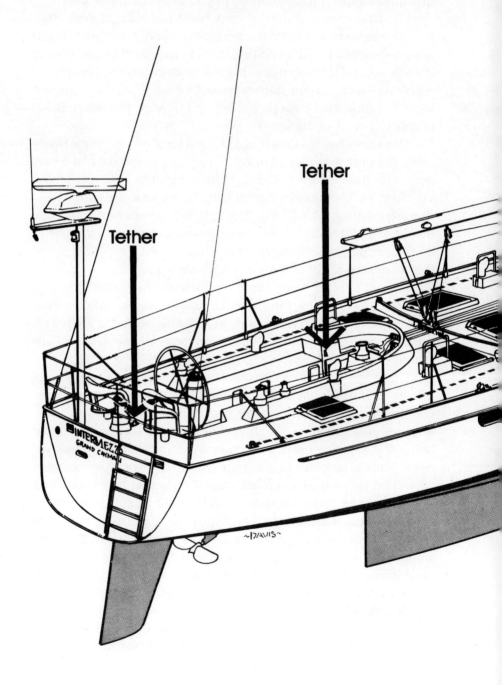

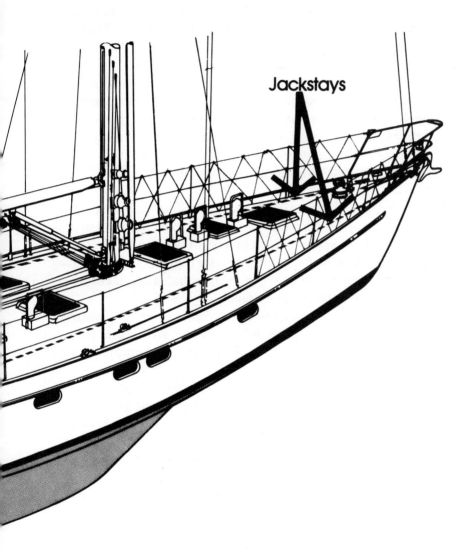

Jackstays

The safety harness system we use on our boats will work on any size vessel. You need a padeye for tethering the harness at the helm and companionway. Then a jackstay (a plastic-coated stainless steel wire) is run from a padeye on one side all the way aft, forward and around the inner forestay, and back aft again. This wire allows you to remain attached while working anywhere on board.

On *Intermezzo* we also attached a 15-foot line to a padeye at the companionway entrance that allowed us to remain hooked up even when we were down below. We could come on deck, take a look around, perhaps go aft to read the taffrail log, and return below without having to think about where or to what to attach ourselves. It was handy for the children during the day-time as well. Their rule was to hook up before entering the cock-pit at all times. As the cockpit was more secure on *Intermezzo II* and the children were older and more responsible, this rule was only enforced in the evenings or if they were on deck without an adult close by.

The second way to minimize the risks of falling overboard, or simply falling, is with secure handholds. Your boat should have handholds anywhere you will have to work. They can be dinghy rails, cabinside handrails, standing rigging, mast bars, or handrails over dorades. *Life lines are the handholds of last resort and should never be totally relied upon.*

When you move from hold to hold, you should keep your center of gravity low for maximum stability. With your feet spread, knees bent, and chest hunched forward, you are less likely to be knocked about by an errant wave.

As you work on deck you learn to anticipate the boat's heave and roll. An alert cockpit crew can shout a warning about an unusually large or misshaped wave. But you will feel it as it hits and have time to brace yourself if you are aware of vessel motion. In many cases you can detect a slight change in the pattern of motion just before a big one hits.

While you can concentrate on handholds when you're sim-ply moving about, it's a different matter when there's work to be done. Your attention is diverted and you have to put at least one hand to the ship's business. I like to brace myself to windward of the work so that any tendency for the boat's motion to fling my body to leeward (and overboard) will be checked by my brace.

If a line has to be rove on the boom and the bales are over-board, you have to lean out, a most uncomfortable and poten-tially dangerous situation. In this case, make sure your tether is secured at the minimum length. It may be necessary to hook your knees under the lifelines in these circumstances. (Presumably you inspected the lifeline systems and attachment points with care and seized all lifeline gates in port *before* you began your passage.) If you can head up and sheet the boom inboard to avoid hanging out, so much the better.

Avoid relying upon sheeted sails for support. When you lean against the boom or a headsail clew, even when a steady wind is blowing, you are also betting that the sheet or traveler will stay in place. What happens if it has nearly chafed through or isn't cleated securely?

Handling a headsail in a seaway or heavy wind demands caution. A gust of wind or a sea can catch the partially dropped

Unhappy at having to pose for yet another photo, Elyse demonstrates our jackstay.

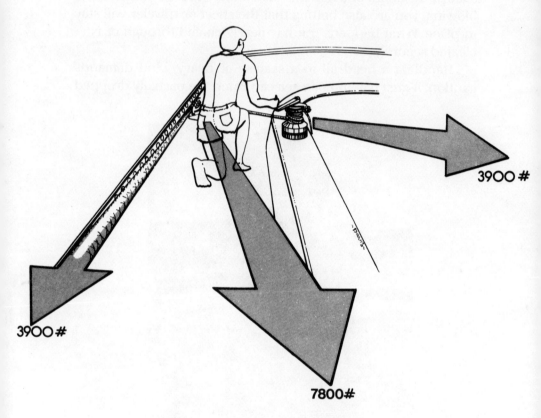

3900#

3900#

7800#

Avoid placing your body in the bight of a stressed sheet. The strains are frequently double the working load, and if something fails, you are in the line of fire.

sail and blow it overboard. Always position yourself so that you are to windward of the sail, and do not stand on the cloth. Not only will it be slippery, but it can take you with it as it goes. If the sail does begin to blow overboard, have a firm idea of when the battle is lost and it is time to let go. At some point the sail is simply going to take off on its own, and you will be unable to stop it.

When you're working the foredeck, watch for flailing sheets and clews. A loose sheet can snap back and forth through a substantial arc. I have lost numerous pairs of prescription glasses and received an occasional welt by ignoring this rule. The place to be when sheets are flailing is to windward.

Sheets or halyards coiled down on deck present hazards to your feet. If you stand on lines that have a load at one end, you are relying on cleats and winches to keep them in check. If something lets go in a hurry or a crewmember casts loose, you won't be caught if you stand clear.

Experienced seamen never stand in the bight of a line under load. When a sheet runs aft to a snatch or turning block and then comes forward to a winch, the load on that block is twice what it is at the winch. If you stand in the open V and the block fails, you are likely to be injured. The same goes for booms that depend upon halyards, topping lifts, or sheets to hold them in check. If you're standing to windward, you are out of the way if something goes wrong.

Good deckshoes are vital to safety on deck. In our experience different brands have widely varying traction depending upon whether the deck is wet or dry and the type of nonskid pattern on the deck itself. Be sure your shoe tread adheres well to *your* wet, angled deck. Then be certain your sea boots have similar characteristics. Some types of sea boots are adapted from hiking or fishing styles and have very little wet deck traction.

All seagoing vessels should have a toerail at least 2 inches high. It provides a convenient bracing spot when working to leeward on a heeled deck and can catch errant winch handles.

GOING ALOFT

At some point in your cruising you are going to have to leave the relative security of your deck and head aloft. The upper end of the rig should be inspected periodically, as well as before and after every major passage. Time aloft gives you a chance to do some preventative maintenance and can give you confidence from knowing the spar and rigging are in top condition.

There is, however, an element of danger any time your feet leave the deck area even when the boat is dockside or at anchor. Accidents brought on by motion or gear failure can be serious to those both aloft and below. Before you go aloft you should make sure you have the right equipment, follow reasonable precautions, and have some degree of familiarity with the procedure.

My favorite means of going up the mast is with a homemade bosun's chair. We drill in each corner of a piece of ¾-inch plywood (in good condition) a 1-inch hole and make a lifting sling by threading ¾-inch three-strand nylon through the holes, crossing and seizing the line under the middle of the seat. Loops spliced into the ends provide a secure point to attach a halyard. The chair bottom should be about 4 inches wider than your own. The sling lines are lead at 60-degree angles. The combination of angle and chair bottom width should be such that your leg circulation is not cramped by the inward pull of the lifting bridle. Some people pad the leg side of their bosun's chair with foam to help prevent circulatory problems.

We also put a safety lanyard through the lifting eye of our chair. It is a length of ½-inch line to which is spliced a shackle. I attach the shackle to a secure bit of hardware on the mast when I am working. It provides a backup in case the halyard slips.

All tools you take aloft should be secured to the chair by lanyards. A bucket attached to the chair is also handy for dropping tools into (even though they are on lanyards). It keeps the tools from becoming tangled in the rigging when you are heading up or down and is a good receptacle for trash and spare parts.

As an extra safety precaution, despite the lanyards, we always make sure no crewmember is anywhere near the glide path of errant tools.

Some of our more cautious friends also hook a chest safety harness to a second halyard when they go aloft. If the primary halyard fails, they will be held by the second. Because I inspected my halyards regularly, I didn't feel the need for the backup, but I always hold on securely to the rigging as I move about.

When I would go aloft for a routine inspection, I carried a basic inventory of tools and gear: rigging knife, vise grip, large screwdriver, and spare running light bulb. The halyard was run through a role of duct tape so the tape was held conveniently right in front of me, ready to use if I found any rough spots that might snag sails.

I also took along a tube of silicone. Where cotter keys or bolts are a source of problems and taping is not practical, a dollop of silicone provides excellent chafe resistance.

There are three basic means of getting aloft once you are ready. You can use a tackle and pull yourself up. I like a three-to-one purchase with ⅜-inch line (easy on the hands) and a ratchet block at the top. The ratchet block allows you to rest between heaves with very little strain on the line. This method should be an in-port procedure only.

Second, someone on deck can winch you up on an external halyard. You can pull on the halyard to assist the deckhand.

The preferred system, though, is to put the halyard tail on the electric windlass and let it do the heavy work. This is the method that Linda and I employ. I feel it is safer than hand work,

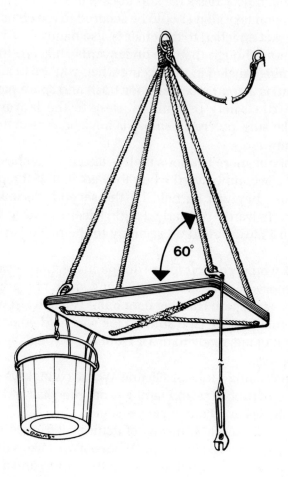

Here is an inexpensive yet functional bosun's chair. Note the tethered tools (for safety) and bucket. The lanyard shown at the top enables you to secure yourself while working, just in case something slips on the halyard.

and because it is so easy, we tend to make more inspection trips to the masthead.

A number of our cruising friends have mast steps to get aloft. They are quicker to use than a halyard/chair rig, but they provide less security once you get where you're going as you must hold yourself on as you work. You should always employ a safety halyard and chest harness when you climb mast steps.

Learning to work aloft is not unlike taking your first scuba diving lessons. Neophyte divers, if they are at all anxious, will use a large amount of air and emerge from an easy dive exhausted because of anxiety. The same happens aloft. If you are tense and hanging on for dear life, you will find it more difficult to work aloft, and you will tire quickly.

Familiarity and paying attention to some basic rules are the keys to overcoming the problem of fear. You must be in good physical condition. Working aloft in port can call on a fair amount of exertion. If something does go wrong, your life may depend on your muscles. Working aloft at sea definitely requires strength and dexterity.

Assuming you have the luxury of a power winch or crew to hoist you aloft, the major job you will have is maintaining good control of your body's movement as you are pulled up. This means securing good handholds, working from one stay to another. In port, my favorite system is to tie an external spinnaker halyard (rope) securely off the mast and hang onto it as I travel up. It provides an easy handhold and minimizes my motion.

Any motion felt on deck is magnified aloft. If the deck heaves a few inches, the masthead will swing through a few feet. The wake of a small runabout that barely moves you on deck will push the masthead through a wide arc. When motion is a factor, at sea for example, standing rigging will provide a more rigid framework for bracing than an external line such as I use in port.

Your travel upward should be at a slow, even pace. Anticipate how you will circumvent obstacles. You will need to swing out and around the lower shrouds, intermediate supports, and the cap shrouds. Gravity will tend to pull you towards the mast, and you will have to haul yourself out a bit to keep clear of obstruc-

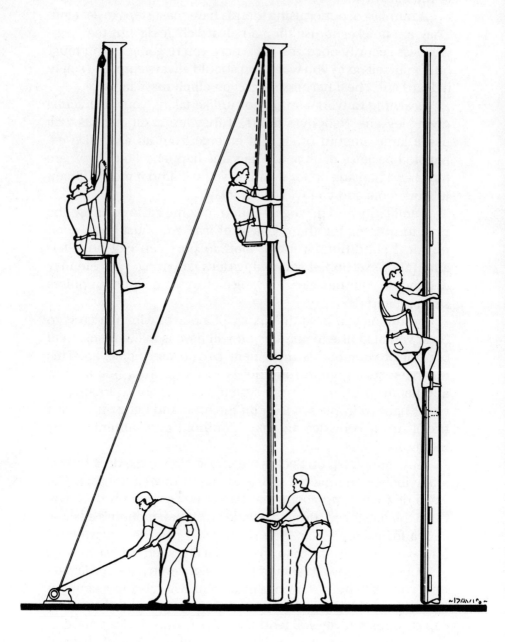

tions as you move up.

During routine inspections I find it easiest to go all the way to the masthead in one trip and then have the deck crew lower me slowly while I look things over. The deck crew should start to slow the pace at which you are being hauled up when you are about 6 to 8 feet from the masthead. With a power winch this is especially important. Communications from masthead to deck can be difficult, and if a motor is grinding away, all but impossible. When Linda winches me up, she stops the motor when I am 6 feet from the masthead (we mark the halyard tails to signal this point) and then inches me up slowly. This way we prevent the end of the halyard from jamming in the block and me from becoming jammed between rigging and the spar.

When I work aloft in port, I wrap my legs around the spar or stay to keep my body in position, leaving both hands free for work. At sea I often need to hold on with my hands as well as my legs. When a sail is set so I can't get a good grip with my legs I'll wrap them around the shrouds, leaning back toward the spar to work.

Another approach is to tie a lanyard from you to a shroud to hold you away from the mast. You can then twist your body, grab the spar with your feet, and keep both hands free to work. The more movement there is aloft, however, the more likely you are to need both feet and hands to stay in one place.

When a sea is running, you must anticipate its affects aloft. Work in advance of the roll, hold on while motion takes over, and

A power winch provides the ideal way to go aloft. If you are going to the masthead, it will be better to take the halyard tail through a turning block at the mast base and then to a winch to avoid being caught between halyard tail and mast at the top. If you are using maststeps, it is best to have someone tail you with a halyard to a saftey harness, or if you are by yourself, tie off with a safety line when you are working. Another approach is to use a tackle with a ratchet block. This system works best with 3-inch ball-bearing blocks and at least ⅜-inch-diameter line.

then work again when the roll momentarily stops. It is frequently easier to work aloft with a bit more rather than less sail
on, because more sail sometimes dampens motion. Conversely,
on occasion we have kept only the headsail up so I could get a
good hold with my feet around the spar.

It may be necessary to work on the headstay or backstay,
away from the spar. Perhaps a backstay link plate needs taping,
or you want to check the headstay wires for damage. In these
cases, go to the masthead, hook onto the stay with a short, heavy
tether, and then have the deck crew lower you down the stay.

If it is necessary to go aloft when the boat is heeled, perhaps
even hove-to, keep your tool weight as low as possible. The more
weight there is aloft, the more heel angle you will experience.

Working on the masthead itself is possibly the most difficult
chore aloft. The bosun's chair can come within only a few feet of
the top, so you are forced to stretch. It may be necessary only to
shorten the lifting sling on the chair to get you close enough
safely. Be wary of standing in or scrambling out of the chair to do
the job. A bosun's chair is most difficult to get back into.

The deck crew should remember that the crew aloft will tire
quickly. It requires a lot of effort just to hang on, let alone perform the tasks at hand. The crew aloft should be brought down
as smoothly and quickly as possible.

It is particularly at this stage of the operation that the importance of experienced deck crew becomes apparent. Mishandling
the tail to the winch can quickly lead to an override. If an override does occur, the crew aloft will have to take his or her weight
off the halyard until the override is cleared, a most annoying
procedure at best. Fewer wraps on the winch will be wanted to
lower the crew than to raise him or her. The line should be
evenly flaked out on the deck and fed smoothly to the winch, not
only to avoid overrides; jerky, stop-and-start motion is very tiring
to the person aloft.

As the bosun's chair nears the deck, the descent should be
slowed, gently. Your leg circulation will have been cramped, and
it will be difficult to hold your balance on deck. Always hold
yourself firmly to rigging or the spar after you have come to rest.
Once your body is secure, step out of the chair, remembering

that the vessel can still roll under you.

After a few trips aloft, you begin to relax and enjoy the view. It is spectacular. The color, visibility, and waves breaking beneath your long, slender hull are breathtaking. Linda often has to remind me I have a reason for going aloft besides the view.

After awhile the urge to capture these vistas on film may become overwhelming. One of the prerequisites is a 28mm (wide-angle) lens. On most double-spreader rigs, if you hold onto the upper spreader and aim the camera in the general direction of the deck, you will get some reasonable shots. Remember to keep your legs and hands out of the lens's view.

You must have the right gear and a bit of practice under ideal conditions before you decide to go aloft at sea. But with experience, good physical conditioning, and a knowledgeable hoisting crew, working aloft can be a real treat.

CLEARING THE DECKS

Where to store gear is a problem most cruisers face. Sails, covers, awnings, spare ground tackle, dive gear, and even outboards, not to mention spare fuel and water, sometimes end up being lashed on deck. It is a dangerous and unseamanlike procedure, but one many of us accept as necessary from time to time. The problem comes in assessing the danger. At the dock or in a calm anchorage, gear on deck looks well secured, of no major concern. But offshore with solid water sweeping on board, the gear not only may be lost but can wreak havoc with deck structures and crew if it comes adrift.

Some years back the powerful ocean-racing sloop *Sorcery*, a C&C 61, was rolled 360 degrees in a Force 9 to 10 gale while crossing the Pacific from Japan to the United States and dismasted. She was carrying spare diesel fuel on deck in 44-gallon drums, several of which washed overboard. One did not. It ended up in the cockpit, on the leg of a young crewmember. She suffered a severe compound fracture and was lucky to survive the ordeal.

All that weight on deck also compromises a boat's stability. The boat will be more tender than she would be if her gear were stored below or eliminated altogether. Reducing stability at best means an uncomfortable ride. At worst it may make it impossible to sail off a leeshore.

Join us now for a trip along the coast of Central America. A short, steep swell lifts our bow as we motorsail northwest towards Mexico and the Gulf of Tehuantepec just 50 miles ahead. *Intermezzo II* is making good time under main, yankee, and iron genoa. The southerly breeze, what little there is, barely keeps the sails filled and our motion steady.

Sailing directions, cruising guides, and yachting folklore all give the gulf and its infamous northers quite a reputation. Even the southbound ships we talk with speak of it with respect. Linda is nervous. All these comments about steep seas and high winds has her adrenaline flowing before there's even a hint of action.

"Don't worry," I say reassuringly. "We don't have to deal with a Gulf Stream or the Agulhas Current here, and there isn't sufficient fetch for a good sea to build. Besides, we can always duck into shore if it blows too hard." Given some of the really bad conditions she has been through, I can't understand her concern. "Regardless of what sort of weather we get, it can't be as bad as what you've already seen." Linda sees that as small consolation.

I make a turn around the decks, checking fittings, lashings, and sheets for chafe: best to do it now when the seas are calm. Even though we have never had solid water on deck, I throw an extra line over the dinghy.

Dinner is succulent roast chicken, fresh beets, and lobster salad, served early. Before Linda secures the galley she makes a double batch of popcorn. Popcorn is the mainstay of our existence when things get tough. The crew of *Intermezzo II* is ready for the norther.

The wind begins to swing to the northeast, a sure sign of action to come. The breeze, still light, is too far forward for headsails, as our apparent wind is almost on the nose. I am forced to douse the yankee. An hour later there's more wind though, and we are sailing; Mr. Perkins takes a well-earned rest as *Intermezzo II* charges ahead on a close reach. The wind finally plateaus in the 25-knot range, and with the yankee back up and a reef in the main, *Intermezzo II* is rapidly eating up the miles. Sailing like this, she is a thing of beauty. Her long waterline and powerful hull sections are at their best, and her steam gauge shows a steady 9.7 to 10 knots.

We are fortunate that the boat has ample stowage in her forepeak and engine room. Our decks are clean of extraneous gear, except for the dinghy nestled to port alongside the mast. We have not always been so lucky. On smaller boats we've needed to use more of the interior volume for living space, leaving less for boat gear, and the decks have not always been so ready for sea as *Intermezzo II*'s.

One of the difficulties in recognizing the change in your vessel's motion that results from all that gear on deck is that the gear accumulates slowly. Because the change is gradual, usually you don't notice the difference in how she handles. If you have a lot of weight topside, try leaving it at the dock for an afternoon sail. The difference in stiffness and boatspeed will be enormous and readily apparent.

It is 2200, and the wind is beginning to build again. In the last 2 hours the barometer has risen 4 millibars. The high-pressure system caught behind the mountain range at the head of the gulf must be ready to spill over. I ask Linda to come on deck and bring with her my foul-weather-gear top. As I slip into my slicker I explain the coming sail changes.

"Take the boat off the pilot. Hold her as high as you can without tacking. I want the jib to luff inboard. As soon as I drop it, head off a bit to keep from getting into irons. Once I have the yankee secured, I'll hoist the staysail. Flip the pilot back on then, and start to trim in the sheet." It sounds easy enough, but with the wind gusting into the forties and a very steep 8- to 12-foot sea running, it will take a fair amount of skill on the helm to keep the yankee onboard and the foredeck crew relatively dry.

A flat section of sea comes our way, and Linda begins to head up. I clip my safety harness to the jackstay and quickly move forward. The yankee halyard is first flaked out on deck and knotted at the bitter end. The jib begins to luff. "Hold her just like that!" I holler aft.

I release the halyard and the sail drops halfway, and then wind pressure starts it climbing the headstay. I have to go to the bow to haul it down. It is a struggle to get the sail tie around the head and halyard. I work aft along the rail, securing the sail to the stanchions. Our bow netting takes care of the rest. In another minute the heavy staysail is up and luffing. Still dry, I move aft to help Linda winch in the last few feet.

"Don't you think you should stow the yankee?" Linda asks.

"No, it will be okay. The seas aren't coming on board, and besides, I might get wet the next time."

We tack to port to close with the weather shore, seeking the calming influence of land on sea. The wind continues to build. With it now blowing a steady 40-plus knots and gusting into the fifties, we understand from whence the steep seas have come. *Intermezzo II* blasts through the waves with little motion but much noise as the bigger waves try unsuccessfully to impede her progress.

Every now and then we pick up solid water. The waves, influenced by shore, head straight on our bow, and the tops of the bigger ones roll down the deck. *Now* I would like to stow the yankee in the forepeak, but working by myself up forward in these conditions would be very difficult. I decide to chance riding the situation out until we are closer to shore and in smoother water.

Twelve miles from the weather shore haven we run into an enormous fleet of fishing vessels out working the shallow banks. Linda counts 40 radar targets at one time. We will have to stand offshore, outside of them. We are stuck in the heavy seas.

In leaving a sail lashed on deck with the possibility of weather making up, I have broken a fundamental tenet of seamanship. A good seaman always assumes the worst and prepares as if it is about to overtake him. The situation in which I find myself should never have occurred. When I dropped the yankee, I should have removed it from the headstay and stowed it. I have been lulled into complacency by the seakeeping ability of our boat, and I have underrated the weather.

Dawn arrives, and the wind seems to increase in the gusts, but as we close the shore, the seas are rapidly moderating. The fishing fleet is behind us, and land is just a few miles to windward. In another hour I go forward. The yankee partially trails over the side. Six hanks have been wrenched loose from the headstay, broken in half by the force of the sea. The sail is torn from leech to luff in two spots, and there are a half-dozen other rips. Two of our stout lifeline stanchions are bent at right angles from the sail and sea pressure. It is not a pretty sight.

I have no one to blame but myself. With just 5 minutes of preventative work on the bow when I first changed headsails all this would not have happened.

There is no place for complacency on a boat. The sea is unforgiving and must never be underestimated.

SAILING SHORTHANDED

Most of today's yachts have aboard a crew that is much smaller than was considered safe even a decade ago. Modern sailhandling aids; lighter-displacement, better-tracking hulls; and reliable self-steering have freed the skipper from the necessity of a large crew. Now the largest number, by far, of successful long-term cruisers are two-person teams. If there are other souls aboard, they are usually children. Closer to home, while social requirements may dictate a larger crew, the lack of watchstanding chores makes it possible to look soley at the number of hands required to sail and moor when making crew size decisions.

GENERAL CONSIDERATIONS

When Linda and I began to plan for extended cruising, we weighed the pros and cons of taking along crew. We had several friends with whom we had raced for many years, and if one of them could have gotten away, we might have taken extra help. But finding someone whom we didn't already know who could live in harmony with us and our two children while cramped in a 50-foot boat seemed to be a major project.

Linda at the helm of *Intermezzo II* during one of our many brisk sails (35 to 40 knots in this photo) around Cape Hatteras.

The obvious advantages of having more crew came in sailhandling, navigation chores, and watch-standing; there is an enormous difference between doing 3 hours on and 6 hours off and doing 3 on and just 3 off! And we had to consider the possibility of an emergency. If something happened to me, another crew would mean help for Linda. On the negative side was mixing unknown personalities in a fixed living space. Even at 50 feet, *Intermezzo* would have been cramped with a nonfamily member aboard. Personal space for stowage would have been further subdivided, and more important, our individual turf would have been reduced. Simple things such as good reading places, cockpit corners, and sea berths that were fine for our crew of four would have presented problems with another person aboard; someone would get the dregs.

The final argument for starting off without another crewmember, however, was that we realized we would probably be sailing only one out of ten days, at the most. The rest of the time we would be at anchor. And while there are advantages in having extra crew offshore, on the hook, regardless of how compatible we were, crew would be a liability.

So we went as a family unit.

Deciding to cruise shorthanded meant special preparation in a number of areas. First, both Linda and I had to be able to handle the boat alone in an emergency should one of us be incapacitated. In this we felt comfortable because, I reasoned, the worst that would happen is that we would travel a little slower. Even if we had to use only the mainsail, we would still get there eventually.

Second, I already knew how to navigate, but Linda still had to learn; a course in celestial navigation taught her the rudiments, and practice advancing our dead-reckoning position during watches brought home the basics of piloting.

My biggest concern was losing one of us overboard. As a result, as we mentioned in an earlier chapter, we adopted some very stringent rules about when to wear safety harnesses, and we installed jackstays.

I considered it more likely that the negatives of sailing shorthanded would hit us in the comfort and convenience areas.

Steering, for example, was a question. Since it is primarily self-steering that makes shorthanded sailing feasible, what would happen if it went out?

Aboard *Intermezzo* we carried two self-steering systems: an autopilot and a windvane. There were times when one or the other had a problem, but both never malfunctioned at the same time.

On *Intermezzo II* we started out with just an autopilot. I felt that the boat's high, broad stern wouldn't lend itself to a vane. At the last minute I realized I should carry a backup pilot aboard, but by then it was too late to arrange to have one sent to us. On our second Atlantic crossing, when we were 26 days out from Cape Town, South Africa, and just four days from Antigua, the pilot went into hibernation. Linda and I were forced to steer watch after watch with occasional help from the kids. We weren't involved in a life-or-death situation, but we were happier to get the hook down in English Harbour than in any other anchorage we visited. Shortly afterward we bought a backup pilot.

When we docked both *Intermezzo*s I pulled out an extra-long but unallocated dockline, just in case. I also pulled two extra fenders from their locker to use if a problem developed.

COMMUNICATING WITH HAND SIGNALS

One of the most difficult problems that arises when sailing shorthanded is communication between the cockpit and foredeck. Just how difficult it can be was brought home to us in a forceful manner one blustery morning off Baja California. A northeasterly gale had sprung up without warning, leaving us on an exposed lee shore.

We were most anxious to get the anchor up and put some sea room between ourselves and the coast. Because of the 40 knots of wind and the rising sea, we had to resort to engine power to bring *Intermezzo* forward on her chain. As the wind would blow her bow off, Linda, at the helm, would correct with the rudder. Since she couldn't see the chain angle from her position, I had to direct her from my position at the bow. She had to play the throttle constantly in the gusts and waves to bring us slowly ahead, yet not override the chain. It was a real balancing act. At the bow it was my job to watch the chain coming aboard and control the anchor windlass while at the same time trying to *shout* aft to Linda to head to starboard, speed up, turn to port, slow down, and so on. Because I was facing forward most of the time, Linda could rarely hear what I was saying above the wind and engine noises. There was considerable confusion between us. That we were able to get the anchor aboard safely and work out to sea was due more to luck than good seamanship. That our marriage and cruising plans survived was a miracle!

That experience convinced me to work out a system of communicating by hand signals, and in our years of cruising we eventually came to use three types. Our anchoring, sail trim, and docking procedures all benefited. Anyone who has watched a crane being operated on a construction site will recognize some of the signals used.

To direct steering under power we hold an arm out straight athwartships to tell the person at the helm to head in the direction the arm is pointing. To request that the helm be centered and that we move forward, we swing the arm fore and aft along the centerline. To indicate reverse, we put our palm up facing the helm and motion aft. A horizontal rotating motion of the forearm and hand indicates come ahead. To ask for increased engine rpms, we spiral our fore finger upwards in a circular motion. Just the opposite, the finger spiraled towards the deck, means slow down. A vertical series of chops with the hand facing outboard means put the engine in neutral. When everything is secured the universal cut across the throat tells the helm to shut down the engine.

For quiet sail trimming, we use a modified version of our steering signals. Circular motion of the arm and hand indicate ease the sheet. A palm facing aft with a pushing motion means trim, and a vertical chop says secure.

Docking requires the helm to signal the line handlers. We normally have a bow line, two springs, and a stern line to throw. The helmsman holds up one finger for the bow and gives a wave when he or she wants the bow line to be tossed. The bow spring gets two fingers, the stern spring three, and the stern line four.

If you don't have deck illumination or if you are trying to protect your night vision by using minimum light, these signals can also be adapted for use with a flashlight. Pointing to port or starboard indicates turning direction. Swinging the light fore and aft on the centerline means steer ahead. Power forward is indicated by a series of quick flashes aimed aft—but not directly at the person steering. Speed up is a spiral motion upwards with the light, and slow down is a spiral motion aimed at the deck. Engine neutral is another sequence of flashes aimed aft.

From time to time we had problems with the person aft at the controls missing signals because his or her attention was elsewhere. When you are depending on hand signals to complete a task, it is obviously important that both parties maintain concentration. Hand signals, ours or your own variation, are not difficult to learn or to employ. In fact, what is necessary are a few practice sessions with your crew without the pressure of actual need or an anchorage of bystanders. An orderly, well-organized, and *quiet* ship is the result.

While our original impetus to develop a system of hand signals was a situation in which the wind made it impossible to communicate, over the years signaling rather than shouting became a habit, and we did it even in calm weather.

As long as you consider what problems can arise as a result of your sailing shorthanded and think out in advance a reasonable means of coping with them, there is, in our opinion, no pressing reason to take crew.

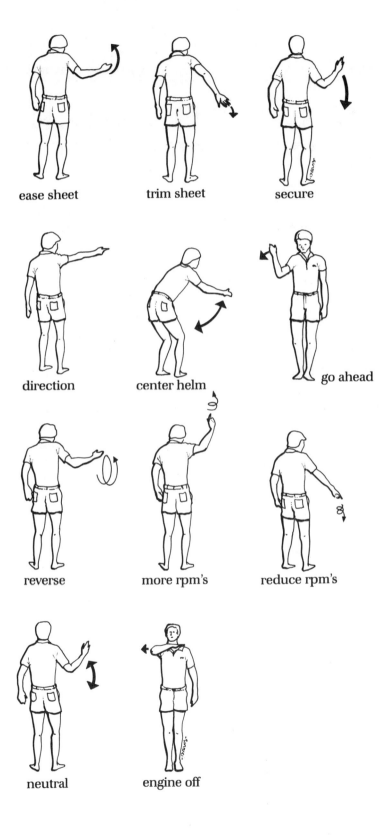

ease sheet

trim sheet

secure

direction

center helm

go ahead

reverse

more rpm's

reduce rpm's

neutral

engine off

HOW TO HANDLE SPINNAKER POLES

Another difficult operation in sailing shorthanded is handling spinnaker or whisker poles off the wind. Handling a heavy, awkward pole on a heaving foredeck can be daunting to even a fully crewed ocean racer. And yet with the proper gear and a little practice, two people can handle the largest poles with a minimum of risk even in heavy weather.

When I first looked at *Intermezzo*'s two spinnaker poles I felt they would never see action with a jib, let alone a chute. They were what are known as "penalty" poles: extra long to accommodate a bigger spinnaker for downwind racing. At 18 feet in length and 6 inches in diameter, they were enormous.

Yet they had one advantage; because large diameters made them very stiff, their walls could be thin, and thus they were light for their length: less than 25 pounds. I could pick one up with ease and from time to time amazed docksitters with my feats of strength and agility by carting these apparent monsters about the foredeck.

Moving a pole in harbor is one thing. Working with it at sea is another. Linda and I evolved a system that eventually led us to treat this gear as we did everything else aboard: with respect and caution but without fear.

The biggest problem was in actually attaching the pole to the mast. Whenever it was possible we hooked on the pole in port when we expected a downwind passage. The inboard end was held securely on the mast while the outboard end would be hooked to the lower railing of the bow pulpit. The only problems with this arrangement were that in this position the pole restricted how far we could open our forward hatch and fouled the staysail sheet if we were hard on the wind.

Setting the pole from here was easy. The topping lift, pole-car lift, foreguy, and afterguy or sheet all had special marks for the initial set. I would start by taking up the afterguy to its first mark. This meant it was slack at first, but as the pole was raised, the guy would begin to pull it aft, preventing it from banging onto the headstay. The foreguy was likewise preset. When the pole was fully hoisted, the foreguy prevented the pole from banging the side shrouds.

With the guys in position, I would attach the topping lift and then take a minute to double-check that the lead of the jib or spinnaker sheet through the pole end was untwisted and clear of the guys and topping lift. From experience we knew that the line should be run through the end of the pole. Attaching the pole to a clew ring could make it impossible to trip the sail clear in a strong breeze.

Then I would hoist the topping lift one-third of the way up, cleat it, and hoist the pole butt two-thirds of the way up. Next I took the topping lift to its final preset mark and then cranked the butt end the rest of the way up to complete that phase of the operation.

As the pole lifted, the afterguy would tighten, automatically pulling the pole aft. If it had been preset properly, the pole would end up close to where we ultimately wanted it. With the exception of the initial attachment on the mast, setting the pole was a one-man operation.

Gybing required a bit more forethought. We started out using the twin-pole system common in big-boat racing in heavier going. But we soon found that it was usually easier for us to "dip-pole" gybe most of the time. With the inner forestay removed, the pole would be tripped from the sheet, hoisted on the inboard end, dropped at the topping lift, and swung down behind the headstay, where the new sheet or guy would be attached; the pole would then be winched home. Gybing was a two-person operation and involved a bit of coordination if the headsail was not to collapse or wrap around the headstay.

If the breeze was up or a sea was running, we would first hoist the second pole and then gybe the headsail or spinnaker, leaving the first pole in position until the sail was drawing. If another gybe was likely, the unused pole was left rigged, with the outboard end lowered and secured to the pulpit.

Intermezzo sailed with genoas and jib topsails, neither of which necessitated a high-pole position, so it was possible for us to use a double car and single track on the front of the mast. The high clew of a yankee jib would make it impossible on most boats to reach the car, so twin tracks would be required if two poles were to be used.

When *Intermezzo II*'s rig was in the planning stage I decided right off to have vertical pole stowage. This arrangement would allow us to keep the pole stowed on the mast out of the way when we headed out to sea, yet permit us to set it easily without having to worry about getting the butt end into the mast socket. Given her very large 25-foot-long pole, we needed all the help we

could get!

On *Intermezzo II* Linda and I were initially so intimidated by our foredeck chores that it took us three days of downwind sailing on our first passage before we tackled a pole set. We found that with the pole stowed vertically, we could hoist it so the outboard end would just clear the lifelines at the shrouds and the loads of the topping lift and butt lift would almost counterbalance. The mast car could be hauled down by hand, and the geometry of the pole and topping lift was such that only a few final tweaks were necessary to get the pole into proper position.

Because of weight, budget, and windage, I opted for a single pole rather than twins as on the old boat. The decision turned out to be a mistake. *Intermezzo II* was too big for comfortable dip-pole gybes, and while we did gybe in strong winds, twin poles would have been more expedient for the two of us.

We also found, as have most experienced cruisers, that vertical mast stowage is fine in port and when running or broad reaching. But in a crosswind or in upwind sailing the poles should be stowed on deck. The weight and windage aloft significantly detracts from weatherliness and stability, not to mention speed.

The structural requirements of whisker poles, which should be used with a jib or genoa only, are often underestimated. The pole may have to see heavy-air downwind work. You may end up reaching with it set with the wind on the beam and the headsail occasionally collapsing. And it could be rolled into the water in a heavy following sea. The differences in cost, weight, and windage between a properly sized spinnaker pole and a lightweight whisker pole are slight. A whisker pole does not belong on a bluewater cruiser.

Another aspect to consider is a storm pole. If you are caught out running in conditions requiring the use of a storm jib, your normal pole may be too unwieldy. Yet a storm jib set downwind without benefit of pole will eventually destroy itself through collapsing and filling. One solution is to use a reaching strut if you have one available. Or consider having aboard a short pole, one just a little longer than a reaching strut, especially for use in severe weather.

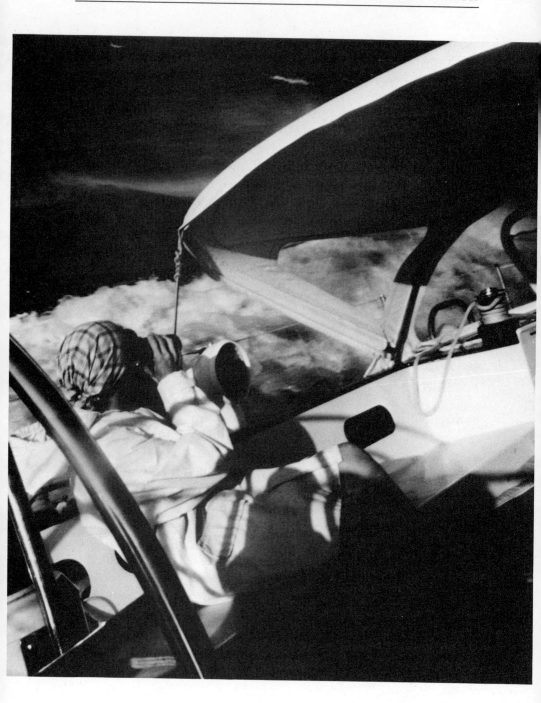

STANDING

WATCH

Because Linda and I decided to cruise without additional crew we knew that standing watches during passages could well be among our more tiring times aboard. Over the years we used a number of different combinations of time on and time off. We discussed the systems used by cruising friends and adapted several, but we never really settled on an ultimate system. Instead, we would look at the particulars of each passage ahead of time and then decide how we would divide up the hours.

For us, the most important consideration involved navigation. I like to be on deck at important waypoints, when it is time to do celestial observations, and whenever the situation calls for tight maneuvering. Whatever system we used had to be worked around these requirements. Next in consideration were Linda's responsibilities with the children and in the galley. And finally, the length of the passage itself affected our choice of watchkeeping system.

Vicki Carkhuff photo

Watch Systems

We have found that on intermediate to long passages it is best to stick with a formal watch system. Even if the off-watch isn't tired, he or she should take time as the clock indicates. Often Linda or I would not feel tired at the end of a watch and think about giving the other a little more sack time. But as much as this extra rest would be appreciated, it would mean that the person extending the work would ultimately be more tired on the next round.

When we started passagemaking we used a 4-hour-on and 4-hour-off approach. The watch was long for the person on, but it generated good sleep (usually) for the one off. Later we switched to a three-and-three pattern. In most cases it seemed to work out better.

As Elyse and Sarah became older, we started letting them (together) take short watch periods during the day. By the time they had reached ages seven and ten, they could keep an eye on things for us during the mid-morning and mid-afternoon and occasionally after dinner, as well. That extra hour or two added to our sleep really felt good.

On two long passages when we were forced to hand-steer because of pilot or vane malfunctions, we found spending any longer than 2 hours on the helm real drudgery and so worked on a two-and-two system; it was tiring, but under the circumstances it was the best system for us.

At night Linda usually took the 1900 to 2200 stretch, I took over until 0100, Linda came on again until 0400, and I stood the last watch, until 0700. This timing allowed me to catch a round of stars as well as the joy of sunrise, while Linda could catch sunset.

Short passages I found more difficult and tiring. Since the beginning and end of each trip involve a lot of navigation, on the short ones it was impossible to work out a systematic approach to watches. While Linda can fall asleep at a moment's notice, it usually takes me two or three days to change my body clock to accept a new sleep pattern. For me, the first days of each passage meant spending a lot of time in the sack with eyes closed and brain open. Therefore, on the shorter passages, or when I wanted to be awake at specific points for navigating, we modified the system to a catch-as-catch-can basis.

Because of our division of responsibilities (I was always ultimately responsible for navigating the boat), before I went off watch I always left written instructions in the log as to course, apparent wind angles, expected windspeed, and the range of wind that the rig should carry. I also noted any special instructions dealing with navigational waypoints, for example, whether I was expecting a shallow spot to come on the depthsounder or perhaps a radar return. I also wrote down the parameters for each instruction. If they were exceeded, in either direction, Linda woke me.

Being dry and comfortable are prerequisites to good watchkeeping. Your cockpit, dodger, and cushions should be laid out with an eye towards sailing, rather than in-port use. You should be able to brace yourself easily on either tack. A low-density red light should be available for reading.

AVOIDING COLLISION

One of the biggest concerns of the person standing watch will be shipping. And although most ships stand reasonable watches, when it comes to avoiding collisions, they are on the lookout for other ships, not small yachts. To compound the problem, from a cruiser's perspective, during daylight hours a small sailboat or powerboat will frequently blend in with the sea, rendering it almost invisible to a large ship until the two are very close. If the ship's watch leaves the bridge unattended for a moment, the yacht may be missed entirely. Radar doesn't help much, either. The small blip of even the biggest radar reflector can easily be lost in the echoes of waves if any sea is running.

At night when you display a masthead tricolor light, your chances of being seen are better. But if there are several other vessels about, you can bet the watch aboard the ship is busily plotting the others' coordinates, course, and speed, which leaves little time for a strange soft light on the horizon. From a practical point of view, the responsibility for avoiding collision with large ships rests with you.

Simply identifying the presence of a ship is, of course, only the first step. You must be able to identify what the ship is doing and its approximate course and speed, while factoring in other special considerations such as the other commercial shipping it may have to avoid. If you don't pay careful attention to identification lights at night, it is easy to become confused, as the following story illustrates.

A light northwesterly breeze pushes the yacht towards the tip of Baja California. With main, mizzen, reacher, and mizzen staysail set, the 45-foot ketch is making good time tonight. The bow wave sings a gentle song, while the occasional whoosh of a porpoise coming up for air keeps the watch alert. To port 10 miles away looms the outline of Cedros Island. With a gibbous moon and clear sky, it is clearly visible.

From time to time the skipper checks the compass and the self-steering and then has a look around the horizon. It has been 10 days since the boat left San Francisco heading south. In the last three days, not a ship has been sighted. Yet there is plenty of traffic out there.

A curious porpoise breaks the water's surface next to the cockpit. As it gulps in air, the skipper of this ketch is startled into wakefulness. For a second he isn't sure where he is; then, realizing he has fallen asleep, he quickly stands up and braces himself against the mizzenboom with his right arm. Ahead, just off the port bow and under the foot of the reacher, he can see the glow of lights. Quickly he scans the rest of the horizon and then settles back to study the lights forward. There are two clusters that appear to be separated by some distance. Without bothering to reach for the binoculars, he decides the two clusters are a tug and a tow. Somewhat groggily he thinks to himself, "I've got plenty of time. If it is a salt barge coming out of Scammon's Lagoon, it can't be making more than five or six knots." He ducks below for a moment to get the coffeepot brewing, but something troubles him as he reaches for the propane valve. He realizes he

Stanley Dashew

Many a quiet watch has been interrupted by the unexpected and noisy antics of these playful friends.

hasn't made a positive identification of the lights; he didn't pick out the steaming or towing lights. The coffee now forgotten, he fumbles in the companionway for the glasses and rushes on deck.

One method of checking a ship's heading in daylight is to study the relative positions of the bow and bridge on the ship. If the two are aligned, the vessel is heading directly for you. If the bridge or aft masts seem to be swung out towards you, it means the heading of the ship is forward of your bow. If the bow appears closer than the stern in angle then the vessel is heading astern of you. However, the relationship of these angles is similar to compass bearings; if they stay constant, regardless of bow and bridge orientation, you are both on a collision course.

It is more difficult to interpret another vessel's movements during daylight than at night. Coincidentally, this is the period when watches are the most lax aboard ships and when many cruisers fail to keep any lookout.

You must be able to determine quickly if a collision will result should you and the other vessel maintain your respective courses, and if so, what action you should take. Taking relative bearings is the simplest method of answering the first question. Using your compass, note the bearing of the approaching vessel. If this bearing remains constant over the next few seconds, the two of you are on a collision course. If the angle gradually widens, the ship will pass by your stern, and if it is closing, it will pass you by the head.

The lights are much closer now. The skipper's first fear is that he will be caught between tug and tow. Then, with a jolt, he realizes the lights aren't a tug and tow at all but a single giant cruiseship. The massive deck illumination has hidden the running lights. Without bothering to pick out the steaming lights and positively discern the liner's course, he throws the autopilot off, puts the yacht about, and then turns on the engine to assist. But the ship seems still to be bearing down on him.

What do you do if you are on a collision course? If there is room, we always prefer to take the ship's stern, rather than try passing by the head. Commercial shipping generally moves at 14 to 20 knots, and the rate of approach is usually deceiving. By

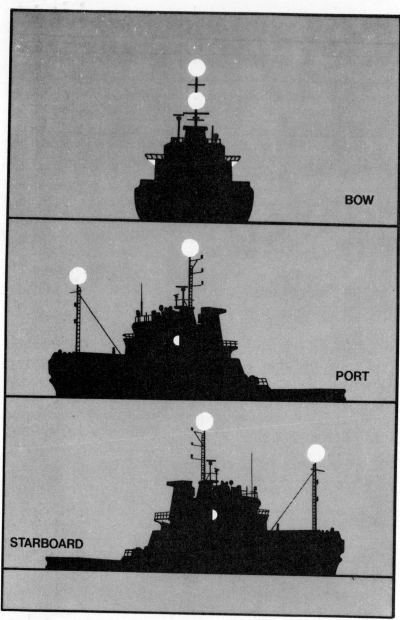

It is vitally important that crewmembers be able to interpret correctly the range lights of other vessels. Shown here are the basic lights of a cargo ship. Two lights, one on top of each other, mean the vessel is heading for you. Bow light to port of the aft light indicates a port heading. If the bow light is to starboard, the vessel is heading to your starboard. Remember, if the angle between your course and the ship's course remains the same, you are on a collision course.

taking the big fellow's stern, you have more flexibility about your own course, to the point where you can reverse it if necessary.

The liner is so close now that without his binoculars the skipper can pick out the steaming lights. They are lined up on top of each other; the ship is heading directly for him! Once again the helm is put over, and this time he gets clear, but the liner passes close enough astern for him to feel the throb of the engines.

Had the skipper of this ketch used his binoculars when he first sighted the lights, he would have been able to tell both the type and heading of the vessel, rendering the last-minute maneuvering unnecessary.

It is easier to pick out a ship's intentions at night than in daylight. The steaming lights, mounted on the bow and a high mast amidships or aft, give pointed indicators of its course. Lined up on top of one another, they are like range lights. You are looking down the centerline of the ship. If the bow light, which is lower than the aft light, is towards you, the ship is on a heading that will cross astern of you. If the bow light is away, the ship is heading past your bow. And if the relative bearing stays the same, you are on a collision course.

A radar provides you with a means of identifying problems at a greater distance than your line of sight. A bearing cursor can be placed on the vessel target. If the ship stays under the cursor, you are converging. In clear weather, however, when a ship is closer than a few miles, never rely on radar; use your eyes instead.

In heavy weather when our own maneuverability is limited and in crowded waters, we try to call approaching traffic on the VHF radio to advise it of our position and ask what avoiding action the master of the ship thinks we should take.

In crowded yachting centers avoiding collision presents different sets of problems. Around the breakwaters of many of today's major marinas there are often significant traffic jams on the weekends. Not only do you have limited space and maneuverability, but also you have to be ready to contend with the unexpected. You can't assume that the other fellow knows the Rules of the Road. Here the easiest course is to sail defensively

The alignment of the foremast on this tanker to the port of the bridge
(to starboard of the observer) means the ship is heading to port of the
observer.

Vicki Carkhuff photo

and to know the fastest ways to maneuver your vessel in an emergency. For example, if you are beating or close reaching, you will head up more quickly if you ease the headsail sheet, than if you use the helm alone. Trying to bear off in any sort of a breeze without letting the mainsheet go is like taking the slow boat to China. And most boats will go head-to-wind more quickly than they will fall off, whether you release the mainsheet or not.

Understanding how to read the lights of other vessels and to discern their movements during day and night is an easily learned skill. Paper models can be used for practice interpretation. Once you have confidence in your own skills, be sure that your crew also learns how to interpret crossing situations. And if they are in doubt in the presence of another ship, be sure you are on deck yourself. Even when you are in the open sea and the right-of-way vessel, always assume you have to get out of a big ship's way. If your own maneuverability is restricted, don't assume the ship will give way until you have had radio confirmation of that fact.

VISIBILITY AT NIGHT

Of course, you must have good night vision to stand an effective watch at night. Being able to see on a dark night is a combination of learned skill and proper environment.

The first criterion is that your eyes be kept in the dark. Exposure to light closes down the pupils in much the same manner as the lens of a camera closes down in sunshine. After even a brief exposure to light, you lose accurate night vision for 15 to 30 minutes.

In order to minimize the possibility of accidental "blinding" aboard our *Intermezzos*, we installed a set of red-coated bulbs, smaller than our usual lights, throughout belowdecks each time we headed to sea. The red color reduces the impact of light on night vision, although it still degrades your vision to a degree.

Some cruisers install double light fixtures with a rocker switch. Set in one direction you have normal lighting; set in the opposite, you have night lighting. Switching on the wrong lights accidentally is common, however, so we preferred switching bulbs.

Lying on the afterdeck of the Solomon Island coaster *Bona*, I am trying to grab a few winks. The deepset throb of propeller and diesel vibrate their way into my body. Tired, frustrated at sleep that won't come, I am nonetheless pleased to be aboard. Linda and I have just had the special experience of visiting the Outlier Islands of the southern Solomons. Because these primitive outposts of Polynesia are encircled by fringing reef, without benefit of harbor or protected anchorage, we are perhaps the first modern-day cruisers ever to visit them. Captain Lanello and his ship have made it possible. On their annual inspection with health officials, police, and insect-control officers, they have offered us their hospitality.

With the excitement of the day behind us, I am now a bit concerned about *Intermezzo*. It is the first time we have ever left her unattended overnight. And while friends ashore (who are also caring for Elyse and Sarah) have said they will keep an eye out, they are landsmen. Even knowing *Intermezzo*'s two big hooks are well set in sand, I still worry.

Unable to rest, I go forward to the wheelhouse. It is the blackest of nights. A strong southeast trade wind is blowing, and low clouds scud by, reflected in the starlight. The moon has already set.

The captain and first mate are having a lively discussion as I enter. "That be the north end of the big island," says the mate, shaking his finger for emphasis.

"No she don't," replies the captain. "It is the reef to the east."

I peer out the window but am unable to see anything. Even though the lighting on the afterdeck is subdued, my night vision is not yet up to the task. I know from experience it will take at least 15 minutes before I can begin to see in the dark.

Slowly my eyes begin to pick out the horizon. By looking out of the corners of my eyes, rather than directly ahead, I can see the white line of surf off the starboard bow. Captain Lanello is right. It is reef rather than island. From his bridge, 15 feet above sea level, he has seen the reef on this moonless night at better than 4 miles. I pick it out at 2.

A few minutes later we can see the briefest outline of palm trees to the north. That will be the island, at a range of 4 to 6 miles easily visible even to an "amateur" like me.

We alter course now, heading for the channel between reefs that will take us to Lom Lom Island and *Intermezzo*. Having seen in daylight the narrow, irregular course that we must follow, I am glad we have a heavily built steel hull under us. But to our island captain and crew, this is no more than a routine passage. Without radar or other navigation aids, in clear weather and foul, they regularly navigate at night in these waters, with only an occasional scratch.

If a moon is up, especially if it is behind you or opposite the direction you are looking, your range of visibility will be greatly extended. High land can be seen at 15 or more miles in clear air. Even with overcast, 4- to 6-mile visibility is possible. If the moon is ahead of you, though, trying to see is like looking into the sun.

The "glare" of the moonlight tends to mask your targets until you are much closer.

Atmospheric conditions also have a great impact on night-time visibility. Clear, dry air is best. Moisture-laden air or air polluted with dust or smoke will reduce the range of visibility.

As we approach the narrow channel, our skipper climbs atop the wheelhouse for a better look. I walk outside towards the bow. From time to time he shouts a command to the helmsman. Over my shoulder I notice a dark blotch on the horizon. Suddenly I realize that right at the critical juncture we will have to deal with a rainsquall. Captain Lanello has seen the clouds as well and calls down for his slicker.

We continue powering towards the opening between reefs. I

With a steel hull and aluminum superstructure, the Solomon Islands trader *Bona* was quite comfortable in a seaway. Note the spotlight above the bridge. It was used on a regular basis when navigating at night through coral.

am distinctly uneasy about the prospect of piloting its narrow confines on a moonless night with rainsqualls about. But at the last minute our captain orders engines slowed and allows the squall to overtake us.

In 15 minutes it has passed by, and we continue. I notice that the residual moisture in the air has cut my own range of sight in half.

From time to time we can see the flicker of a fire or pressure lamp on the island behind the eastern reef. When we're just 3 to 4 miles away, they show up well. I know from comparing sightings against what appears on *Intermezzo*'s radar screen that the lights of an oceangoing ship can be seen 8 to 10 miles off in good conditions. A yacht with a masthead tricolor and a 25-watt bulb when lit will show up at 4 miles. Conventional running lights at deck level are visible from ½ mile to 2 miles. The loom of city lights can sometimes be seen as far away as 40 or more miles, especially if there is a high cloud cover off which they can reflect. Lighthouses, too, can often be seen well outside normal range by their loom against the clouds.

A good-quality, *clean* pair of binoculars aids night vision greatly. It helps to pick out distant lights and the silhouette of land against the horizon. In moonlight, a pair of glasses can help you see almost as well as in the daytime. However, some binoculars that work well in daylight don't have good light-gathering qualities. To be sure you are getting a pair that works well in both situations, try them out at night, preferably in an area with low light levels.

Civilian versions of the military "night scopes" are also available. These specialized binoculars and monoculars gather starlight efficiently, magnify it, and use it to illuminate otherwise hard-to-see objects. They are almost as expensive as radar, which is a better overall investment, but if their cost ever drops within range of a pair of high-quality binoculars, it would be ideal to have a pair aboard.

The reef on our port side is steep-to, and we make for it rather than try to ride the center of the channel. One-quarter mile off, our course is adjusted to parallel, and the skipper turns on his powerful spotlight. I am amazed to see the edge of the reef outlined clearly, a brown line with occasional lighter blotches, meandering along our side. The spotlight, situated on a small mast over the captain's head has very little glare, and we still have some night vision on either side of it.

The use of spotlights at night is common with commercial vessels. They are used not only in clear water with steep-to reefs but also in the higher latitudes for spotting logs, rocks, and tide rips. Specialized models are available with anti-glare lenses.

There are two important factors to remember when using a spotlight. First, the higher it is, the better the viewing angle is and the less glare there is. Second, any rigging that it passes over will reflect the light, destroying night vision and reducing the viewing range of the spotlight itself. While situating a crewmember with the spotlight in the rigging will help the height, it can cause a problem with reflection.

On some boats a servo motor-operated spotlight unit

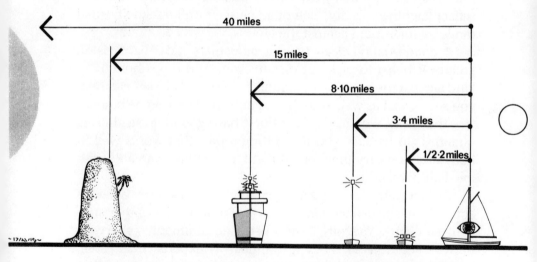

The range of visibility will vary with atmospheric conditions, but in clear air the loom of city lights on clouds can be seen for 40 or more miles. A good-sized ship can be seen at 8 to 10 miles. A masthead tricolor is visible at 3 to 4 miles, while hull level running lights may possibly be seen (if you are lucky) at ½ to 2 miles. Remember that the higher you are, the better your viewing range. Climbing to the lower spreaders will make a big difference in how quickly you can pick out a low object.

mounted at the masthead can solve most of the problems with glare and reflection. Lightweight, powerful units are inexpensive, and with the exception of their electrical wires, relatively lightweight. Mounted at the masthead, they provide excellent viewing range without interference from the rigging. A good-quality light will show up objects at a distance, still leaving you with some night vision for the darker areas.

Being able to see at night is an acquired skill. By practicing with and without aids, you learn to interpret outlines and shadows. As experience and confidence builds, more and more becomes visible in what would otherwise have been unusable light. Close to home, where the terrain is familiar and dangers are known, is where you should learn and practice. Having confidence in your skills can sometimes mean the difference sometimes between safety and disaster.

All this watchkeeping business sounds good in the abstract, but what do you do when it is 0300 in the morning and your eyes are getting heavy? When a watch tends to drag on, a cup of hot coffee or chocolate really helps you to stay awake. We kept a thermos full of hot water on hand and refilled it before the next watch came on deck. Many cruisers tend to snack through the night . Linda and I have found popcorn provides the ideal balance between ease of preparation, caloric intake, and oral gratification.

The other side of the equation is being able to relax and fall asleep after coming off watch. Linda's warm milk recipe works wonderfully as a natural sleeping pill.

Sleepytime Milk

4 cups milk

4 teaspoons honey

1 teaspoon vanilla extract

dash of freshly grated nutmeg

Heat 4 cups of milk to warm. Do not boil or scald.

Add 4 teaspoons of honey and 1 teaspoon vanilla extract.

Stir until the honey is absorbed, pour into four mugs, and serve.

Freshly grated nutmeg sprinkled on top adds a nice flavor, but isn't essential.

Something about the chemical reaction that takes place when the milk is warmed produces a relaxing effect. We also find wearing a set of eyeshades helps induce sleep. So does a back rub...

Believe it or not, watch-keeping at night is one of the joys of passagemaking. You have the sea, wind, stars, boat, and your thoughts completely to yourself. It is a time for thinking, reading, or just sitting back and enjoying the interplay of elements. There is no comparable "time-set" in our modern-day, onshore life. Both Linda and I find it is our favorite time at sea.

Others prefer daytime watches. Perhaps it is the fact that one tends to relax more during the day when visibility is better. But before you adopt this laidback approach, let us tell you a couple more sea stories.

STAYING ALERT

Seven bells ring out from *Intermezzo*'s clock. Eleven-thirty, I think to myself. Another half-hour and the sun will pass overhead. A large wave lifts our stern, and *Intermezzo* begins her graceful descent into the trough below.

Surfing down these substantial South Pacific seas has become commonplace the last 3½ days. It has been blowing like stink from the southeast, and we have covered nearly 200 miles a day since departing Bora Bora.

Suvarov atoll lies ahead, if only we can find it. Without a reliable celestial observation since our departure, I have been working strictly with omega. Omega and my dead-reckoning track put us within 30 miles of the reef. Once the sun moves overhead, into our eyes, visibility will drop to where we will be forced to alter course to make sure we don't miss the inviting lagoon.

Suvarov is one of those spots cruisers dream about. One narrow entrance gives way to an emormous mid-ocean lagoon, more than 20 miles across, within which there is a small, semiprotected anchorage. With only a few acres of dry land

Suvarov has been the off-and-on home of hermit Tom Neal. Of late, it has become a stop for South Pacific yachtsmen enroute to the Samoas and Fiji. Tom's hospitality, abundant lobster on the outer reef, and a wrecked Taiwanese fishing vessel with full diesel tanks await.

Braced against the dodger, I lift my binoculars as we rise to a sea. Just ahead and to port I can see a faint change in color on the underside of the clouds. Trying to steady the glasses with one hand and brace myself with the other, I scan the horizon. If there is color it must be the reflection of the lagoon.

Linda is on deck now, too.

"Over there," she points. "Just to port of the pulpit. Aren't those trees?"

"They sure are," I yell with delight. "We found it! It won't be long now. Go below and flip on the radar, please. I want to check our distance off the islet with the trees."

Linda drops down the companionway to warm up the radar while I continue to take stock. Secure in knowing our location, I begin to relax. Continuing onto Samoa, some 900 miles distant, without a positive position fix wasn't at the top of my list of ideas for having fun. I would much prefer having a calm night's rest between clean sheets in a stationary bunk.

The trees continue to grow in detail as we surge forward, while the radar whirrs overhead as it warms up. I anxiously await word from Linda on our distance off. We are on starboard tack, running square, and I figure we will have to gybe. But I don't want to head down too soon and have to gybe back.

"I can't get the set tuned in!" comes Linda's reply to my inquiry. "You better come down and adjust it."

"Just a minute. Nature is calling."

I step to the leeward shrouds of the mizzen, fumbling with the layers of my foul-weather gear. Our stern raises to a particularly large sea, and as it starts to roll under, *Intermezzo* heels momentarily to windward. There, just under the main boom and directly in front of us ¼ mile off is a large white ribbon of breaking reef.

Instead of being north of Suvarov and having a clear run down to the pass and islet, we are south, and have 6 miles of reef

Popcorn is an essential ingredient for successful watch-keeping aboard our boats.

under our lee.

Had I taken the 2 minutes necessary to drop below, adjust the radar, and read our distance off the islet we would have been thrown ashore—a precipitous, and premature, end to our cruising plans.

Having a watch on deck whenever land or other dangers are near is a fundamental tenet of seamanship. Of the few yachts that get themselves into difficulty cruising, a majority do so because they have not been keeping adequate watch.

During our final approach to Suvarov had I not taken that last moment on deck disaster would have been the result. Going below to check the radar under such conditions now means the off-watch comes on deck to keep an eye on things.

But just being on deck doesn't in and of itself protect you. The watch must be alert to potential dangers. When making strange landfalls or traveling in areas where navigation aids, charts, or pilots are suspect, the watch must concentrate.

Move with us now to the eastern shore of Malakula island in the New Hebrides. It is a beautiful, sunny day, as *Intermezzo* motorsails through a calm sea. We are heading for a rendezvous with cruising friends at Santo Harbor on Espiritu Santo Island.

We are 4½ miles off the island, enough distance to give a wide berth to charted shoals 6 miles ahead. From radar, visual observations, and dead reckoning, we know our exact location. The sun is behind my right shoulder, and I have excellent visibility.

Sitting comfortably at the entrance to *Intermezzo*'s companionway, I look up from my reading now and then to check our progress and scan the horizon. At 6.5 knots, I think to myself, we'll be able to anchor in time to get the awning set and a swim in before dark. With that thought I drop back to the world of the occult and am reabsorbed in Carlos Castaneda's latest Don Juan work.

I am startled out of my concentration. For a second I am confused, and then I realize what it is. The water has changed color. From the safety of dark blue it has turned to pale green. Standing up, I can see coral beneath our keel. The water is rapidly shoaling.

I grab the autopilot control and hit hard starboard, but it is too late. Already we are in stag coral and *Intermezzo* scrapes along the tops of the branches now and then.

Linda is on deck now. The first scrape has brought her running.

"Grab the wheel," I yell. "Head her southeast."

I climb quickly to the lower spreaders to look for a way out. All around us is stag coral. Many patches must be less than 7 feet deep. If we lose way, slow down at all, *Intermezzo* will be trapped. The folding prop will never her moving again.

"Give her full throttle, Linda. It is our only chance."

Intermezzo's little Isuzu diesel surges ahead, trying to increase our speed. We heel slightly as the apparent wind builds.

"Starboard thirty degrees. Now port ten. Hang on, we are going to break through stag coral."

With a sickening jar and shudder, our keel crushes the shallowest coral. We are through the first patch.

I wrap my left hand around the hand hold tapped securely into the aluminum main mast. My right hand grasps the intermediate shroud.

I bend my legs to absorb the shock I know is coming. "Hard to port!" Our bow swings quickly off and then breaks through a spot slightly deeper than the rest.

Three more times our way is blocked, and we are forced to punch through. After what seems like hours but in reality is less than a minute, I see the water drop down through the blues. We are free!

Both of us are shaking now as we rush to assess the damage. Linda checks the sump for water while I inspect the rig. Unbelievably we are watertight, and the rig seems completely intact. I put Don Juan's conversations away for a while and resolve to truly keep my eyes "on the road" when we are close to land.

The next day in Santo I mentioned the "new reef" to the harbormaster. "Oh yes," he replied, "that area tilted up about thirty feet in the earthquake last year." So much for relying on printed aids to navigation.

Most cruisers learn their lessons the hard way. We are no

exception. Generally speaking, the more experienced a sailor is, the less he will rely totally on any electronic or printed aid. His eyes, ears, nose, and sense of motion are the ultimate arbiter of safe passage.

Obviously you cannot maintain an absolutely alert watch every minute of every passage. But when land or other obstructions are close, vigil should never be relaxed.

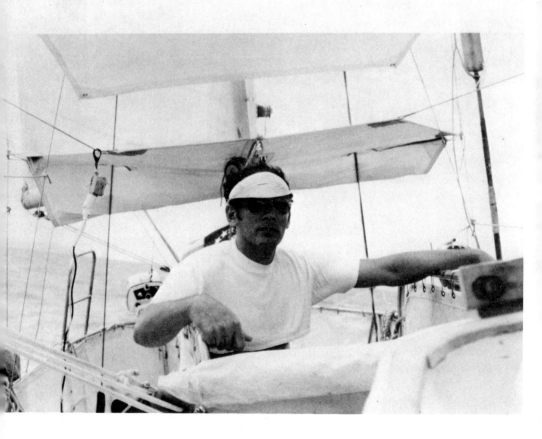

On *Intermezzo* we kept watch from the companionway. With handrails and weathercloths on each side, this relatively high perch gave us good visibility. The only drawback came in wet going where full protection was difficult to come by.

RESPONDING TO THE INNER SENSE

Since we have been on the subject of watch-keeping, perhaps we should talk briefly about a subtler form of staying alert aboard your yacht. Just as a mother can miraculously detect the faintest cough or cry from her children through closed doors at the far end of a house so too can those attuned to their yachts detect seagoing messages at an almost subliminal level.

Every yacht speaks to her crew in a variety of ways. If they are alert, their senses attuned, the subtle messages a boat transmits can save much grief, effort, and expense. Sailing yields one form of music, while machinery in use, another. There are also those soft indications transmitted from the sea.

The key to receiving and understanding these indirect messages is to note carefully any changes from the norm your senses register. The change may be so slight as to sit just on the edge of consciousness, teasing your awareness. I find occasionally it comes almost as a mental tickle, a frustration I can't quite grasp.

Over the years I have learned to focus my awareness in-directly, to come to grips with stimuli from the flanks. Having learned the hard way, I always try to identify the message before proceeding on some new endeavor.

Anyone who has been involved with high-performance machinery will recognize instantly the slightest change in en-gine hum or vibration. A difference in the low-decibel sound level or frequency of vibration, while almost undetectable by it-self, is easy to sense when it's set against a background of expectation.

The situation is similar at sea when the diesel is running. There are few stimuli competing for your attention, and while you don't need to concentrate on the noise itself, you should have in the back of your mind an awareness of exactly the right "tune" the engine and its accessories should be singing.

A slight change in rpm could signal different engine loading or perhaps a fuel problem. A small difference in vibration pat-terns can give early warning of propeller, bearing, engine mount, or accessory malfunction. Even a loose V-belt gives out a signal.

Smell is a potent message-carrier. When you first board a ves-sel, a potpourri of scents assaults your nose. Bilgewater, leaky heads, overripe vegetables, mildew, stale bedding—each has a message that can be classified. Eventually these odors form a backdrop against which your senses can measure interlopers. A whiff of acrid smoke caught on deck means trouble in the elec-trical department. Perhaps a circuit breaker is overloaded, and the wiring is beginning to burn. Leaking diesel, oil, propane, gas, or paint stores all can be detected well in advance of explosive levels.

At sea, under sail, we knowingly or otherwise depend upon a symphony of sound to create moods to help us with trim, to tell us when we are overpressed or not moving well. If you want to demonstrate just how important these sounds are, try sailing with ear protectors.

The importance of sound to performance was made abun-dantly clear to me in the late 1960s in a *Yachting* magazine One-of-a-Kind regatta. I was racing our 32-foot D-class catamaran, *Beowulf V*. This very sophisticated go-fast machine was backed by equally as sophisticated computer performance sailing programs.

On board were some of the first digital readout sailing instruments, but we found that if we had to look at the dials, interpret the data, and then react, we lost too much time. With all our computer backup and sophisticated design, we still had to sail *Beowulf* V by the seat of our pants, which we did, well enough to be ahead in the regatta by the third race.

Sports Illustrated magazine asked us if we would mind having a helicopter follow us around the race course to shoot some photos.

"Not at all," I said. "Just don't mess up our wind, and stay out of the rigging."

The chopper and photographer found us during the first broad reach of the modified Olympic course. We were sailing with big drifter and main, at an apparent wind angle of 28 degrees. In the 12-knot winds *Beowulf* V was doing her normal 22 to 24 knots. I was steering from the trapeze, while Norm Riise (my computer expert) and Rick Taylor (resident sailmaker) rode the main beam and controlled the sheets.

We had all raced together off and on for years, and little verbal communication was necessary. With *Beowulf* V generating so much apparent wind, each minor change in true wind velocity or direction necessitated major corrections in helm or sheet. It was like riding a knife edge. A little too much power and over we would go; too little, and the speed would drop in half within seconds.

The noise of the chopper's engine and rotors behind us was overpowering. None of us could hear a thing. We quickly discovered that we totally depended upon sound for our input on sail trim and steering angle. The bow wave, the wind, and the fins all had messages for each of us. Unable to hear, we were unable to sail. That we kept ourselves upright and moving while the chopper was on our tail was a function of luck. Overall our time for the leg was substantially slower than it was in any of the other races of the series.

It was an interesting observation, but of no major significance then, as we chose not to make a habit of having helicopters fly in our rigging! But offshore, in larger vessels, with subtler sounds, I have learned to listen carefully, especially when I'm down below.

The ever-present theme of wind on sail and rigging, sea against hull, gurgle of bow and quarter wave, can hide notes of change that can mean something's amiss. On deck, background noise is overpowering. Below, masked by insulation and structure, the sounds we seek to warn us are also muted.

The chattering of a leech or luff of a headsail both send signals. At night we frequently trim by sound alone. In heavy airs any change from the norm is cause for investigation. In these conditions improperly led or sheeted sails lead to damage in short order, but fortunately, they protest their maltreatment loudly and immediately.

Structural sounds have a different theme. Some vessels creak and groan rhythmically as they are worked by the sea. More modern vessels, especially those of fiberglass, rarely talk unless there is a problem. A loose bulkhead or an overly flexible hull will frequently make itself known well in advance of disaster.

In the spars and rigging the type of sound is different. Here it is the sharp retort, perhaps barely a crack above the ever-present background noise. But a snap or crack indicates structural failure that must be dealt with quickly if the rig is to be kept intact.

Motion sends another type of message. Below, in the relatively quiet confines of the cabin, you may feel changes in motion that are the first indication of your vessel's need. Perhaps her gentle gamboling becomes a higher stepping pitch, gradually building until it is impossible to ignore. If you pay attention early, you may be able to change sails or head off on a new course that will be difficult to effect later.

Vibration is often another indicator. You may not hear a luffing jib or chattering leech, but you surely will feel it. At anchor the vibration of mast and shrouds lets you know when the wind picks up.

The sea sends its calling card as well. Perhaps you have changed direction slightly, or maybe you are feeling swell from a nearby reef or land.

On the opposite side of the equation, when you are anchored snugly and there's no sea noise, the sound of wind in rigging becomes omnipresent. Even a gentle breeze sounds overpowerful. Many is the time we have debated the wisdom of heading out when the noise on deck seemed to indicate prudence, only to switch on the anemometer and see it register just 12 or 15 knots. Then there is the anchor chain on the bottom. Listening to it tug at the bow or rattle over the seabed gives warning of shifting position or dragging.

The key to sensing your environment lies in knowing the norm and then being able to sift the variety of signals for the one that calls for action. It is not a difficult skill to learn. It requires only time and the patience to endure the frequent false alarm.

TOWING DINGHIES

Conservative seamanship dictates that dinghies not be towed offshore. The risk of something going amiss and the dinghy's being swamped or damaged is too high. If a problem does arise with a sea is running, getting the dinghy back aboard is virtually impossible. But on short hops between anchorages in semiprotected waters and with the right setup and preparation, most cruisers indulge in the convenience with no problem.

A number of factors affect a dinghy's towing performance. First is the design of the dink itself. Inflatables create substantially more drag than rigid dinks. They have more wetted surface, and their soft bottoms create resistance. But they are less likely to broach and swamp. A moderate- or narrow-beam dinghy is more stable under tow than a squat one. It has more directional stability because of its hull shape. The second consideration is the towing power of the mother ship. Many small auxiliary sailboats have the power to tow their dinghies in nice weather, but when the wind and sea pipe up the extra load presents a problem. The increased drag of the tow can overpower the rig or engine of a small yacht.

I learned this lesson many years ago the hard way. We were enroute to Catalina Island off southern California in a small catamaran on a blustery fall day. At the last minute I decided to tow my Dad's 10-foot fiberglass dink so I wouldn't have to beach the cat once we arrived. Sailing out of Los Angeles, we had the situation well in hand, but as the afternoon wore on, the sea and breeze built. Finally, as we neared the island, we found we couldn't make reasonable progress to weather. The drag of the dink was too much. Coming about was also a problem. Because the extra drag held back our stern, we couldn't make it through the eye of the wind. Our upwind performance had deteriorated so badly I was afraid that if I gybed, the ground we lost to leeward would make it impossible for us to return to the Los Angeles breakwater entrance. The situation was finally resolved in a somewhat unorthodox manner. We caught the dink square between our stern, and using it as a brake on backwards drift, we were able to blow our bow about with the jib. Admittedly, our dink was out of proportion to the mother ship, but an inflatable behind a small auxiliary sailboat can create the same problem in heavy going.

Towing downwind can present problems, too. Cruisers are

The dink should be towed on the back of the next following wave crest. A sheet or dock line can be knotted over the tow line and dropped aft to act as a drogue. Even though it is pulling from the bow, it will slow the dink sufficiently in most cases to prevent its broaching.

frequently lulled into towing their dinghy on a nice day. Then the wind picks up. As seas build, dinghies, because they are lighter and accelerate quickly, tend to surf down the wave faces towards their mother ship. We have seen dinghies careen madly down a sea, swerve past the stern of the towing boat, reach the limit of the painter as they pass the stern, and then be jerked into the topsides. This scenario usually ends up in a swamping. The violent changes in direction are too much for the lateral stability of the smaller boat. A surf fisherman becomes the likely beneficiary of this kind of stupidity.

Over the years we have evolved some guidelines to reduce the risks of towing our dinks. First, we never tow offshore or inshore where there is risk of a sea making up. We pick days when the weather appears to have settled and trips that will be only a few hours at most. Next we remove all gear from the dink—especially the outboard motor (if we are towing in protected waters, we sometimes break this rule and leave the outboard on, but then we tie it securely in the tilted-up position). We also make up a special towing painter, one that is long enough to hold the dinghy behind the wave crest following our stern in case a sea gets up, making it necessary to let the dink further aft.

We have found that floating line works best as a painter. It minimizes the chance of fouling our propeller.

Towing eyes have to be extremely stout. In fiberglass dinghies I like to glass into the bow a substantial backing block through which the bolts for the eye pass. The towing eye should be near the waterline to reduce the painter's tendency to pull the bow over into a broach. When we tow an inflatable, we pass a line through the molded towing eye in the bow and fasten it in the form of a bridle to eyebolts in the solid stern. This setup has the advantage of allowing us to tow from the proper point but puts the loads into a hefty chunk of wood. (Most cruisers who don't practice this system with their inflatables end up replacing the towing eyes every year or so.)

How we handle the tow once we've set everything up depends on the dink and on sea conditions. We usually start out towing a rigid boat about three dink lengths behind. As a sea begins to build, we drop the dink back to the back of the wave behind our stern. The aim is to have the dinghy always trying to climb over the crest. If the dinghy behaves erratically, we find tying a length of dockline over the painter and letting it slip aft to act as a drogue calms its movement. Even though the drogue pulls from the bow, it has always worked well. If you do deploy a drogue, don't forget to pull it in when you reach your destination; otherwise it will surely find its way into your prop.

On *Intermezzo II* when we anchored or maneuvered in tight quarters our dink was always pulled up snug to the stainless steel boarding ladder on our transom. That kept it off the topsides and the painter out of the propeller. Yachts with conventional transom sterns cannot avail themselves of this technique. In that situation, we find it better to tie the dink alongside to keep it out of the way.

Inflatables sometimes tow best snugged right up to the

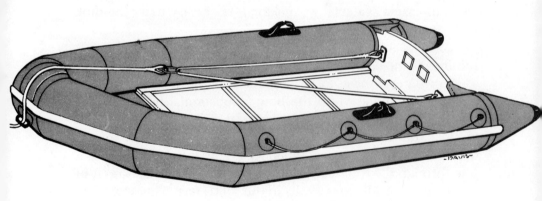

The loads on an inflatable when towed are much higher than they are on a solid dinghy. A bridle rigged through the bow eye to the transom will increase the bow eye's life span considerably.

sternrail, with the bow lifted clear of the water. For this to work the freeboard of the towing vessel has to be low enough so that the dink's bow can be held snugly against the transom of the mother ship. On larger boats the dink can be held instead to a special padeye bolted to the transom.

One of the major risks to the dinghy when it is being towed is filling with water. Whether it comes from spray, broaching, or errant wave tops, even a small amount of water makes a large difference in overall towing weight, rapidly increasing the strain on the gear. To reduce this risk, consider strapping a full, tight-fitting cover on the dink.

Finally, even though we never start towing unless the weather is fair, we always rig the dinghy's lifting sling. That way, if conditions deteriorate, we have a chance to get the boat aboard before it is too late.

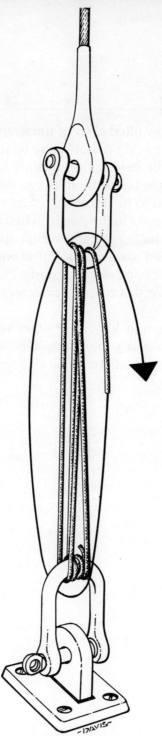

Two large shackles and a binding of light line will carry an enormous load. Take the breaking strength of the line you are using, divide by 10 for a safety factor, and then multiply by enough turns to equal the strength of wire you are replacing.

COPING WITH RIGGING FAILURE

Cruising mast failures are rare. When they do occur it is usually the result of rigging fatigue. And while losing a spar is something most of us would rather not think about, advance planning, coupled with a modest inventory of spares, can usually save the mast before it goes over the side.

Fortunately, it is normally possible to diagnose potential problems before they become terminal. One must be prepared to relieve the over-strained fittings and repair the jury rig quickly. Under pressure at sea is not the time to be thinking about how or with what repairs will be effected. That should be done before you leave port.

As a result of many years of racing with skinny rigs (and occasionaly losing same), I am in the habit of checking our cruising rig carefully. Daily at sea, I survey the lower swages, toggles, and turnbuckles. Except for peace of mind, until now my inspections have never yielded results.

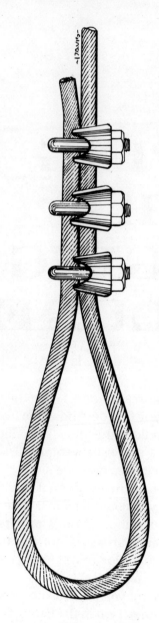

Cable clamps can be used for temporary light-load repairs. Be sure that the cast part of the clamp is on the long side of the loop (the side that takes the direct load of the rig).

Today we are sailing the Indian Ocean, 300 miles from Durban, South Africa, smack in the middle of the ship-killing Agulhas Current. *Intermezzo* has just weathered her third southwesterly gale. My morning rounds turn up broken strands of wire at the swage of the after lower shroud on the mainmast.

Before leaving on our trip we had modified the lower and intermediate shrouds so they were the same length and then put a spare wire aboard, just in case.

Going aloft to remove the offending wire, I am stymied by a frozen clevis pin. Try as I might, it is impossible to free. From my lofty perch I can see the approach of a heavy line of clouds. Another black southwester is on its way. I consider leaving the shroud as it is, but not knowing the intensity of the coming storm or how much good wire is mixed in with the bad, I feel it has to be changed. I have no choice but to hacksaw through the ⅝-inch stainless steel pin. While it would be an easy chore with a vise, I am exhausted working aloft after the fourth hacksaw blade finally makes its way through. After a last tired heave, the new shroud is in place. Minutes before the storm hits, the turnbuckle is tuned and the rig once again secure.

For 36 hours the wind howls at above 50 knots. One nearby yacht is rolled over and another knocked down severely, twice. If I had not made my morning rounds, if I had not stowed the spare shroud, if I had not had a good inventory of hacksaw blades...?

In addition to checking the deck end of the rig, I like to go aloft every third or fourth day (weather permitting) and look at the tangs, terminals, and wire halyards.

To be fully prepared for rigging failure, we always carried aboard our *Intermezzos* a small inventory of spares. Several shackles of the largest possible size with a pin that fit through our terminal eyes were very handy. They could be used as toggles or with many strands of light line in lieu of a turnbuckle. Quarter-inch Dacron rove through a shackle 20 times will carry the working load of 5⁄16-inch wire for a short period. Toggles, turnbuckles, clevis pins, and a spare mast tang or two were also in the spares kit.

One piece of the largest wire, long enough to be used as a

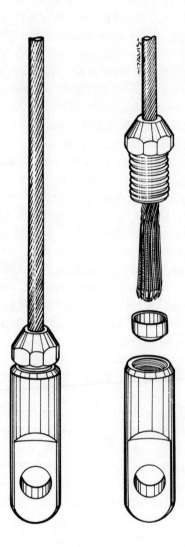

Sta-Lok and Norsemen replaceable rigging terminals are ideal for repairs. They are easy to use and are stronger and longer lived than swages.

backstay or headstay, also served as a cap shroud. It already had the proper terminal affixed to one end. By using a Norseman or Sta-Lok terminal at the deck, it is ready to reeve in a minimum amount of time, cut to the proper length, and prepare the appropriate bottom end.

Before we started voyaging I practiced the actual installation of removable terminals ashore with an experienced rigger. I have found that up through ⅜-inch wire they can be assembled with wrenches. Beyond this size a vise is needed.

Cable clamps can also be used in some cases. Rigid 1 × 19-inch wire cannot be bent around thimbles, and so if a joint is required, the cable clamps hold the two pieces of wire in tension together. It is an approach to be used in the last resort, as only a small percentage of the wire's strength will be retained by the connection.

Cutting standing rigging requires specialized tools. Up through ⁷⁄₁₆-inch wire, cable cutters can be used. We carried Felco C-16 cutters, and with the right technique they will make it through. What is required is an abrupt downward thrust on the cutters. Technique, rather than brute force, carries the day. Once you have practiced, it will become easy. But don't expect to make it through on a heaving deck if you haven't done your homework.

If your rigging runs over ⅜ inch, you should consider hydraulic cutters. A compact unit by Huskie Tools, available at most rigging shops, will make quick work of wire up to ¾ inch. For rod rigging lots of 32-tooth high-carbon steel hacksaw blades used with deliberate action will be necessary.

When we sail with removable terminals (Norseman or Sta-Lok), we carry spare cones for each size. I have learned the hard way to be sure, before I leave port, that turnbuckles and clevis pins are free moving.

If a piece of standing rigging breaks, it doesn't have to mean the loss of a spar. Here, speed and the proper reaction is all important. In order to be prepared for the worst I try to review each possibility and how we should react.

The headstay is the least important of the standing rigging. The luff wire of the jib will give the mast temporary support.

Heading downwind and releasing the vang will relieve pressure. Losing a lower shroud, if there are fore-and-aft lowers is also not immediately critical. The spar must be watched for pumping, and a quick tack is in order. Failure in a single lower, intermediate, or cap shroud requires a crash tack. If you are heading upwind there isn't to time worry about sheets or runners. The helm has to be put down instantly.

Losing a backstay is the worst scenario. If it happens when you're heading upwind, immediately cutting the headsail sheet will allow the mainsail leech to hold the masthead aft. Spare headsail halyards or the topping lift can keep the masthead from whipping until a new backstay is in place. If you are off the wind when the backstay goes, cutting the headsail sheet and heading up is the only hope.

When a structural failure threatens the rig, keeping the mast up requires quick thinking and preparation. In most cases the spar can be saved. A jury rig can be installed that will get you to port without assistance. Even if the spar goes over the side, you will still have the wherewithall to use a spinnaker pole, boom, or mast stump to build a get-home spar.

There are many ways of jury rigging if you lose a spar. Sections of the broken mast or boom can be erected and used with a deeply reefed main and storm headsails. Another approach is to make a bipod with spinnaker poles. A jib, flown on edge, is one of the sails which will work here. If you break your boom, a spinnaker or jockey pole can be used as a splint.

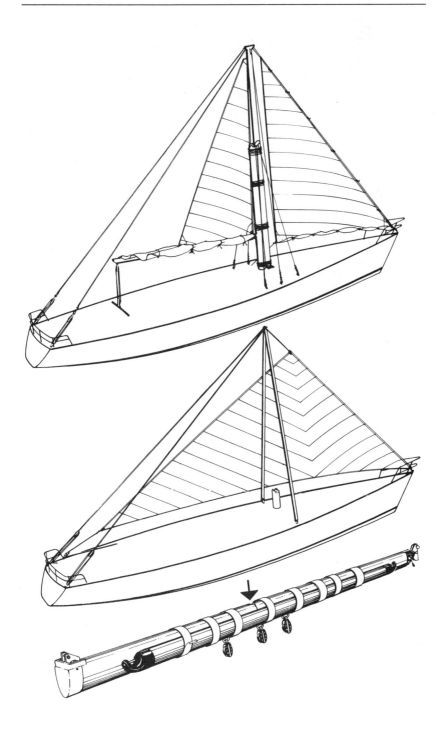

UNDERSTANDING HEAVY WEATHER

Heavy weather is a main topic of discussion wherever sailors meet. While the actual number of times you will sail in truly dangerous weather are few, those storms you do encounter evoke strong memories for a long time afterwards.

Our own experiences may provide some frame of reference. We have been past Cape Hatteras four times, around the Cape of Good Hope twice, across the Agulhas Current and the Indian Ocean once, and through the notorious Tasman Sea twice. Yet with all this "exposure" we have been in only two potentially dangerous storms for a total of just three days. In addition, we have weathered four other severe gales for a total of six days. That's not much time over the course of traveling some 150,000 sea miles.

Heavy weather is as much a frame of mind as a physical state. What Linda and I may consider moderately uncomfortable from the cockpit of *Intermezzo II* we would have put into gale category on our first *Intermezzo*. The same goes for relative levels of experience. The more time you spend at sea and the better you know your boat, the less mental pressure the wind and sea will exert and the more restrained and constructive your reaction to these pressures will be.

WHAT IS HEAVY WEATHER?

What constitutes dangerously heavy weather? Strong winds are what most people think of first, even though they, of themselves, cause the least problems. Directional stability and how long a storm takes to develop are as critical as actual wind strength. Strong, shifting gusts of wind are not nearly as damaging as the sudden passage of a front with its attendant long-term windshifts.

We have experienced a gradual four-day buildup of wind velocity to the 60-knot range in which the wind blew constantly from one quarter and created boisterous but not dangerous sailing. Had the wind come up more quickly or shifted midway through the storm, conditions would have been completely different and far more difficult than they were.

Thus, wind velocity itself is not a paramount concern. It is important, however, when planning how you will deal with bad weather to understand the genesis of the wind and what it can be expected to do as a storm matures. For example, if a stationary or slow-moving high is creating the storm, you can expect wind direction and velocity to remain stable. If a tightly knit front or low is generating the disturbance, knowing what sector you are in is vital. If the wind is already blowing and the front hasn't passed, you can expect a major windshift. On the other hand, the frontal passage itself may have announced the onset of the gale, in which case the odds of its becoming dangerous are much reduced.

Far more important to the safety of your boat is what happens to the seas. The affect of wind on water, in combination with certain other factors, is what forms the major worry in heavy weather. Wave shape more than size is the problem. A large wave of long period with a mature, gentle slope holds little danger. But a small, steep wave can pack a very dangerous wallop.

Wave shape is influenced first by the wind. If the wind has risen slowly, the sea will rise gradually also, assuming there are no other negative influences on wave shape. If the storm comes on with a bang, the seas initially will be steep and only later stretch out.

Wind also influences the direction of the waves. When the wind abruptly changes direction, a new set of seas will develop. It is the affect of the cross seas on a boat and on other waves that can be so dangerous. Waves from a disturbance elsewhere may also affect the sea in your area. A long gentle swell crossed with a locally generated wind wave can create dangerously unstable wave systems.

Next there is bottom contour to consider. Waves pass relatively undisturbed in deep water where there are no undersea obstructions; they exhibit a regular pattern. But undersea ridges, mountains, or continental shelves create turbulence at the sea surface.

Then there is current to contend with. When it is running with the wind, it will calm the sea. But if it is running in any other direction, it will create havoc with wave shape.

Rounding the Cape of Good Hope, Cape Agulhas, and Cape Hatteras carries the same problem: the seabed drops off steeply from relatively shallow water, and there are opposing currents and frequent frontal passages with windshifts—all nasty conditions by themselves, let alone in combination. That's why they are such dangerous places to sail and why cruisers should pick the most favorable time of year and then the best moment in that time to cross these bodies of water.

Is Your Boat Built for Heavy Weather?

So much for the external environment. What seagoing characteristics should your boat have in order to handle heavy weather? First, regardless of the type of boat you choose, you must prepare it in detail for what may come. Then, you should have aboard a good selection of storm canvas. Next, you have to be familiar with the use of your storm canvas.

If you are in the market for a boat and planning to go offshore, then her (and your) survival in extreme heavy weather must be at the top of your priority list. Since most production boats are not built with these conditions in mind, you may have to look a little further, or buy a somewhat smaller, really well built yacht so you can be sure that your vessel will stay intact, come what may.

Any sort of window, house, or deck structure is suspect. Since all boats have some windows, make sure they and their frames are massively strong. Stay away from large expanses of window. A powerful 58-foot Alden Boothbay Challenger was lost in 1982 off Cape Hatteras because of doghouse window failure. Three of her crew ultimately didn't survive the ordeal.

Belowdecks you must be able to move about from handhold to handhold with ease. These must be placed in such a way that you can exert good leverage against them and be able to hold on tightly. A person's hand should close completely around the holds. Remember that children and women have less reach than most men and may require different positioning of holds.

Bunks for all crewmembers must be secure enough to protect them in case of a rollover. Midship pilotberths are ideal, since they are usually compact and impossible to roll out of when fitted with lee cloths.

Bear in mind that the majority of disasters that occur to small boats offshore happen, for the most part, because the crew gives up. They assume the elements are too powerful to deal with, perhaps even finally abandoning their vessel for the apparent security of a liferaft. In most of these cases had they been better prepared, continued the fight, and not left their yacht until she started to really sink beneath the waves, they would have been far better off.

The psychology of dealing with storms is not to be under-rated. It is at the heart of most of the maritime disasters about which we read. Staying cool under pressure, taking action when required, and avoiding the inertia that keeps you moribund while events take over are the keys to staying afloat in good condition. Confidence in the inherent soundness of your vessel, proper preparation for offshore sailing, and carrying the gear necessary to handle storm-force conditions lay the foundations for this attitude.

To achieve this state you must acknowledge that there is a bottom line in the trade-off department. Many design features that are nice for living at anchor create problems in bad weather at sea. This statement applies to sail-handling gear, interior lay-out, and rig and hull design. No salesperson talks about storms, reefs, or unpleasant conditions when you are buying your boat. And while life-threatening storms are rare, you have to know deep down that you have the best combination to take what comes. If your cruising confidence is based on this proposition, you will be far better off physically and mentally.

The psychology of sailing in heavy going has a major impact on how you deal with the elements. If you or your crew are frightened by the wind and sea, you will have a greater tendency to put off actions that may be necessary to reduce risk to the vessel and her crew.

The constant evaluation of conditions and tactics and the moves you should make during a blow can easily lapse while the tumult is at its worse. Precisely when crew and skipper may be psychologically impaired is when action is most required.

This problem starts with lack of seagoing experience. How do you know if you are in a really dangerous storm? Veteran sail-

Linda took this shot in the mid-Pacific with her Instamatic! We had been running in Force 10 to 12 conditions for three days enroute from Bora-Bora to Suvarov atoll.

ors, those who have experienced truly severe weather, can evaluate their environment and the boat's capabilities. But sailors caught offshore in a blow for the first or second time have yet to earn their stripes.

The first thing to remember is that in a well-found vessel truly dangerous conditions are a rarity. If you have picked your time of year to passage, stayed clear of major currents and shallow seabeds, and prepared your vessel well, there is little to fear.

There are important physiological considerations as well. Maintaining a comfortable body temperature is critical. Discomfort leads to inaction, morale drops, and fear grows. Staying warm in temperate latitudes is easier to accomplish than staying cool in a tropical blow. The right clothing and air circulation systems (dorades, fans) are necessary. Nothing is more enervating than trying to relax in a wet bunk. Every effort must be made to secure the interior from water.

Seasickness is exacerbated by physical or psychological discomfort. We have always made it a habit to take seasick preventatives before the onset of bad weather. Even those in the family with "iron stomachs" turn to and down pills, just in case.

Being able to perform normal functions below is important. If you can eat, use the head, wash, and change clothes in some reasonable manner, your mental outlook will be better than if you cannot. Just washing your face and brushing your teeth can be a major morale booster.

Having galley supplies that lend themselves to consumption under inclement conditions is a good idea. Linda has always laid in a store of nutritious foods that fulfill the primary heavy-weather requirement of being easy to prepare and to consume. Crackers, nuts, popcorn, dried fruit, granola bars, prepared sandwiches, casseroles, and stews have also withstood the tests of time and many thousands of heavy-weather ocean miles.

Rest is perhaps the most significant item in maintaining mental preparedness. Being well rested before a storm, and being able to nap or sleep during it, will leave you in the best possible physical and psychological shape.

Leadership is important, too. More experienced crewmembers can reduce the anxieties of novices aboard. Levity is always a good way to ease tension.

There are positive aspects to a real blow. Consider the stories that can be told afterwards. It takes only one storm every 10 years to keep you going at the club bar. Sarah and Elyse used to use heavy weather as an excuse to "close" school. If we were heeled they could slide on pillows from one side of the saloon to the other. The challenge also exists to photograph the conditions. Perhaps you could sell a cover photo to a magazine? Just think how that poster-sized blowup of yourself fighting the wheel will look in the hall! If the seas are tumultuous, the shot will be even more dramatic.

All through any storm, the skipper and crew must bear in mind that contending with heavy weather is an ongoing proposition. Constantly evaluate conditions and how the vessel and crew are doing. When the time arrives to change tactics, you must be ready.

PREPARING FOR AN IMMINENT BLOW

At sea, faced with a blow, there is little you can do to prepare a vessel that wasn't prepared before you left the harbor. There are, however, a number of items to check and backup systems to ready.

I like to start with a look for potential leaks. Cockpit locker gaskets should be in good shape, and the hasps fixed in the closed position. Dorade cowls should be removed and caps fitted. Storm covers should be placed over skylights and deck hatches. Are the fasteners in good shape? How about the corners of the covers themselves?

Fit storm windows before it starts to blow. Even in the best conditions, they are cumbersome to put on, and doing so on a heaving deck can be dangerous.

Check the mast boot. If it is suspect but still dry, duct tape may just keep leaks to a minimum. The chain pipe should be sealed shut and fastened with a bolt.

Next, inspect the rigging. Look for missing cotter keys, check the rigging wire where it exits swages, and make sure turnbuckles are seized so they won't unscrew.

With a pair of binoculars have a look aloft at the condition of the sails. Pay attention to those areas subject to chafe: near spreader tips and after lower shrouds. Check the slides, too. Look over the gooseneck on the inboard end of the boom. Are cracks developing? Are cotter keys or bolts in place?

Check and double-lash spinnaker poles, dinks, anchors (even those with chains attaching them to windlasses), and any other gear.

Take a look at the self-steering control lines. If you are using an autopilot and chain/cable steering, make sure the chain is in good condition and that the cables haven't begun to deteriorate. The emergency tiller should be handy.

Rig a jackstay and rope handholds, and examine and make accessible your safety harnesses.

Below, lockers should be checked for loose gear. Nothing is more annoying than a rolling bottle or can. Old towels make excellent locker stuffers. Cushions and underseat lockers need to be secured with tie-downs. Bilges should be pumped dry and strainers emptied. Are the companionway hatch and slide lock bolts working?

Storm canvas should be dragged out of storage and secured where it is easily accessible. And, of course, prepare to shorten sail.

SEA ROOM

Okay. We have talked about the concept of heavy weather in general, gotten ourselves psyched up, and prepared our vessel for the worst. Now comes the single most important consideration in evaluating heavy weather. I am talking about sea room.

Sea room, or the lack thereof, will determine which approaches you will be able to use in your contest with the wind

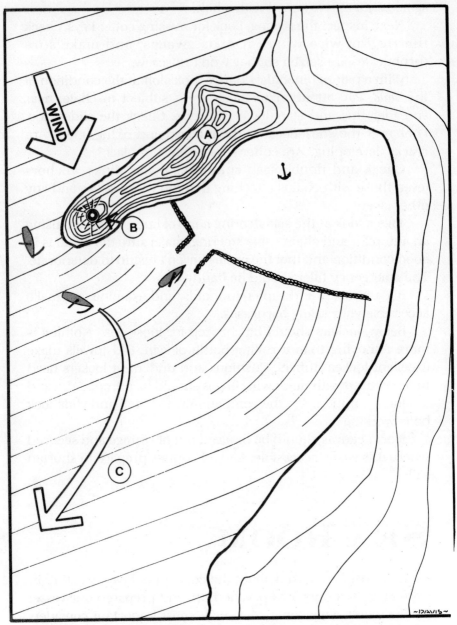

What makes a good landfall in heavy weather? A high headland (A) for easy daytime identification, a powerful light (B) for a night approach, easy escape to leeward (C), and a protected upwind entrance.

and sea. The question arises immediately, What is adequate searoom? That depends upon a series of factors. Foremost is the weatherliness of your boat. If she is set up for heavy-weather beating and is close-winded, you can take a chance of being closer to a lee shore than can a vessel that is unhandy on the wind. The less weatherly your boat is, the more sea room she needs.

Next is the weather system. The harder it blows (or it is expected to blow) and the worse the sea conditions, the more distance off you should be.

Navigational hazards also have to be factored in. A low-lying coast that is difficult to pick out from a distance will warrant a greater safety factor than a steep, easily visible shoreline. You have to consider sea depth and bottom contour as well. Sea conditions may be much worse in shallow water or where the depths change suddenly. Although land may be far off, these treacherous areas of turbulent ocean may have to be regarded in the same context as a lee shore.

Current, of course, is another element. If it is opposing the wind, you will want to stay out of it as much as possible.

In making your analysis take the formal weather forecasts with a grain of salt. It is always prudent to assume the worst, especially where large temperature changes may be involved, such as where the warm Gulf Stream influences continental cold fronts.

You must also consider what would happen if there were a gear failure of some sort. Perhaps steering will let go or the rig will be compromised. If this occurs extra room you will need to make repairs while you are drifting helplessly to leeward. While nobody expects such a mishap aboard a well-found vessel, it is best to have enough sea room to take a problem in stride.

The equation becomes more confused when there is a potential haven close by but to leeward. Now you are faced with trying to make shelter, giving up sea room in the process, or standing offshore in uncomfortable and possibly dangerous conditions.

I suspect that most problems that occur as a result of heavy weather begin at just this decision-making point. If you give up your sea room and then find you are unable to negotiate the harbor entrance safely, the danger to vessel and crew has been substantially increased.

On the other hand, nothing feels better than rounding up into the wind in the lee of a breakwater as your hull stops its wild ride in a calm harbor.

The question, then, is one of evaluating the risk in finding your harbor of refuge and then entering it.

Factors that have to be considered initially are those of navigation. How difficult a landfall will it be within the context of the navigation gear aboard and skills of the navigator?

What sort of visibility is required? If overcast threatens, can you make a safe landfall without sunlight? What about a night-time entrance? Remember that the risks from a mistake are greater in heavy weather. There will be less time to recover, and your vessel will be more unwieldy. If you find yourself on a lee shore, you may not be able to claw off.

How about entrance conditions? Will there be a breaking bar? Some harbor entrances that are safe in moderate seas become dangerous when the waves really start to pound.

Once you have gained the harbor mouth, what sort of maneuvering will be required in the channel? If the harbor itself is straightforward, this may not pose a problem. But if there are rocks or shoals, or twists or turns, handling your vessel may be difficult in the conditions that will exist.

Before running off, consider too that while present conditions may make gaining a harbor appear a safe alternative, weather may have deteriorated substantially by the time you arrive.

It is also a good idea to ponder the unthinkable. Just what sort of risk does crew and vessel face if you are driven ashore? If the coastline is made up of gently shelving sand or mud, waves are relatively small, and your yacht is of heavy construction, risk to life and property may be minimal. But a rocky shoreline in heavy surf can make short work of boat and crew.

Just what sort of a harbor is ideal? First would be one that is easy to find, even in bad weather. Next would be one with minimal wave action at the entrance. Then I would look for a port with an upwind entrance. Beating or reaching into a harbor leaves you in more control than running does.

If the harbor mouth is situated behind a headland, which provides both a prominent landmark as well as a sheltering lee, risks will be reduced even further.

In heavy going offshore the novice sailor may equate safety with land. But to the experienced, conservative seaman just the opposite is true. Unless there is an easily gained harbor of refuge close by, he or she will put as much distance between the boat and any *potential* lee shore as is possible. After conditions have moderated, or at least stabilized, is the time to return.

If there is a doubt as to whether or not you can make a safe landfall, it is generally better to stand offshore.

Stanley Dashew photo

EMPLOYING STORM TACTICS

Your tactical approach to dealing with severe weather at sea will be dictated by a series of factors. First, as we have alluded to in the previous chapter, is whether you have sufficient sea room. Then you have to consider the weather and what it is likely to do. Obviously the characteristics and preparation of your yacht and crew will also have a place in the decision-making process. Usually at the end of the list of considerations is your final destination.

BEATING

Let's look at your options if you're first trying to work upwind when conditions start to make up. Beating to windward in heavy weather is most uncomfortable, even on the largest vessels, and can usually be avoided. In most situations it will pay to wait out the weather in port or to heave-to offshore until conditions moderate or the wind shifts to a favorable angle. But occasionally schedule, potential further deterioration of

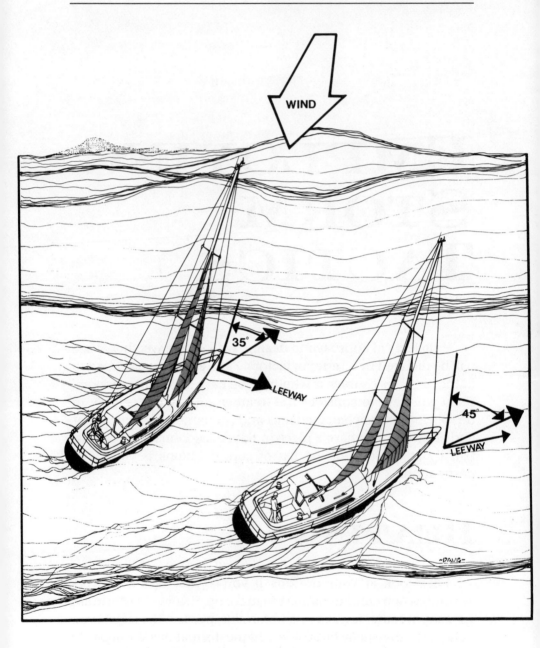

Sometimes falling off and reducing sail will result in better progress to windward when you are fighting big seas. Motion will ease and leeway is reduced.

weather or a threatening leeshore make passive tactics untenable. You must then be ready to take on the sea at its worst angle—on the nose.

Making a sailing yacht go to windward in heavy conditions is an entirely different prospect from normal uphill work. The loads of wind and sea that the vessel must overcome are increased substantially at the same time that the aero- and hydrodynamic configurations of her design are at a big disadvantage.

Windage increases dramatically. It goes up with the square of the increase in windspeed. Thus, in 40 knots of wind there is 77 percent more wind drag than in 30 knots of wind.

The boat's keel, hull, and rudder are designed in part to provide lift to overcome drift to leeward. In smooth water they can do this job relatively efficiently. But when the seas start to bounce the vessel around, the keel stalls out, ventilates, and operates under a handicap. If large steering corrections are required, the rudder will be working overtime, too.

All the factors that you consider when beating in moderate conditions are even more important in heavy weather. Windage should be your priority. Roller-furled sails should be brought down on deck. They contribute enormously to drag. Next to be removed are weather cloths. Perhaps the dodger can be folded. Moving weight below and clearing the decks also helps reduce windage.

There is not much you can do on the spot to reduce drag that results from your boat's underwater configuration. But if a hard beat is in store you will be happier if you've stayed ahead of this important area of maintenance. Having a clean bottom and a folding or feathering prop is of paramount importance. In many instances, this one factor alone will make the difference in the boat's ability to make any forward progress.

The next important consideration is the sailplan. Sails must be very flat and be able to hold their shape. They should be sheeted so that the leech is looser than the foot. A tight leech on a headsail will stall the boat, make her heel over, and retard progress. The sailplan should also have a low center of effort.

A variety of storm canvas should be aboard. Having a range of headsails from which to choose is very important. The mainsail must be easy to reef. There should be an extra-deep reef for extreme conditions as well as a storm trysail.

In order to generate power in the rig to overcome the enormous amount of drag and resistance built up by the wind and seas, many yachts must carry a relatively large (for the conditions) press of sail. Picking the right combination of sail, boatspeed, and discomfort is tricky and depends on a number of factors. Chief amongst these will be the amount of keel area in your boat, her stability, and how your hull shape and pitching center react with the sea conditions.

Yachts with efficient underbodies and keels sporting plenty of lateral area can make progress upwind under bad conditions, if they are sailed *slowly*. If the keel is designed for racing or lightish airs, you will be forced to sail at a speed high enough so the keel doesn't become overloaded and stall out.

Our first *Intermezzo* was typical of the latter type of design; built as a racing boat, she was relatively fast (for her type) to windward. She had a minimum-sized keel because of the racer's concern with wetted surface, which made it necessary for us either to go full speed to windward or to heave-to. If we tried to pick a more comfortable in-between course, her fin stalled out, and she would make great quantities of leeway.

Having learned the hard way, we have since made an effort on the vessels we have designed and built to pay a slight light-air penalty in order to have sufficient keel area to allow us to sail slowly to windward under adverse conditions. This design trait can be used to advantage in less than storm conditions as well.

If you are caught out and have to make progress uphill but don't have prior experience, you are going to have to experiment to see what works well for you. From the standpoint of comfort you will want to carry as little sail as possible and to go slowly. But if you start drifting to leeward, you will have to add sail to increase boatspeed and water flow over the keel.

Success to windward under adverse conditions is also a function of the tactics you employ. It may be best to carry a little more sail than is comfortable for the gusts in order to keep moving in the lulls. In the stronger gusts you can pinch up some.

Usually it will be necessary to keep the boat driving just off the wind to make headway through the seas. A vessel that normally sails at 35 degrees apparent wind angle may have to fall off to 40 or 45 degrees to continue progress.

Remember that your heavy air is most probably the result of frontal weather, which means you can also expect substantial windshifts. It may be better to heave-to for the moment and await the windshift that will free you. Or perhaps it is best to pinch for the time being, knowing you can sail off when the wind begins to swing.

HEAVING-TO

When the time comes to take a rest or just hold station, you will want to consider heaving-to. If you do so properly, your vessel will lie quietly with her head 40 to 50 degrees off the wind, rising and falling rythmically as seas sweep under the hull. Drift, both forward and to leeward, will be minimal, and if the seas are on the steep side, the slick that develops to windward of the hull can, under some circumstances, reduce the chances of waves breaking on board.

Heaving-to has a much wider application at sea than just coping with bad weather, of course. If you need to delay your arrival because of poor visibility or low tide, it will probably be more comfortable to heave-to than to slow down so much that you haven't enough way on to keep motion reasonable. Over the years we have frequently hove-to for dinner, a hot shower, or a good night's sleep when conditions were a bit too bouncy. We have also hove-to while undertaking difficult maintenance chores.

In heavy weather, heaving-to can be a useful means of holding station while giving up a minimum amount of room to leeward. If you are beating or reaching and the wind and sea are making life difficult, you'll notice an amazing difference in motion when you stop forward progress.

Heaving-to is also useful in advance of a storm you know you

Heaving-to requires a balance between the sails and helm to keep the
boat lying as close to the wind as possible (A). As the wind increases,
sail area will have to be reduced and the center of effort moved aft, or
the bow will tend to blow off to leeward (B).

can't avoid. It will give you a chance to check your gear, to rig storm canvas, and most important, to get a good rest.

If you are considering heaving-to for more than a short period, you'll need to weigh several factors. The first is navigational. If there is any current about, you will want to be relatively certain of the direction the current is traveling and any dangers that may exist in that direction. Remember, current will have more relative impact on your drift when you are moving slowly or not at all than when you are moving fast.

Be certain to maintain a good watch if land or reefs may be nearby. Even if you think you have enough offing, check the horizon periodically. Your last fix may not have been accurate or your drift may be quicker than you think.

However, pay close attention to the storm's likely path if you are contemplating heaving-to because of approaching stormy weather. Maintaining speed may get you clear more quickly than staying in one place. In some cases moving on and taking a pounding may be the more conservative approach.

There are an infinite variety of ways to heave-to. And as sea and wind change, you will have to modify the particular combination that works on your own boat.

Reduced to the simplest components, heaving-to is maintaining a balance among the forces generated by a shortened rig, a rudder, and the wind. By moving the balance, or center of effort, in the rig aft, by reducing speed, and by putting the helm down so the bow wants to head up, you effectively stop your boat.

If there is too much helm, the bow may go through the eye of the wind and tack. If there is too little, or if there is too much headsail up, the bow may lay off downwind, and you will slowly forereach.

Having the right-sized sails for the wind strength is critical. In light to medium winds, single-stickers can make do with a full or reefed mainsail. On *Intermezzo* we often employed just the mizzen to hold us in position, although we found that as the wind increased we had to add a small headsail to balance it. In moderate-force winds a staysail with reefed main usually worked well. In general, when wind forces increase, sail area has to be reduced proportionately, so that in heavy air you may be down to only a storm trysail or a trysail in combination with a storm jib set on a staysail stay.

As the seas make up, it becomes more important to be sure your bow is being held up. If your hove-to position is abeam or downwind of the seas, a breaking wave can be very dangerous. With the bow in the proper attitude, a breaking sea will exert less force on your boat, and cabinsides and other deck structures will be less vulnerable.

You can gain practice heaving-to in a variety of conditions close to home. The first step is to tack, but leave the jibsheet cleated. As you come about, put the helm down so the bow wants to head up. Way will mostly stop, but because of the normal-sized headsail you will be forereaching slowly ahead. If you drop the headsail, your bow will come much closer to the wind. If the boat wants to tack, ease the helm a bit and or slide the mainsheet traveler to leeward.

As the wind strength increases, try reefing the main and using the staysail or storm jib in conjunction with differing amounts of helm. Gradually you will build up a logbook with a number of combinations entered.

LYING AHULL

When wind strength increases to the point where there is simply too much wind force to heave-to, lying ahull can be a convenient, albeit potentially dangerous, way of "playing possum" with the elements. Shorn of sail, with only natural windage, most yachts will lie head downwind in a broad-reaching attitude if the helm is lashed to leeward.

Lying ahull is only a short-term, stop-gap tactic. While it has the advantage of allowing the crew to stay below, it also has shortcomings. First, it is very uncomfortable. Motion will be extreme, and any form of traffic aboard will be difficult. Your vessel takes a tremendous buffeting from the sea with no sail to steady you. Second, drift to leeward will be rapid, and third, once the seas begin to break, you are in a very vulnerable angle to the waves, with no way on with which to adequately steer clear of dangerous crests. Under these conditions lying ahull becomes the most dangerous of storm tactics.

Of the four people we have spoken with recently who have experienced being rolled in a small yacht, three said they were lying ahull when the boat rolled over. In two of the three cases, rigging or structural failures had occurred, and given the circumstances they felt lying ahull was the best tactic to employ. Hindsight, however, had convinced all three sailors that they would employ more active heavy-weather tactics the next time around.

If conditions are such that you feel lying ahull may be a safe compromise, keep a wary eye out on the development of the storm and its seas. You will want to change tactics *before* waves start to break on board. If you wait until it seems dangerous, the first of the breakers that might give you warning may also roll you over.

Assuming you have been lying ahull because it is unsafe to run off before the storm, the last tactic available is forereaching.

This approach is a rarely used although valuable heavy-weather tactic when sea conditions deteriorate to the point where heaving-to or lying ahull are unsafe and a lee shore makes running off impractical.

FOREREACHING

Forereaching is really an active form of heaving-to. You proceed forward, as close to the wind as possible, maintaining just enough boatspeed to head up into breaking seas when required.

Balance among boatspeed, apparent wind angle, and wave angle are critical. If you're moving too fast, a plunging, wildly uncomfortable, and potentially dangerous ride may result. If you're moving too slowly, reaction time to breaking waves will be inadequate.

The most important factors are wave angle and shape. It is

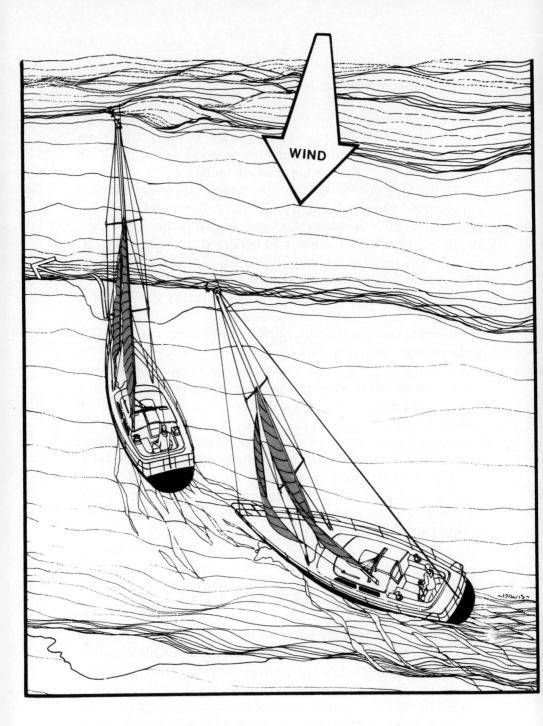

If you are beating into breaking seas, you will want to head higher, putting the bow as close to straight through the crests as possible, and then head off the wind as you punch through. Care has to be exercised to prevent your being caught aback.

not unusual to find the waves almost straight-on to the bow on one tack and somewhat abeam when you're on the opposite board. I feel that if they are breaking dangerously, I want them as close-on the bow as possible to reduce loading on the hull as it penetrates the crest.

In forereaching *the balance of your storm canvas must be similar to that of your normal sailing rig*. The center of effort should have the same or slightly more lead over the center of lateral resistance of hull and keel. Leeward helm, however, should be avoided at all costs, as you'll need to luff quickly into the biggest seas to avoid being smashed broadside.

The helming technique in forereaching is much the same as that practiced on racing yachts when beating in big seas. You want to keep up speed by heading off in the smoother patches of water and heading up into the breaking crests. This tactic allows your bow to split the wave, keeping any boarding portions, you hope, on the foredeck.

You must take care not to be caught aback on a new tack, with the waves more abeam. If this occurs, the headsail will hold your bow well off the wind and your hull will be in its most vulnerable position.

Forereaching can be carried out successfully with a powerful windvane. We used this approach in the most dangerous gale *Intermezzo* ever weathered, off the southern coast of Africa. A combination of Aries servo-pendulum vane and a fully balanced spade rudder made it possible. We maintained a speed through the water of 3 knots as our course varied from 25 degrees to 50 degrees from the wave faces. Occasionally a very large breaking sea would rumble aboard, making contact at the bow or mainmast cap shrouds. *Intermezzo* would shudder, stop, and then head off down the backside of the wave.

Sometimes the storm staysail would luff violently as we were flung too close to the wind, while Linda and I waited anxiously to see if we would be taken aback. But during the 36 hours of this 50-knot gale in the middle of the Aghulas Current, we never had a problem. Had conditions on deck been less chaotic or had we had an extra crewmember aboard I would have preferred to suffer the discomfort of hand steering, but given our situation, that

Intermezzo II driving hard downwind in 60 to 70 knots of wind in a Cape Hatteras norther. This photo was taken after we had rounded the cape and seas had subsided!

Sean Holland photo

was not a safe option.

One risk of forereaching, especially under self-steering, is being dropped from the face of an overly steep wave into the trough. This can occur if boatspeed is too slow and angle to the waves too flat. On a well-built, flushdeck yacht such a fall could be tolerated without serious damage, but boats with abovedeck superstructure could be seriously damaged. If this potential for damage exists, forereaching should be employed only where running off is out of the question because of a lee shore.

There is no single rule for dealing with heavy weather. As conditions change, as wind strength increases and seas build, become unstable, or mature, you must constantly modify the tactics you employ to deal with the elements. At some point dangerous wave shape may make running downwind the safest alternative.

RUNNING OFF

The traditional method of running off in heavy weather has meant going as slowly as possible, while towing some form of drogue to keep your stern to the seas. This method has the advantage of allowing the crew and vessel to assume a passive attitude. You are at the mercy of the elements but no direct action is required. The crew lie in their bunks, listening with apprehension as the big ones hiss by, safe from the tumult on deck.

The body of seagoing lore supporting this approach was based on the experience of heavy-displacement, low-freeboard yachts with long keels and attached rudders. This type of vessel is difficult to steer downwind in heavy going, doesn't take kindly to surfing, and is at extreme risk in a broach. With this design there is no choice but to adopt a slow-down approach to the elements.

But the majority of today's cruisers sport moderate- to light-displacement hulls, detached rudders, high freeboard, and relatively low centers of gravity. As a result, they can tolerate more downwind speed, can be controlled better, and are not as subject to danger if they do broach. Thus on a modern-design vessel, it becomes possible for the crew to remain active participants in the downwind contest.

Assuming you have sea room to leeward, running off at speed under control offers one of the safest ways of dealing with breaking seas. Within limits, higher speed can mean more, not less, control, *and it is steering control that is the secret to this safety*.

With greater boatspeed, an overtaking wave, if it boards you, will have less impact. Boatspeed, as long as there is attendant maneuverability, means the helmsman can steer away from breaking crests and across dangerous troughs at the least risky attitude.

The key, then, is the physical ability of the crew to control the speed and direction of the vessel as they play on the wave faces. In deciding upon the right amount of speed, you first have to understand the handling characteristics of your boat under heavy-air downwind conditions.

The single most important element of design is hull balance. If the hull is balanced, your boat maintains the same amount of weather helm as she heels over. The more unbalanced your hull is, the more weather helm she generates as she heels. Moderate-beam yachts without large stern distortions tend to be balanced, while yachts with fat sterns or excessively broad beam are unbalanced.

Hull balance is important for two reasons. First, even in smooth water a balanced hull will steer more easily. Second, one of the biggest risks in running downwind in heavy air is that of being slapped on the stern quarter by a wave and being spun around. If you are spun around, the apparent wind builds, and the boat quickly heels. The helmsman has to exert force on the rudder both to head back down the wave face *and* to counteract weather helm from heeling. The less weather helm there is, the easier will be his or her job, and in an ultimate situation, the better will be the odds for survival.

The steering system is the next important ingredient. The better it is, the quicker will be your response on the helm. Balanced spade rudders generate the most turning force for the least amount of effort. A skeg-hung rudder with a counter-balance projection comes next. Vessels with keel-attached rudders have the least efficient helms.

You also need an efficient means of transmitting the helmsman's force to the rudder. Low gear ratio cable-steering systems with roller-bearing blocks have little friction. Worm-gear steering, on the other hand, has substantial amounts of friction and is slow.

Underwater profile and displacement go hand in hand. A heavy, smooth-tracking design with a long keel and lots of deadrise is less maneuverable than a lighter design with fin keel and cutaway forefoot. Maneuverability is the cornerstone of safe speed downwind.

Freeboard and vertical center of gravity are next. Lighter weight vessels with higher freeboard are able to endure more of a broach and recover through a wider range of sea conditions. If you can take a knockdown without immersing a great deal of your deck, you are less likely to be tripped and rolled by the drag of the deck edge. Keel shape plays a part, too. A deep-keeled yacht may trip on her fin where a shallower design might just skid off to leeward, much the way a dinghy whose centerboard is up does on a power reach. The lower your vertical center of gravity is and the stiffer your vessel, the better she will behave in a broach and the less she will tend to heel when slapped by seas. Late International Offshore Rule designs are at some risk here due to their excessively high centers of gravity and limited range of stability. Conservative seamanship indicates that a vessel should be able to heel at least 125 degrees before rolling over, but some racing designs will hardly make it to 90. If you are sailing one of these in heavy conditions you will have to pay extra attention to crew position and helming. High vertical-center-of-gravity designs should be buttoned up and be made watertight very early into any sort of a blow.

The last characteristic of design that affects downwind storm tactics in an important way is stern shape and its relationship to the rudder. Some modern yachts with broad sterns and rudders hung well aft when heeled have little rudder left in

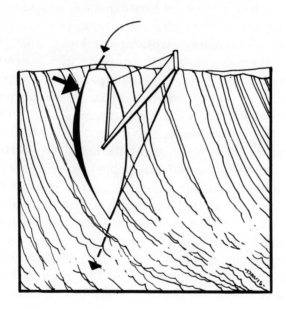

A broach is usually started by a wave catching the stern. The better your steering control, the easier it will be for you to correct the course back downwind *before* the broach occurs.

the water with which to turn back downwind.

In assessing what heavy-weather tactic to employ you must also assess the human element. An easily steered design means that you will be able to use self-steering longer. That means the crew, when called upon, is better rested. The pool of steering talent is important, and their collective strength must be rationed against the expected period of dangerous steering conditions. This applies to other heavy-weather tactics as well, of course. If you sail shorthanded, as most of us do, you will want to be sure that all your working crew can physically handle the steering loads.

Fortunately it is not necessary to be caught offshore in a severe blow to learn how to steer off the wind under difficult conditions. The quickest way to proficiency is in a performance planing dinghy. The dinghy sailor's equivalent of a winter gale in the Gulf Stream won't even rate small-craft warnings in a 30-foot family cruiser.

Scaling up, larger craft can find adequate testing grounds close to home where a strong breeze runs against a fast-flowing tide. If the water is shallow, so much the better. The short, steep waves, especially if you put up a larger than normal sailplan, will give you an idea of what may happen offshore with more wind, bigger waves, and storm canvas.

Even a broach, properly prepared for, can be sloughed off. Heeling a well-found vessel to a 60-degree angle or more, when there is no second breaking wave, isn't a major cause for concern. If you stay dry below, have storm shutters in place, and have an easily managed rig, a little extra adrenaline may flow, but not much else.

Having examined your boat's design and your crew and practiced in moderate conditions, you must finally look to the condition of your yacht. Just as it is important upwind, a smooth, clean bottom means you can attain the necessary speed with less sail, and the hull will respond better. But just a moderate amount of growth on your hull and rudder will reduce substantially the speed at which you can travel and still maintain control. Likewise, the less payload you carry and the lower it is stored, the safer you will be. If you have a feathering or

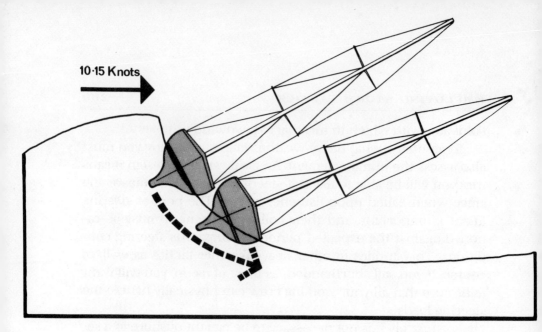

10·15 Knots

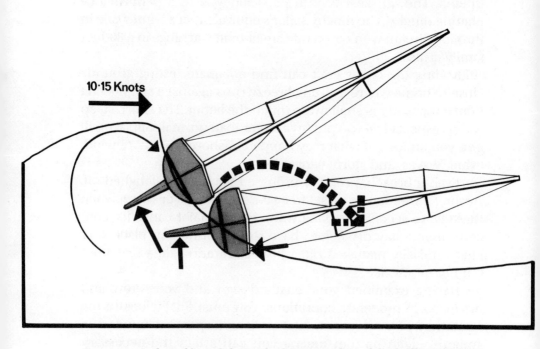

10·15 Knots

In a wave-induced knockdown the biggest risk is of the hull tripping on the deck edge as it is shoved to leeward. Yachts with higher freeboard will fare better in this situation. Open to debate is the different effect a wave-induced breakdown has on deep keels and shallow keels. We feel a shallow keel is at less risk, but recent tank testing indicates the there may be little difference in the behavior of keel types in this situation.

folding prop instead of a fixed wheel, so much the better.

Heavy weather and dangerous seas are relative terms. What may seem to be survival conditions to a neophyte out of sight of land for the first time is often just a brisk sail to more experienced sailors. Vessel size has less to do with safety than comfort. How, then, do you know the proper downwind tactics to adopt without having prior experience?

Within the context of the level of your crew's skill and your vessel's handling characteristics, wave shape and size are the most important considerations. You want to maintain enough speed to have fast steering response. Windspeed complicates the decision about which canvas to carry. If it were constant in angle and velocity, the boat could be trimmed up for the chosen speed. But the wind is constantly changing, and it is the lulls that are the most dangerous. Boatspeed drops, you lose steering control, and you lose your ability to react ahead of a breaking sea, to steer out of the way of a crest. As a result, in many situations it is less dangerous to carry a bit too much sail than too little. *Adequate speed must be maintained for good steering control.*

A major factor that controls the application of these tactics is sea development. A storm that comes on suddenly with high wind speeds will initially generate very steep waves. So too will a current opposing the wind. Underwater obstructions or a shallow seabed produce similar results. In both a mature storm and one that develops gradually, the seas will be large but stretched out. Regardless of a wave's ultimate size, it is the breaking crest that does the damage. A large but stable wave holds little to fear.

If you have been hove-to, forereaching, or lying ahull and the seas begin to break, you will have to consider running off. If only an occasional sea is breaking you will have more options in boatspeed and angle. During this period of a storm, carefully weigh the course to be steered while you still have some flexibility. Windshifts, lee shores, changing currents, and bathrythmic contours that may cause sea changes all have to be considered.

Where a lee shore is present, even though far off, or where a lee shore may be created by a windshift, do everything possible to avoid giving up room to leeward. Maintaining sea room may

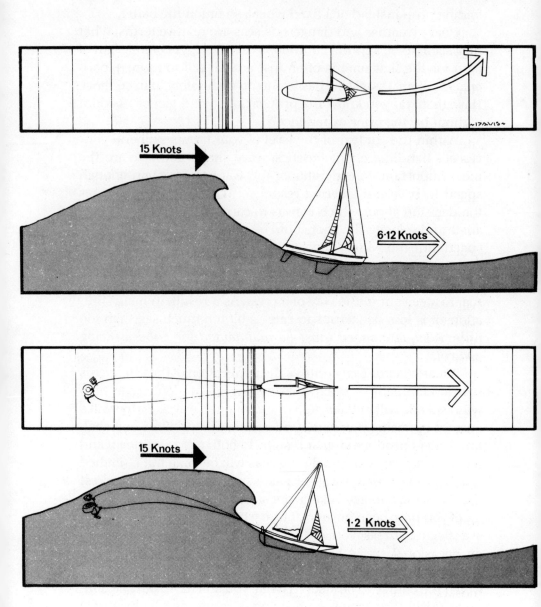

The faster you travel (as long as you're in control!), the less likely it is that a breaking crest will catch you.

mean broad reaching across the seas, in which the helmsman will have to keep an eye out for the occasional breaking crest and head off downhill in front of it.

In the absence of the need to steer a specific course, the best downwind route is usually between a very broad reach and a dead run. Keeping the wind slightly on the quarter will be more comfortable. Boatspeed can be held in the moderate levels as the risk from going too slowly relates directly to the severity of the sea conditions.

As the seas steepen and more begin to break, it becomes safer to sail in the higher range of your controllable speed spectrum. Your steering has to be more adept, but you are less likely to be caught unawares by a crest and knocked down or spun around. With a windshift or secondary wave system imposed on the first, the situation becomes more complicated. The combination of two wave trains coming together at divergent angles will occasionally create highly unstable breaking seas. The more normal wave-to-wave pattern will also be affected, and you may have to adopt a course change that keeps the most dangerous series of seas primarily aft of your stern quarter, while not letting the other system catch the bow and induce a broach.

Under "normal" heavy downwind steering your major moment-to-moment concern will be with quartering seas trying to slap the stern and spin you broadside to waves. You will hear and see these seas before they hit, which gives you time to align your stern with them, or if you are late, correct course back downhill before you are broached. Up to a point, the slower you are moving or the harder your vessel is to steer, the more you will have to anticipate the needed correction.

Even at night, with heavy overcast, a breaking crest will usually be visible in enough time for you to take avoiding action. The mass of white water on the face of the wave is visible under the most inclement of nighttime conditions. Of course, the sounds it makes don't change at nightfall.

That the helmsman stay alert is obviously a prerequisite. He or she must be securely tethered to the vessel, and in the best of all worlds, dry, and well rested. Remember that these factors, too, directly relate to your ability to steer your yacht.

At some point you may find you have too much speed and need to slow down. Where seas become extremely steep or troughs deep so that the vessel can't be controlled, whether because of helmsman fatigue or design inadequacies, you must take a new approach. Towing warps or drogues will reduce boatspeed but they have the inherent problem of being relatively fixed. Once a long bight is deployed astern, it is next to impossible to shorten or bring it aboard should a lull in the wind make a speed increase necessary. For this reason, where practical, I prefer to run the engine in reverse as an overall means of slowing progress. It gives you the ability to allow boatspeed to increase quickly when a lull threatens.

The period immediately after the passing of a storm is potentially the most dangerous. The seas remain rough long after the wind has gone; in fact, shorn of wind pressure, they quickly become unstable and more liable to break. Your boatspeed drops and the crew relaxes, happy the storm has passed. It is now that sail must quickly be set to keep boatspeed up. It will be several hours before the seas settle down.

Yachts at extreme ends of the design spectrum will require different handling. Very heavy vessels with attached rudders will be uncontrollable under the same conditions that will allow a more moderate design to be surfing gaily ahead of the waves. But design doesn't change the basic approach to dealing with extreme conditions. Yachts of this type should still be run at the best speed *commensurate with steering control* within the context of *their* capabilities.

At the other end, extremely light small yachts with unbalanced hulls and high centers of gravity of the type fostered by recent IOR changes may accelerate too fast on a breaking face to be controlled by any but the finest helmsman. They are caught in a design-induced conundrum: too fast and they may spin out and be rolled; too slow, and they will be caught by a breaking crest and smashed down in the trough. On the other hand, ultra-lights with balanced hulls and low vertical center of gravitys are so easily steered that they can be handled by less experienced crew with a higher degree of safety.

The type of sailplan to be deployed and the ease with which

it can be changed under adverse conditions will have a great impact on the success of your tactics. A low center of effort that is balanced in the same general area as the normal rig is required. Sails must be able to be set and led efficiently, with good shape control. Carrying a storm jib on the very end of the bow, for example, puts the hull-to-rig relationship out of balance, reducing maneuverability. The Cruising Club of America has recently recognized this factor by requiring entrants in the biennial Newport, Rhode Island, to Bermuda Race to be able to set storm jibs or staysails on an inner forestay. A storm staysail on its own or in combination with deeply reefed main or trysail is ideal. Split rigs are usually safer this way as well, rather than with a jib and jigger setup. *Roller-furling systems are not acceptable alternatives to proper storm canvas.*

In the final analysis, you will rarely encounter truly dangerous conditions offshore. These tactics, if employed at all, will more likely see action in the context of completing a voyage in the quickest, most comfortable way. Preparation, forethought, and practice under moderate conditions will give you the tools to deal with the sea on an even basis.

AVOIDING HEAVY WEATHER

Heavy-weather tactics make for a lively discussion. But most of us would rather keep the debate focused in the abstract. Most dangerous heavy weather can be avoided by understanding how weather patterns and seasons relate to the boat you are sailing.

LOCAL SYSTEMS

There are three basic types of weather patterns to which sailors should be alert. The first deals with locally generated winds of short duration. These are often associated with summertime thunderstorms, local fronts, or nearby mountain ranges.

In most cases the characteristics, expected velocity, and warning signals are well known to local sailors. Information is usually available as well from nearby weather bureaus and harbormasters and is often mentioned in guidebooks or the pilot.

The summer thunderstorms that pepper the Chesapeake Bay, Long Island Sound, and Florida coastline are good examples. Sailors living in these areas can watch the thunderheads develop firsthand. When these miniature fronts sweep out from the land there is less warning, although even then they are usually visible from some distance, leaving time for sailors to seek shelter or reduce sail. And while wind velocities in a summer thunderstorm can be substantial—as much as 75 knots—the duration is short, and they rarely generate the waves that would damage a seagoing yacht.

Topography can also generate substantial winds. Winds aloft can trip on mountaintops and swoop down to sea level, resulting in heavy localized velocities. Again, these downslope winds do not usually generate large seas. Perhaps the best-known example of this phenomenon takes place in the Hawaiian Islands. The tall mountains bring the high-speed components of the trades roaring down to earth. Exhilarating sailing (as long as you are on a stiff, dry boat!) is the result. The lesson here is that if you are sailing along a mountainous shoreline with an offshore breeze, expect the wind to increase by canyon and river mouths and to decrease where the mountains edge the shore. The rule of thumb is to hug the shore as close as possible. Winds may be less, and the short offshore fetch will prevent wave buildup.

An especially dangerous type of localized offshore breeze can be generated by stationary high- and low-pressure areas rotating asynchronously; the wintertime "Santa Ana" winds on the northern Mexican and southern California coastlines are but one example of this effect. The switch from light pleasant sailing to roaring northerlies is usually abrupt. If you are anchored in an exposed location, say the northeast side of one of the offshore California islands, when the Santa Ana arrives, you will suddenly find yourself on a dangerous lee shore.

The right ingredients to create a Santa Ana-type condition can exist for weeks with nothing untoward happening. As a result, many sailors in these areas tend to ignore the potential danger. At night a high barometer and a clear, sharp sky are precursors. During the day abrupt shifts in temperature and a definitive dirty cloudline towards the mainland are telltale signs.

WEATHER PATTERNS AND SYSTEMS

Of greater concern to more cruising sailors than locally generated weather patterns are longer-range weather systems, which on a macro-scale are to some degree predictable. For example, weather patterns vary tremendously over the course of a year, both in potential damage they may cause and in their predictability. As a general rule, summer months, whether north or south of the equator, offer the mildest weather, except where tropical storm development can occur. Equinoctial weather (spring/fall) can be the worst in terms of speed, movement, and development, making equinoctial gales among the hardest to predict. Winter storms are generally easier to predict, if a bit colder and windier.

The first element that should concern a cruising sailor is the quality of any weather forecasts he or she is likely to receive. With weather satellites, automatic ocean buoys, and myriad other devices at our disposal, forecasting today has a lot going for it, but there are still problems. Timing is a big one.

The wind howls through *Intermezzo*'s rigging as she tugs at her mooring lines. Snugly secured to the Point Yacht Club dock in Durban, South Africa, she is weathering yet another southwesterly gale. For three weeks now, we and a number of other visiting yachts have been waiting for a clear stretch of weather— just enough of a breather to allow us to travel the 230 miles down the coast to East London. Every night we crowd around the club television to listen to the latest weather report and study the synoptic map. It's not that we really want to leave. The club facilties are wonderfully located, tucked behind a lovely park in the middle of a beautiful, modern city with laundry, supermarket, and library only a few blocks away; we could stay forever except that new ports beckon.

My Dad at the helm of the 68-foot cutter *Deerfoot*. Note the safety harness being worn even though conditions are moderate.

Two hundred thirty miles doesn't sound far in the context of the 13,000 sea miles we have covered the last year, but this short passage is likely to be among the hardest we will do. Late spring and early summer in this part of the world bring a succession of fast-moving high-pressure systems. These compact highs generate strong southwesters that by themselves wouldn't be too bad. The real problem is the Agulhas Current. Running southerly at 3 to 8 knots, it opposes the wind, creating mountainous, steep waves in the process. Add a sharp drop at the edge of the continental shelf and swells arriving from the Southern Ocean, and you can understand why professional mariners consider this coastline the most dangerous in the world. Even though we have a lot of faith in *Intermezzo*'s abilities, we prefer not to put her to the ultimate test. And so we wait.

You have to understand the problems of disseminating weather data to fully comprehend a forecaster's plight. Most weathermen, if they could talk to you in real time, would do a relatively accurate job. But it takes them time to assimilate the data they receive and then to prepare their reports, which still must be sent to the broadcast stations to which you listen. Weather systems can move, combine, and develop rapidly. A frontal system that looks moderate at 0600 may have turned into a dangerous gale by 1200. If the weather report is broadcast at 1130 you may be 6 or 8 hours from knowing what the forecaster thinks, which means you must also keep an eye out for yourself.

Using external sources of weather analysis—radio broadcasts, weatherfax, television, and printed charts—should be a part of your total approach to forecasting, but the cautious skipper evaluates what he or she sees locally, too. Cloud formations, barometer readings, wind direction, wind velocity, nature of shifts, temperature, and sea state all are excellent indicators of what you can expect. Combined with the externally generated reports, they provide an excellent basis for predicting your future.

High- and low-pressure systems generally move in a northwest to southeast direction in the Northern Hemisphere and a southwest to northeast direction in the Southern Hemisphere. If you are sailing on the East Coast of the United States, then there are hundreds of stations feeding data to the weatherman about what is coming at you. On the other hand, systems arriving from at sea on the West Coast of the United States, in New Zealand, or at the bottom of Africa, for example, come as much more of a surprise.

Right now we are wondering what surprises may be in store for us. *Intermezzo*'s tanks are topped off, the fridge is full of fresh supplies, and our heavy #3 jib is bent on the headstay. A light northeaster teases us, and the forecast guarantees two delightful days of clear weather. A fair breeze and fair current should make quick work of the 230-mile passage. If we are lucky we might even make it farther down the coast before the weather breaks.

Three other yachts hastily make their preparations as well. It will almost be a race. We cast off and pull out of the raft-up in front of the club. With a last round of farewells we motor clear and head for the breakwater. *Intermezzo* lifts her head as the first swells sweep by. Before long she is plugging along at 5.5 knots under the drifter, main, and mizzen staysail. While South Africa has a reputation for unreliable forecasts, my own instincts have jived with the reports of the professionals, and I see nothing outside the harbor to make me change my mind.

Assuming you have mastered the basics of reading weather maps and external weather signs, you should be able to formulate for each passage certain weather signs. A key ingredient is time. If you are on a tight schedule, you may be tempted to take more risks. Better to allow the weather system to pass or leave the boat and attend to business, moving her later on.

One of the axioms of coasting the southern end of the African continent is that you either stay close inshore or go far outside, beyond the influence of the Agulhas Current. I have decided instead to play the current for as much speed as possible and duck inshore if we get caught in a southwester. Twenty-four hours later I am beginning to wonder about my tactics. Our fair breeze has gone around to the south but remains light. We are some 30 miles offshore, and our transmission has chosen an inopportune moment to quit.

We are now beating, heading directly for shore. The weather

forecast hasn't mentioned a blow, but a rising barometer and the windshift are not good signs. At our 2.5 or 3 knots of speed, even a slow-moving high will be able to catch us. I go forward and change up to our heavy #2 genoa. It will keep us moving, and with a reef in the main we should be able to carry it to 30 knots of wind. Getting across the continental shelf and out of the current is now my chief concern.

Of course, you never can be 100 percent certain of the weather you will encounter. You can reduce risks but never totally eliminate them. Any passagemaking planning must, of course, take into account the characteristics of vessel and the area through which you'll be traveling. Are there intermediate ports you can use in the event that weather threatens to overtake you? How difficult are the entrances? Can they be negotiated in foul weather, with a sea running, or at night? Will you be on a lee shore? How seaworthy is your boat? How fast can she move under power (including range) and under sail? The wind often dies in the approach path of a major storm system, and with good powering speed/range you can scoot out of harm's way. Finally, how prepared for heavy weather is the boat and crew?

Intermezzo is pounding hard. Bone-jarring shudders run stem to stern as she crashes through the almost-vertical seas. It seems only minutes ago that we had a calm sea, and now it is blowing 25 to 30 with 6- to 8-foot waves.

I am torn between reducing canvas and thus putting our speed at a more comfortable level and pressing on before the wind makes up even more. Pretoria weather hasn't dignified our blow with a forecast, but I am concerned about the continuing rise in the barometer.

Coastal journeys entail less risk weatherwise than longer offshore passages. Weather data is apt to be more reliable and harbors of refuge closer at hand. Thus, weather factors are not quite as important as they are when you journey offshore, when you will be at risk with the elements for many days. Because frontal systems can move so quickly, it is impossible to predict an entire offshore passage free of bad weather. Most sailors play the odds; they pick the best season for voyaging and then try for the clearest shot within that time.

Picking the right time of year in part means minimizing risks from cyclonic storms, or hurricanes. In the North Atlantic, for example, the hurricane season runs from June through October; within this broad period, however, are wide year-to-year variations. There were few hurricanes there in 1983 and 1984, yet the normally docile eastern North Pacific racked up major cyclonic disturbances in record numbers. Hurricanes can occur out of season as well.

Looking at the averages, however, allows you to take the path of minimum risk. You want to thread your way between winter gales and summer hurricanes. In most of the world, that leaves the end of spring and the beginning of fall for serious offshore passages.

There are two approaches to picking the final departure time. One is to wait until a clear period appears to be developing. It may result from a lull between weather systems, in which case powering may be the best way to move. Or a slow-moving high-pressure system or even a double high may bring temporary stability to the area. A high tends to block any deep lows before passing on, but beware: highs can also deal wind.

A second approach is to wait until a favorable, somewhat stable weather system exists and then ride it as long as possible. This is the "better the devil you know than the one you don't" theory.

A major factor to consider when you are working up strategy is the direction you are sailing relative to the direction the weather is moving. In general, westbound vessels sail into weather and eastbound ones away from it. If you are heading east then, the weather overtakes you. This means there's a much longer period between changing systems. If the low or high is moving at 15 knots and you are going 7 in the same direction, the system will come closer to you by only 190 miles a day. If you are heading towards the weather, the rate of approach becomes 528 miles a day.

That is the basic problem we face coming down this awful African coast. We and the weather are on a collision course. "I'm starting to see the coast on the radar," Linda calls up from below.

"Looks like we are sixteen miles off."

Twelve miles until the shelf, I think to myself. Nothing to do now but hang on.

With the wind still building, I am forced to shorten sail. We tuck a reef into the main, and our motion eases somewhat. But I am concerned that *Intermezzo* might drop off a wave face into the trough. Perhaps the genoa should be furled in favor of the storm staysail?

We seem to be crossing varying areas of current velocity. At some points the seas even out a bit; then just as we relax, they become nearly vertical again.

I can see the coastline now. The coastal mountaintops are lost in cloud. Before long we'll reach the shelf.

On a passage that runs the same direction as the weather, you may get two or three days grace, enough time to complete many voyages without undue hardship. But if you are heading towards the system, a day may be all the time you have before a major shift in conditions.

Revolving storms that start out as tropical lows are particularly potent systems to watch. These storms have different characteristics in various parts of the world, and while they tend to display set patterns in formation, speed direction and movement, wind development, and size and have some degree of predictability, they do not follow the same patterns as open weather systems. For example, western Pacific typhoons are generally larger and have higher windspeeds than their Atlantic or eastern Pacific cousins, and they follow less of a seasonal pattern. Western North Pacific typhoons have been known to develop in all months of the year with some degree of frequency, although they tend to occur more often in summer months.

If you choose to make a passage where the potential for one of these lows to develop is greater than you would like, you must maintain a careful watch of weather reports. You need to decide in advance how cautiously to play this cat-and-mouse game with disaster. Sailors do make successful passages between revolving storms, but reliable power and good range are prerequisites. You have to be prepared to turn tail and run if the storm begins to head in your direction. It is often possible to dip towards the equator to avoid tropical lows, since they rarely move into the equitorial zone. And you must be prepared to head away from the storm's expected path, even if you must turn away from your final destination. Finally, you must always keep in mind that storms are to some degree unpredictable and can jog suddenly or reform quickly after seemingly having died.

Be careful about the type of landfall you are going to make when tropical storms are about. Overcast skies with heavy rain can extend many hundreds of miles from the storm center. If good visibility is required to close with the land, you may have to wait.

As sailors gain more experience offshore, they tend to treat passages that expose them to potential heavy weather with more respect. One result is a tendency to power when the wind dies; the simple fact is that when the potential for heavy weather exists, the less time you spend at sea, the less likely it is that you will be caught. We have gradually evolved from the purist's point of view, never touching the starter button on the diesel, to the pragmatist's approach. If, when we are at sea and our speed drops below an efficient motoring level, we turn on the engine. It is not pleasant to listen to, but it makes for quick, safe passages.

Suddenly *Intermezzo* seems to right herself and then, taking the bit in her mouth, charges ahead, but without the violent pitching of a few moments before. We are onto the continental shelf and out of the Agulhas Current. Hardening up, I winch in the staysail and reefed main. Ahead I can see signs of civilization dotting the coast. East London, our port of call, isn't far off.

There is no greater joy in cruising than a protected anchorage, a beautiful beach, and a graceful yacht a few yards offshore.

ASSESSING THE SEAWORTHINESS OF MODERN RACING YACHTS

Before we leave the topic of heavy weather for friendlier waters the question of how modern racing yachts stand up in heavy weather has to be discussed.

The transition from the old Cruising Club of America and Royal Ocean Racing Club rules to the International Offshore Rule brought many beneficial developments to the yachting scene. Early IOR designs were stiff, had better seakeeping abilities, were faster, and were roomier than their counterparts from days of old. But competitive pressure and certain characteristics of the IOR rule has forced designers to reduce measured stability, beamy, lightweight racing yachts with insufficient safety factors to deal with the ocean at its worst. These characteristics, coupled with skinny rigs and featherweight hulls (which reduce pitching moment), have changed the IOR type substantially from from what it was in the early seventies.

Today, in 1984, top racing boats are faster than ever. They are also more difficult to handle in heavy going and more subject to damage if anything goes wrong. And while these design parameters may add an edge to offshore racing under normal conditions, they are to be avoided if you are cruising shorthanded.

Unfortunately, many high-speed characteristics of the newer racers have filtered into some of the new, highly popular classes in the 30-foot and smaller category, which have created new problems with their offshore capabilities. First is stability. On the newer designs, very high initial stability is conferred by hull shape and the practice of putting the crew on the rail to windward. Hulls are beamy, which helps form stability directly and also moves crew further to windward.

This is coupled with an attempt to reduce both overall displacement and center of gravity and or measured righting moments. The IOR says that if you have less displacement and a higher center of gravity, you can carry more sail. On a racer, that means boatspeed.

But when the chips are down, these factors turn against the boat and her crew. The high initial stability, low displacement, and high center of gravity mean the boat has a very limited range of stability. In plain English this equates to a boat that loses its stability at moderate heeling angles and will then capsize. There is a further problem in that these same types of designs are relatively stable *upside down*. A knockdown is more likely in heavy going, and if it does occur the chances of a rollover are greater. If that happens, instead of a quick roll right back up again, these boats stay over longer, trapping crew upside down for minutes.

Some years ago when we were in New Zealand there was a giant flap over the Australians' decision to conduct actual self-righting tests before a Sydney-Hobart race. The Kiwis felt this was an attempt to throw out their best boats from the Southern Cross series. Yachts were hove down at the dock until masts were almost touching the water. They had to show that they could stay there and not go turtle. As an old catamaran sailor, I thought this test was ludicrous. Even though the boats passed this "test," nobody bothered to check what would happen if a crewmember or two fell onto the mainsail from his perilous perch on the weather rail.

Before this trend started, under the racing rules designs could go to 160 or more degrees *before losing stability*. Along with common sense, research conducted in towing tanks as a result of the 1979 Fastnet Race disaster indicate that the newer designs are more subject to being rolled over as well as being knocked down than their stiffer forerunners. Lack of range of stability is the main reason for this unhappy state of affairs.

If racing or high-speed cruising instincts move you toward these competitive animals, be aware that very special heavy-weather techniques will be required in their handling and a full complement of competent, experienced heavy-weather helmsmen should be aboard.

Were I racing today, I would applaud the specialized rigs, sail cuts, and materials and the general hull shapes. The newer boats are fast, and they are fun. But lack of hull scantlings and the dangerous range of stability (or lack thereof) have no place on an ocean-cruising yacht.

Another style of yacht has also evolved concurrently that is fast and fun *and* safe. These are some of the ultralight-displacement boats (ULDBs) and their cruising cousins, which have developed on the West Coast of the United States.

Since their primary criterion has been boatspeed regardless of the peculiarities of various handicapping rules, they have tended to be long and moderate in beam and have very low centers of gravity. As a result of the low vertical center of gravity and moderate beam, they steer easily, balance well, and behave nicely in heavy-going downwind. In many instances the hulls are conservatively built. Well-engineered ULDBs, such as Bill Lee's *Merlin* and the Santa Cruz 50s, have sailed thousands of miles without problems.

Step up the scantlings, and you have the cruising versions of the lightweights now making their appearance. These designs have long, narrow hulls, moderate rigs (which makes them easy to handle), and enough displacement left over for really strong hulls. *Intermezzo II* and the series of Deerfoot yachts that have slid down the ways in her wake are but examples of this new approach to conservative offshore design. Even though *Intermezzo II* was considered extreme by some people, her construction was as close to "bulletproof" as you can get. Her scantlings were far in excess of those required by the American Bureau of Shipping or LLoyd's, even though she was much lighter than comparable vessels for which those scantlings were engineered. Having sailed quite a few miles in older designs and in newer ones, it is our opinion that built properly, the more modern, long, narrow, lightweight cruisers are the most comfortable, seaworthy compromise yet.

Whatever type of vessel you are sailing or dreaming about, the important heavy-weather criteria boil down to this: substantial enough scantlings to take the worst the sea can dish out, hull balance to ease steering loads, and a good range of stability to limit knockdowns and rollover potential. If you have these factors working on your side, you are one step ahead of King Neptune in any contest.

The magnificent mountains of Tahiti await those cruisers who arrive in daylight. Some who arrive at night are so eager to taste the delights of this fabled port-of-call that they end up permanently on the barrier reef fronting Papeete harbor.

ENTERING STRANGE HARBORS AT NIGHT

The waning moon outlines the mountaintops of American Samoa as *Intermezzo* reaches towards Pago Pago. We have been at sea for three bouncy but fast days since leaving Suvarov atoll in the northern Cook Islands. An "American" port lays ahead. Skippy peanut butter, real hamburgers, mayonnaise, and other delicacies await.

At 2330 faint loom from the city is visible on the underside of the cloud cover. With our big reacher and a full main both drawing, we are clipping along at just under 8 knots. In another couple of hours we will be there.

"Honey, why don't you come up for a few minutes so I can have another look at the pilot and charts." A minute later Linda arrives on deck, festooned in her standard dog watch outfit of nightgown, yellow slicker, and safety harness.

"I haven't seen any traffic. We're about ten miles offshore, and the breeze seems to be holding. Don't worry about the compass course. Head for the center of the lights. Just make sure we don't close with the land too fast." With that last comment I drop below.

Sitting at *Intermezzo*'s compact nav station, I study the data laid out before me. What a pleasure! U.S. charts of U.S. waters, with the U.S. Coast Guard to maintain the aids to navigation.

It appears that the harbor entrance is distinguished by a set of range lights, several buoys marking a reef we will pass to port, and a light on a rock promontory at the starboard side of the harbor.

Entry shouldn't be too bad, I think. Once we're through the entrance, there will be a turn to port with a large deep harbor, mostly clear of obstructions, in which to find a spot to drop the hook. After a last look at the chart I turn and head back up the companionway.

"How does it look?" Linda asks.

"Shouldn't be too bad," I reply. "I think we might even go in tonight. The chart is detailed, there are range lights, it's a commercial harbor, and we are back in U.S. waters."

Linda is appalled at my suggestion. "I thought we had a rule about strange harbors after dark?"

She did have a point. It has always been our hard, fast rule *never* to venture into a strange harbor after dark. My dad taught me this tenet of seamanship, and for the sake of a few hours of being hove-to, I am preparing to break this sacrosanct rule.

"Well, let's see how things look when we get there," I reply.

The time passes almost as quickly as the trade-wind seas lifting our stern. By 0245 we are directly upwind of Pago Pago harbor, 2½ miles to leeward. The seas are running 10 to 12 feet and becoming disturbed from reflected waves bouncing off the shoreline. To heave-to until daylight will be most uncomfortable.

We shorten sail and work in slowly toward the land. Slightly to starboard I can see the first range light, a white flasher. In another few minutes I pick up the second light. The compass angle looks about right from where we stand. To starboard the entrance light beams away in its preset cadence.

"Sure looks easy," I say.

"Let's wait," is Linda's reply. "It will be light in another couple of hours. Why take a chance? Once we are hove-to I'll warm some hot chocolate. We can make a batch of popcorn, and I'll stay up to help you eat it."

That is an offer I find hard to refuse. We turn our head upwind, reef down the main, and set the small staysail. Once the genoa is rolled away our motion quiets, and I put the helm over. *Intermezzo* heaves-to neatly with the staysail aback. Hot chocolate time!

By 0530 the sky has begun to lighten to the point where visibility is rapidly improving. The mountains to starboard are sharply defined, and we can see the reef breaking to port. We bear off under reduced sail and work toward the harbor mouth.

In the first light of day the navigational lights are still visible. As we work up to windward the "range lights" hove into alignment. What I had planned to lead us safely into the harbor is a combination of a warehouse light ashore and the lighted buoy at the end of the reef! With the sea that is running *Intermezzo* would have been shredded fiberglass in minutes had we adopted that approach.

Relieved that Linda had forestalled such a rash act, I am yet irritated with the U.S. Coast Guard. After all, our tax dollars are paying for proper maintenance. Once we have tied up at the immigration dock, I hail the first man in uniform I find and advise him that the range lights aren't working.

"Well, I guess they haven't gotten around to fixing them yet," is the reply. "Last week somebody mentioned it, too." (Six weeks later when we left American Samoa the range lights still were inoperative.)

That experience strengthened my resolve never again to consider entering a strange harbor at night, even in continental waters. I might go in if I'd had a good look in daylight, but I'd never go in someplace I'd seen only in the dark.

But there may be times when it seems the lesser of two evils to seek a new harbor in the dark. Perhaps your cruising area is so reef strewn and position finding is so unreliable that the risks of standing off are greater than those of trying to make an entrance. Weather may be deteriorating, or a medical emergency may force your hand.

In weighing the alternatives you have to consider a number of aspects. First, what type of charts and pilot data do you have available? How accurate are they likely to be? Are there aids to navigation to be relied upon? To verify the information you have it is best to try to contact a local cruiser via radio. If the cruiser is in the harbor he or she will be able to advise you of the best approach and may be able to talk you in. Be sure to ask also about uncharted dangers, such as a vessel that may have recently gone to the bottom in the entrance.

You also have to weigh the dangers of inadverdently becoming stranded. Is the sea running or likely to make up? How about bottom condition? A mud bottom will be less likely to damage your vessel than rock or coral. Take into account the state of tides. A rising tide gives you some small room for error. If it is dropping you will have little chance to correct mistakes.

You also must take into account the characteristics of your vessel. If she is stoutly built, hopefully of metal, she will be able to take more punishment, for longer, if she grounds. Wood or ferrocement vessels have little tolerance for error.

We had to choose between entering an unknown harbor at night or standing off in bad circumstances during a passage we made in the New Hebrides Islands (now the nation of Vanuatu)—yes, even after vowing in Samoa we would never give ourselves that choice.

Having left Havana Harbor on the island of Efate at sunrise we are now motorsailing northwest toward a reportedly beautiful anchorage on the northwest corner of Epi Island. The quantity and variety of islets and volcanic cones dotting the horizon amaze us all. On the chart many bear the notation "active volcano", and a large area bears the warning "Caution, underwater volcanic activity." It appears that the hydrographers can't keep up with nature.

As the day wears on, a gentle swell begins to roll in from the southwest. The swell itself doesn't concern us, but as a precursor of worse to come it does; we fear our proposed anchorage may become a lee shore. We are caught in a difficult situation. There is no fully protected harbor that we know we can reach safely and in daylight. Havana is too far behind. It appears that

Port Sandwich, on the southeast corner of Malekula Island is our best bet.

We set every stitch of sail *Intermezzo* can carry as we race the sun. A bit of afternoon breeze fills in to help us on our way. If we are lucky, we may just make it.

But then the breeze begins to lighten, and we are reduced to diesel power once again. Linda and I confer; to stand offshore at night, in poorly charted waters strewn with reefs not marked by any navigation aids and possibly containing a new volcano or two seems even more dangerous than trying our luck at the new harbor. We decide to go for it.

On the ham radio we raise the Hasts aboard the schooner *Sunday Morning* in Port Sandwich. They inform us that the entrance is just as it looks on the chart, deep down the center, steep-to on the starboard side, with reef out about 100 yards from shore to port. The chart indicates a gradual shoaling from 20 fathoms to 8 some distance from the reef. Linda and I decide to enter with the radar and depthfinder and then use our eyes and depthfinder to work our way inside to an anchorage.

We head in, and Linda calls the depthfinder readings. As long as we have more than 20 fathoms under our bottom we will be okay. The entrance presents a good radar target, and we favor the starboard side away from the reef.

With the the starboard entrance now abeam, Linda heads slightly to port. I go forward to watch for any disturbance in the water that indicates shallow depths ahead. As the bottom shoals Linda calls off the numbers, "Fifteen, twelve, ten, ten, eight fathoms."

"Back down hard," is my reply, and *Intermezzo* slowly comes to a halt. We will anchor in deep water tonight. This is close enough to the reef. In the morning we will move to the inner recess of the harbor.

ANCHORING

The sound of chatter on *Intermezzo*'s foredeck cuts through the fog of my afternoon siesta. Anchored snugly in Taeohae Bae on Nuka Hiva Island, a port of entry for the French Polynesian Marquesas Islands, I am taking what I feel is a well-earned rest. After all, I say to myself, have I not just navigated us to a perfect landfall after 2,800 miles of ocean?

Respect for this accomplishment is singularly lacking in the crew as the younger members excitedly announce the arrival of a new yacht. Consoled by the thought of the fresh limeade I know Linda has in the fridge, I pick up sun visor, sunglasses, and suntan lotion and work my way towards the deck.

Adorned with proper accoutrements for a tropical paradise, I look to starboard and sight the new arrival. The reason for the excitement is immediately apparent. An honest to goodness gaff-rigged Colin Archer ketch has just sailed her way into the anchorage. Far from equating such a rig with inefficiency and hard work, Elyse and Sarah have visions of bearded pirates, cannons, and broadsides.

The skipper, whom we shall call George, drops his hook to windward and just inshore of us. While he secures his little ship I go below for a pitcher of that cold limeade. Elyse and Sarah are summoned to row some over to our new neighbor.

As I come back on deck I am surprised to see our salty-looking neighbor abeam. "You're dragging!" he hollers over.

Having just set our anchor with full reverse in a hard mud bottom, I find that a highly unlikely event and say something to that effect. George answers back, "But I have let out fifty feet of chain, and the water is only forty feet deep."

After gently suggesting he try letting go another 150 feet, I send the kids across with our peace offering. The zip in our limeade does the trick (along with a little extra rode), and he fetches up hard against his anchor.

At dinner two evenings later our new friend allows as how this is the first time he has ever anchored! As we came to find out in subsequent anchorages, this is not an unusual state of affairs. Anchoring is one seamanship technique at which many of us get little practice. Much of the time our yachts sit at moorings or in slips, and when we do set out for a weekend away, it's off to a reserved space at another marina dock or yacht club. When the time finally comes to get off by ourselves and enjoy the quiet of a secluded cove, our anchoring skills are rusty at best.

DIFFERENT STRATEGIES FOR DIFFERENT SITUATIONS

Four key factors control your approach to anchoring: bottom condition, swinging room, weather, and the protection afforded by your location. What's on the bottom will dictate the amount of scope required, the best type of anchor to use, and your relative security. In soft mud, usually found where there is alluvial runoff, such as by the mouth of a river, a Danforth-type anchor works best, because its large fluke area provides plenty of hold in soft ground. With harder bottoms—sand or stiff mud—plow anchors hold well. The plows and Bruce-type anchors have less fluke area than the Danforth-types and bury themselves into the bottom. Their advantage is two-fold. First, because they are deeply buried, when your position shifts, the anchor crabs around under the seabed to stay in line rather than drag or trip.

Second, their flukes, although smaller, are heavier and are not as subject to bending or jamming as are the lighter, larger flukes of the lightweight Danforth-type hooks. Rock bottoms require a Herreshoff or yachtsman's anchor, and in grass, depending upon the type, you may need a yachtsman's or plow anchor to penetrate through to the seabed.

In assessing just this one factor, it is obvious that no single anchor will do it all. The more experienced you become, the larger and more varied becomes the ground tackle inventory you feel you need to carry aboard. Most conservative sailors carry either a burying or Danforth-type for everyday use, a second anchor of a different type as backup or for special conditions, and a third yachtsman's type as a "once-in-a-lifetime-hope-we-never-use-it hook."

Aboard *Intermezzo* we started out with a 60-pound CQR as the main anchor. A 35-pound Danforth Hi-Tensile hook was mounted under the bowsprit for use in soft conditions or when two hooks were deemed prudent. A Viking 22-pound aluminum anchor was carried aft.

When we were still tied up in southern California, that big CQR looked enormous, and we took some ribbing about its size. But a year and a half later when we had the chance in Suva, Fiji, to trade up to a 75-pounder we jumped at it.

Intermezzo II started out with a 110-pound Bruce as her primary anchor. She had two of the largest Vikings for stern use and backup. These had the holding power of 60-pound Danforths.

Given good holding ground, amazingly small anchors will secure very large yachts. But you can't always count on good holding. In fact, the one thing you probably can count on is being stuck sometime in a tight harbor with minimum swinging room and a lousy bottom. It is under these conditions that you want to drop the biggest possible anchor.

Some cruisers carry a "storm" anchor for heavy-weather anchoring. Our philosophy is to use the storm hook as our basic all-around anchor. When you consider that the holding power of the ground tackle system comes primarily from the weight and fluke area of your anchor, a big hook begins to make sense.

Let's say you have a heavy bow roller and a windlass and you carry 300 feet of 5/16-inch high-tensile chain and four anchors. The total weight of these items may be 650 pounds. If your main anchor is a 45-pounder, it weighs less than 7 percent of the total. What happens if you upgrade to a 60-pounder? The total gain in ground tackle weight is miniscule, yet the ultimate holding power of the system in an adverse bottom has increased almost 50 percent. This is both a weight- and cost-effective means to security. Don't ignore it. As far as anchors go, bigger is definitely better.

How will you know in advance what to expect in bottom condition? Charts and guidebooks usually show bottom characteristics. Depending on its type, your depthfinder can be another good source of data. The shade and width of its track

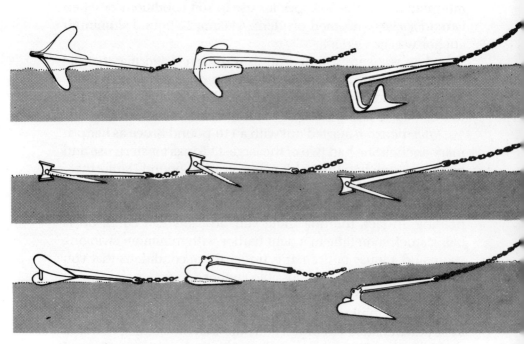

Each of these popular anchors has it's own burying characteristics. The Bruce digs down but leaves some of its stock exposed. The Danforth usually just barely scoots below the surface, while the CQR really dives deep into the bottom.

indicate relative hardness: a thin, firm line on the chart or flasher means hard bottom; a thicker line, a soft bottom or perhaps grass. An old-fashioned lead line with a little wax in its cone is another source of bottom information. Drop the line so the cone touches the bottom; the wax will pick up a sample for you to examine. If you are having trouble setting the hook, bringing it back aboard will also give you an idea of the bottom conditions. If it is clean, the seabed is probably hard. An extremely soft mud will leave filmy traces on the flukes, and a heavily weeded bottom will reveal itself where pieces of greenery catch on the hook or stick in the shackle.

Finally, bottom characteristics will be telegraphed up the anchor rode; experience teaches you the code. Placing your hand or foot on the chain or rode will enable you to feel the interaction between anchor and ground as it digs in. If you feel vibration and an occasional bump coming up the chain or rode, the anchor is sliding on the bottom. If the boat drags back slowly and then the anchor digs in, the bottom is probably composed of soft mud over firm bottom. With good holding, hard deep sand for instance, the anchor will slide a short distance and then dig in hard.

Rock- or coral-infested bottoms require a bit more interpretation. The anchor will slide and bump along, catching occasionally and then breaking loose as the load builds. You want to be careful in this situation not to be fooled into thinking you have a good bite when the anchor is temporarily locked onto a rock or coral head. The holding may be okay in the direction you are pulling, but if the wind shifts a bit, the anchor may break free.

Even where you have a steady trade-wind breeze to hold you, be wary. Although coral heads may provide an initial hold, they are apt to break off after awhile. The action of the chain or anchor grinding the soft coral weakens the head.

How much scope you need depends upon the quality of the holding ground, the size of the anchor relative to the size of your boat, and the expected loads. With a heavy anchor of the burying type, good holding, and moderate conditions, you can be as tight as three-to-one   although you would normally use this

When you are anchoring in coral, always check that your anchor has a firm grip in sand or mud. Jamming a coral head may feel like a good bite, but if the wind shifts or the head breaks, you will be drifting in a hurry.

Using a Danforth or similar style lightweight on a coral strewn or foul bottom can lead to jammed flukes. If this occurs it will be virtually impossible to get the anchor to dig in properly.

little scope only if swinging space were limited. The ideal scope is seven- or eight-to-one. But the nature of anchorage, your proximity to neighbors, or water depth may preclude you from using the ideal. The characteristics of your anchor also affect how much rode you pay out. Some anchors require flatter scope than others. A Bruce and yachtsman's can be used with very short scope. Bruce claims 50 percent holding at a scope of just three-to-one. Danforth types on the other hand, require much flatter angles. Remember, with any anchor the flatter the angle, the more scope you have and the better the holding. Still, there are some situations where no amount of scope will do, regardless of anchor type. We learned this one summer in southern Florida.

An early hurricane threat had sent *Intermezzo II* and crew looking for cover. We had picked out a protected hole some time before, just in case, and in nice weather had found the secret to working our way through the shallow canal into the deeper, protected lagoon. But we had not checked the bottom.

After gaining the lagoon we found we had it entirely to ourselves. I set about cruising back and forth, noting depthfinder readings to check for potential trouble spots and to locate the shallowest place that would allow us good swinging room. We finally opted for a slight rise in the seabed, about 25 yards to the south of the geographic center of the lagoon.

I carefully maneuvered *Intermezzo II* into location and then had Linda drop the 110-pound Bruce anchor. We had room to let out all 280 feet of chain and still swing clear of obstructions along the lagoon's perimeter. Adding our 6 feet of bow height to the 10 feet of water, we had a scope of seventeen-to-one. The Bruce held up through half-throttle in reverse, but then it

When you calculate water depth (WD) for scope or angle, always add in your freeboard (F). If you are anchored in 10 feet of water and have a 5-foot-high bow, you must assume a 15-foot height times your scope. If you want to swing on a five-to-one angle, you need 75 feet of rode, not 50 feet. The catenary (C) of chain reduces scope requirements somewhat.

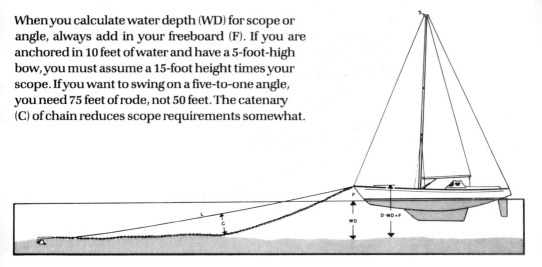

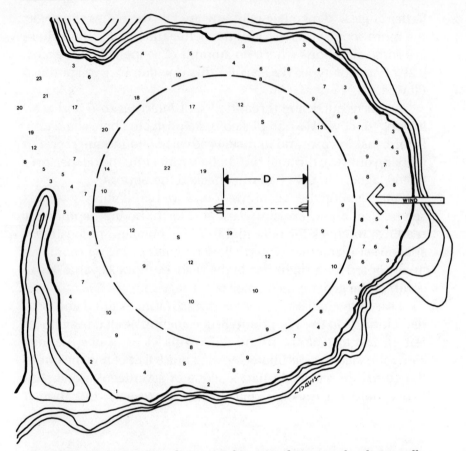

Always factor in a setting distance when you drop your hook. In really soft mud or very hard bottoms the hook may drag a considerable distance before it gets a good grip.

started to drag. Half-throttle developed the load of only 50 knots of wind, considerably less than what we were expecting.

We winched the Bruce back aboard and set one of the 32-pound Viking aluminum hooks we carried for soft bottoms. With only 25 feet of chain and 100 feet of line, the anchor stood up to full reverse, the equivalent of 70 knots of wind. We proceeded to reset the Bruce, as a backup, keeping a third Danforth-type anchor in reserve.

While you are mentally measuring scope against swinging

room, allowance for the distance the hook may drag before it sets must be made. If you have a soft ooze on top and hard mud underneath, it may take 50 or 100 feet with seven-to-one scope before the hook really digs in, depending on your anchor type. Burying anchors take longer to get a good bite, while a Danforth will dig in immediately. In tropical waters you'll sometimes drag the hook for long distances before it will find a sandy spot to dig in, unless you find a clear spot from the surface first. Even if we plan to anchor short, we initially set our hooks on longer scope. The flat angle makes it easier for the anchor flukes to dig in.

Our worst experience with dragging the hook before it set took place on the beautiful island of Raiatea in French Polynesia. We had come to the village of Uturoa to help the locals celebrate Fête. The lagoon bottom was a uniform 15 fathoms deep with the occasional coral head coming within a few fathoms of the surface. Surrounded on all sides by steep-to reef, this lagoon had a well-deserved reputation for the worst holding in the Society Islands. A very hard coral bottom overlaid by a thin layer of sand created the problem. There simply was not enough bottom material to allow a big plow anchor to dig in. And if you used a Danforth, you risked jamming the flukes with coral or having the anchor trip out as the boat swung when the tide changed. The answer was to drop the CQR and drag it until it found a sand

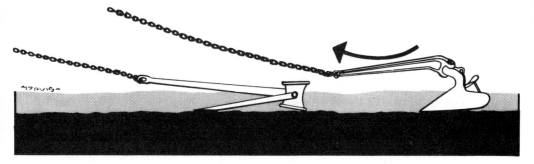

In thin sand over hard coral, typical of many tropical anchorages, the CQR type of anchor may not have enough depth to bury properly and develop full holding power. In the same conditions a Danforth may work just fine. Carrying an inventory of different anchors for different bottoms is the only solution to safe anchoring.

pocket deep enough to bury itself.

An overnight sail from Tahuata had brought us to the entrance pass for Raiatea by mid-morning. With the sunlight behind us, we had no problems entering the pass and then running down the lagoon inside the reef. Turning the corner into the anchorage, we found many old friends waiting. Elyse and Sarah would have playmates, while Linda and I could swap sea and land stories with the assembled cruisers. A famous old bakery along the road into town reputedly offered the best coconut bread in the South Pacific, and we were eager to confirm its reputation ourselves.

Unfortunately the quay was already crowded so we were forced to anchor out. We circled around and around, looking for a shallow spot to drop the hook, without luck. We would have to let go in 15 fathoms. That meant we had to use all 480 feet of chain to get any sort of reasonable scope.

I circled two more times just to double-check and then, positioning *Intermezzo*'s bow in the middle of the anchorage, signaled to Linda to let the hook go. With so much water depth she had to keep the clutch partially on to reduce the chain's exit speed. Once the hook was on the bottom, I carefully backed *Intermezzo*, using as little power as possible, until we had 400 feet of chain veered. Because the bottom was so strewn with coral heads, I wanted our chain laid straight. Using a combination of riding sail and windage to drift us backwards in a straight path was preferable to reversing in a circle!

With all chain finally veered, Linda set the brake on the windlass and then put in the gypsy lock. She came aft to take over the controls while I went forward to interpret the signals coming up the chain. I signed to Linda to put the engine in reverse, slowly. I wanted to apply minimum pressure to the anchor until it started to dig in. When I felt it beginning to hold, we would gradually kick up the revs until we were in full reverse.

It all sounds good in theory, but in practice, Polynesian style, something was lacking. The CQR simply refused to dig in. It would bump and bounce along the bottom and then stop abruptly as it snagged a rock or coral head. Occasionally I thought I felt it biting, but when Linda applied more revs it would start to slide again. Finally we had reached a point where our stern was just off the reef.

After winching aboard all 480 feet of chain (and giving thanks for our electric windlass), we repositioned ourselves well upwind of the middle of the lagoon. I hoped this time to hook in by the time we reached the middle.

In the end, we went through the procedure four times before getting a reasonable bite in a position that allowed us room both to drag and to swing 360 degrees.

Anchoring safely also means making allowance for changes in weather, especially wind direction and velocity. If all the yachts in your anchorage are being held by a gentle northeaster, what happens if it quits? What about the tidal flow and time of change? And finally, picking the right spot to anchor involves

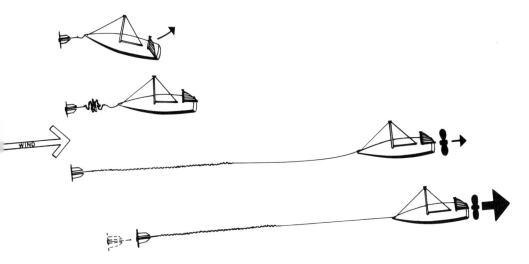

If you are dropping your anchor in foul ground, you will want to pay out scope in as straight a manner as possible, directly downwind, to try to avoid snags on the rode. Unless you can back straight under power it will be better to drift back on the rode, hopefully with a riding sail set to keep you head-to-wind, and then to set the hook under power after you have run the rode out all the way.

looking at how to exit in a hurry should weather conditions force you to leave. Could you get out in the middle of the night? Could the anchorage, protected for now, become a dangerous lee shore? You may have no choice but to stay in an exposed cove, but if that is the case, you will have to keep a wary eye on the weather and not wait until the last minute to leave if the situation begins to deteriorate. When you arrive, don't be in a hurry to drop the hook and leave the boat.

Spend as much time as is necessary to position yourself correctly and set the anchor hard, even if you must raise and reset

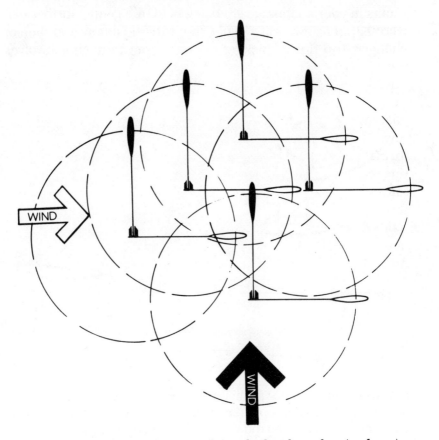

When anchoring near neighbors, always look at how they (and you) will swing should the wind shift. You must take into account whether they are on chain or rope. Those on rope will take a lot more swinging room.

the anchor several times. If you can't seem to find just the right spot, maybe you should anchor farther out or find another anchorage. Never settle for second best where the anchored security of your vessel is concerned. If conditions change, could those vessels anchored nearby drift down on you, forcing you to drag, too?

Once you've picked your anchor, decided on your scope, and determined where you're going to settle in, you still have to drop the anchor. Setting your hook under power is a critical aspect of anchoring for most cruisers. The rode should be payed out slowly as you back down. If your boat tends to circle under power in reverse, drop the hook with a small amount of sternway and then pile chain just behind the anchor. Allow the wind to carry you straight back. At the desired scope, snug up the rode and allow the anchor to dig in under slow reverse. Then when you feel a bite, apply more power to set the anchor securely. How much power is enough? That depends on the boat and propeller. A sailboat with a folding prop requires full reverse rpm. A fixed prop will do a good job at 70 percent throttle, and a reversing feathering prop will give excellent thrust at 50 percent power. Aboard *Intermezzo II*, which had a full reversing prop and an efficient engine, we still used full throttle just to be sure. When the bottom was good, Linda would hold power on for 15 or 20 seconds. If we were not sure of the bottom type, we maintained full throttle for a minute or longer. An anchor that is well dug in sends a high-frequency, constant

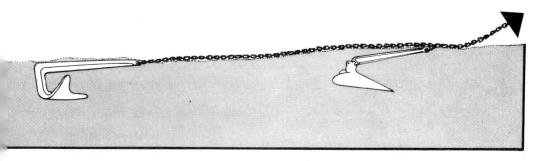

Putting two hooks in line is an excellent way of increasing holding power without incurring the problems of two separate rodes.

vibration up the rode or chain. Or, if you don't have good reverse power, it may just tighten up slowly, then loosen a bit—a sort of rocking up and down motion along the length of the chain. Any other vibration indicates that the anchor is slipping. With enough power in reverse the angle of the rode is straight and remains constant. If it tends to flex, that is another indication that your anchor is moving on the bottom.

Of course, picking the best spot to anchor depends upon

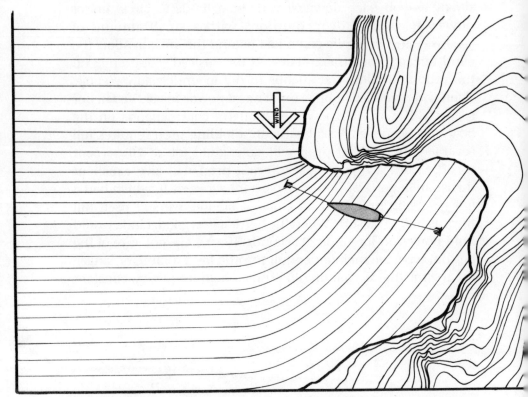

Most anchorages that depend upon a point of land for protection end up with a swell sweeping in at right angles to the prevailing wind. Setting a stern hook will hold you into the swell and ease motion, but be prepared to cut the stern line loose if you have to exit in a hurry. One way of making sure it doesn't foul the prop is to winch it in extremely tight *before* cutting so the line will spring away from the hull when it is cut.

how many and what type of neighbors you have. Boats of different design behave quite differently at anchor. Single-stickers, especially sloops, shear about more at anchor. Those lying-to rope move a great deal more than those held with chain. Boats on light chain move more than ones on heavy chain. The amount of scope out directly affects a boat's swinging radius. Inquire of your potential neighbors what and how much they have out and where their anchor is set.

When the weather looks threatening you may want to increase the holding power of your anchoring system. The simplest method of doing so is with another hook. Once the second anchor and rode are ready to go, power slowly to windward, wide of your first hook and keeping watch on the first rode

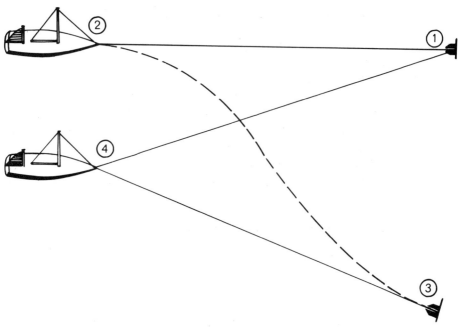

Setting two hooks on their own rodes must be handled with care to avoid wrapping the extra rode around the keel or prop. We like to drop our chain hook first; and after it is set, we power to windward and set the secondary anchor on rope. If both your anchors are on rope, after you set the first anchor, be sure to pull in the slack while powering up to set the second, or better yet set it with the dinghy.

so it doesn't foul your keel or prop. If you are setting a nylon rode and already have the first anchor on chain, take the load on the nylon. It will act as a shock absorber and take most of the strain, leaving the chain rode as the backup system. Another approach is to slide a deadman, or weight, down the anchor chain or rode. The deadman is usually the same weight as the anchor and substantially increases the holding power. It is also possible to shackle two anchors on one chain. Many experienced cruisers prefer this system because it offers enormous holding power without the complications of twin rodes. It is probably the best system to employ if you are leaving your boat unattended. But it is sometimes difficult to get the second anchor back aboard without scratching the topsides. Any time a rope rode is used, be sure to watch for chafe where it passes over the bow roller.

It is sometimes necessary to anchor bow and stern to keep

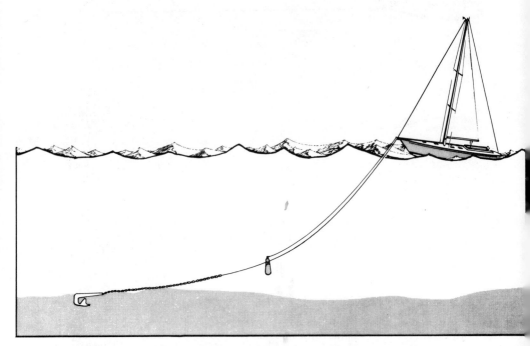

Sending a "deadman" or heavy weight down the chain on a pennant is one means of both dampening motion and adding to the holding power of your anchoring system.

aligned with swell or to avoid hitting neighboring boats in a crowded anchorage. The stern hook is frequently set from the dink, after shutting the engine down.

Handling a good-sized anchor from a dinghy requires technique. We find it best to hang the anchor over the stern with a trip line, piling chain and some rode on the stern seat. I then row towards the desired spot while Linda pays out line from aboard *Intermezzo*. It is necessary to row past the actual spot you want to drop the hook. Once you quit rowing the weight of the rode will pull you back towards the boat, until you drop the anchor. The anchor will tend to glide towards the boat as it sinks. As a rule of thumb I usually row out beyond the actual spot I want the anchor to set twice the water depth.

The stern anchor should be stowed with rode attached, ready to go in an instant, in case it is required in an emergency.

The world-encircling Bermuda 40 *Resolve* with the Carkhuffs aboard await a South Pacific blow with three hooks set.

If you use this system of setting the stern anchor you may have to use the dinghy to pick it up, too. If weather forces a rapid departure, there may not be time to retrieve it. When possible, I prefer instead to set the stern hook by backing down on the main anchor, leaving extra chain, setting the stern hook, and then winching the boat back between the two anchors. This method makes it possible to pick up the stern hook by simply reversing the procedure; there's no need to resort to the dink.

Remember that if the wind shifts to beam-on, the load on the two anchors will be much greater than if you are anchored from the bow only. This means the stern anchor and rode must be able to take as much strain as the main anchor and that its leads and attachment points aboard must be heavily reinforced. And consider ahead of time if you have to exit with a beam wind wether you will have time to recover the bow anchor before you blow off to leeward into another vessel or underwater obstruction.

Should you find yourself in a spot with strong reversing currents, you may need to set two bow anchors, one uptide and another downtide, with your boat bridled at the bow between them.

With the hook or hooks set and your vessel swung back on her rode, take a minute and work two or three bearings on shore. Try to pick landmarks that will be visible at night. If good bearings aren't available, consider dropping a dinghy anchor with a float. With no load on it it will stay put even if you drag,

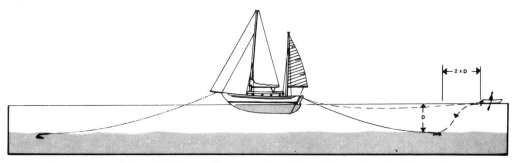

If you are rowing out the anchor, row two times the water depth past the spot you want the anchor to end up to allow for the anchor to drift towards the boat as it settles towards the bottom.

providing a handy, nearby reference in inclement conditions.

In some circumstances a depthfinder fitted with a variable alarm can be helpful as an anchor watch. Modern loran systems are so accurate that they also serve this purpose; in fact, several now come with anchor watch alarms. Radar with good close-in definition will also work well. On vessels equipped with radar we always note what the screen looks like during daylight so we can compare the radar picture with our actual surroundings later. Putting a sketch in the logbook of the what the radar scope bearings and distances off are helps me compare late at night.

Anytime you get ready to leave with two anchors set be especially careful to keep the stern rode clear of the propeller.

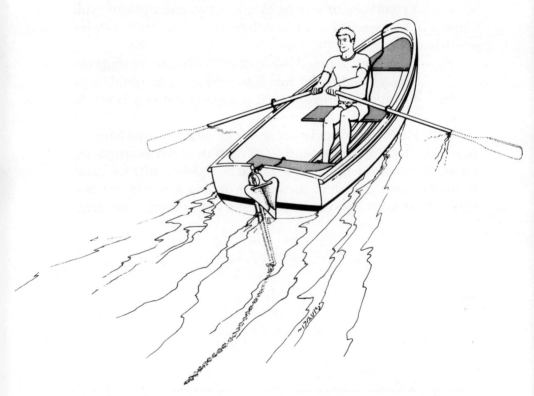

Tying the anchor outboard of the dink to the transom with a trip line will enable you to keep pressure on the oars right up to the moment you cut the hook loose.

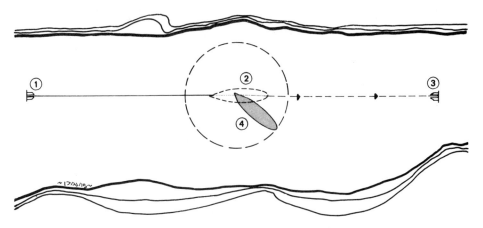

A Bahamian moor made with two anchors, both off the bow, is useful in a tight anchorage with reversing tidal flow. It is necessary either to use a dink to drop the second hook or to drift back towards the end of the first rode to set the second anchor.

REDUCING LOADS

Anchoring in shallow water in heavy weather may require special procedures. Assuming your scope is limited by surrounding vessels or obstructions, you will want to reduce the shock loading of the anchor as the wind gusts and your boat sheers. Nylon rode will do this automatically, but if you are on chain, the surge loads, if they are transmitted to the anchor directly, may just break it free. To reduce the chances of this happening, you should employ some form of shock absorber. Larger yachts occasionally have spring-loaded chain stoppers for this purpose. I prefer to tie light-duty three-strand nylon between the bow cleats and the chain. In heavy winds we use a 20-foot-long piece, which will stretch 4 or 5 feet under load. The chain is left in a loose loop between the cleat and end of the nylon, so as the nylon reaches the end of its stretch, the chain again takes the load directly. This line should be the smallest that will take the load to provide the most elasticity. On *Intermezzo*, a moderate windage vessel, we used a piece of $5/16$-inch nylon and never had a problem. *Intermezzo II*, with perhaps 50 percent more windage, used a ⅜-inch piece of line.

In a really heavy blow, or with a sea running, even if you have unlimited swinging room and lots of chain veered, at some point the chain will snub up tight. Once again, a shock-absorbing system is a necessity.

Another way to reduce loads is to lower the attachment point of the rode to your bow. The lower pull flattens the angle and reduces scope requirements. Our yachts have always had a fitting just above the waterline at the bow onto which we could shackle a pennant in adverse conditions.

Obviously all shackles on the anchor should be wired closed. Chains with joining links and swivels should be avoided at all costs, as they frequently fail. Make sure your shackles are at least as strong as the chain. Inspect them and their attached links frequently for chafe.

As we have said before, anchor rope must be protected from chafe. Under high load, any sort of a burr or sharp edge will cut through rope quickly, so be sure your anchor rollers and chocks

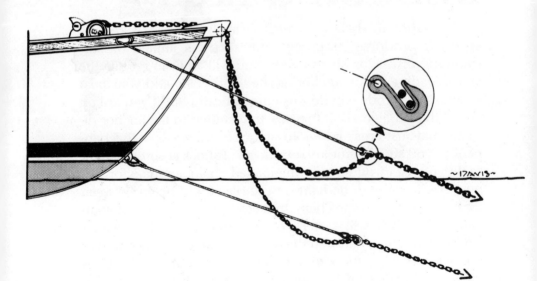

Connecting the rode to an eye just above the waterline reduces the scope required. Note the light nylon shock absorber tied onto the chain.

are smooth. Have plenty of chafing gear handy, and secure it tightly to the rode. As the anchor line stretches and contracts, chafing gear tends to move around, so check the rode condition frequently. If you find it impossible to keep chafe gear on, ease the rode a few inches every half an hour to reduce the possibility of chafing one spot badly. Remember, too, that in adverse conditions you can run the engine slowly ahead or put it in gear during the worst of the puffs to reduce anchoring loads.

Another method to substantially reduce anchor loads in a blow is with a riding sail, as an experience of ours in Papua New Guinea illustrates.

The volcanic calderas surrounding Rabaul harbor trip the bottom edges of the rapidly moving cumulus clouds. As the wind whistles down from the hills in ever-increasing strength. Yachts tug at their anchors, sheering first to starboard and then to port. Aboard *Intermezzo* our chief concern is that one of our neighbors may start to drag down upon us. Even in a secure anchorage there are spots that have less than ideal bottom conditions, and sheering adds to the anchor load already increased by the passing of this summertime front.

About us are all manner of yachts from heavy-displacement, long-keeled boats to modern fin-keeled cruisers; some are built of ferrocement, many of steel, a few of wood, and others of fiberglass. Of the single-stickers, one characteristic is evident regardless of design type or material of construction. They are all weaving back and forth on their rodes.

Sheering is caused by wind action on the topsides and rigging. The boat's tendency to sheer is affected by where its center of windage (without sails) is relative to its underwater center of lateral resistance. In a windshift the bow naturally wants to blow off until it is well off the wind. When the boat reaches a 30- to 40-degree angle to the wind, the rode forces the boat to "tack," and she begins to sheer in the opposite direction.

Sheering produces a very uncomfortable motion. The wind will also cause many vessels to heel considerably, and the quick rolls from side to side as they zoom back and forth on their tethers make getting any sort of rest difficult.

Worse than the discomfort, though, are the loads on the

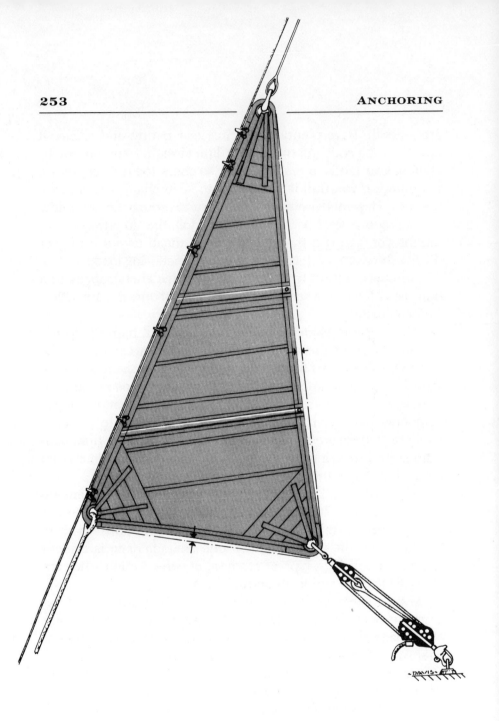

A backstay riding sail is a small but very important piece of gear. It should be made of storm jib weight materials, with full-length battens and hollow edges.

ground tackle system. An increase in direct tension of as much as 150 percent can result. If the holding is less than ideal or local conditions necessitate short scope, the extra loads may break the anchor free.

Intermezzo, however, rides serenely on her double anchors. She exhibits a slight tendency to head off, but then quickly points her stem back into the wind. Aboard, we are comfortable, and all hands except for the anchor watch will sleep well this evening. The secret is her riding sail. Her small, heavily built mizzen acts as a weathercock to keep her bow into the wind.

The ability to deploy a riding sail is not limited to boats with split rigs. Cutters and sloops can rig a riding sail from the backstay by seizing a block about 40 percent of the distance to the masthead to accommodate a short riding sail halyard or simply by using the main halyard. The sheet is led forward, usually to the main boom traveler, a cleat, or padeye amidships.

How large should a riding sail be? A sail the size of a storm jib will do nicely, or use 8 percent of total measured sail area as a rule of thumb. Consider also building in a means of reducing this area. A sail that works well in moderate conditions may tend to overpower you in heavy-weather windshifts. Riding mizzens can be slab or jiffy reefed. The solution several of our cruising friends with backstay riding sails decided upon is to have a second storm-sized riding sail for that once-in-a-lifetime ultimate blow at anchor. It is about half the size of their smallest storm jib.

The riding sail can be sheeted to the end of the main boom or to a spot on deck.

The full-length battens will work best if they are bolted into their pockets.

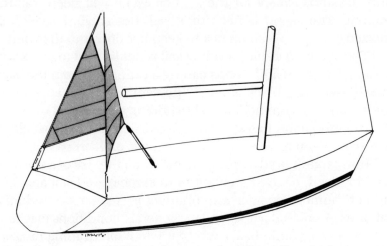

Twin backstays lend themselves to twin riding sails, which are more effective and make less noise than a single sail.

A riding sail should be built from storm jib-weight cloth. While the loads on it will be moderate, it will spend many hours aloft.

We have employed both used sails cut down to suit and new Dacron sails. When our budget has allowed a new riding sail, we have opted for ultraviolet-stabilized cloth, triple-stitched. The cut should be board flat, with a hollowed leech, luff, and foot.

Full-length battens in a mizzen or backstay riding sail will reduce or eliminate chatter in the sail. Solid fiberglass or PVC tube battens work best. We have found it better to bolt the battens into their pockets with locknuts rather than tie them in; ties can loosen or chafe through. Sails set on the backstay should have closely spaced hanks, and top and bottommost hanks should be oversized.

You should *not* use conventional sails and storm jibs as riding sails except in an emergency, in part because of the ultraviolet degradation that results from prolonged exposure. With storm sails, in particular, you will want to know they are at 100 percent strength when you need them.

How large do you go? On our first *Intermezzo*, a 100-square-foot mizzen, which we could reef as needed, worked very well. Aboard *Intermezzo II* we used twin sails to take advantage of her double backstays. These were 15 square feet each. Although the two sails were very small, the inboard angle they formed would hold us rock steady.

There is a light-weather advantage to riding sails as well. When the air is shifty, they will help keep you weathercocked, improving both ventilation and comfort below.

The next time you anchor, try out a storm jib or staysail (temporarily) on the backstay. You will find the difference in comfort amazing.

RETRIEVING THE ANCHOR

Retrieving an anchor in a strong wind takes coordination and practice. You need to use the engine to come up on the chain. But you do not want to override the chain and then have the bow blow off. Thus, the person on the helm will have to follow the directions of the bowman, probably using a system of hand signals, as verbal communication will be difficult or impossible.

The actual technique you employ varies with conditions. If a sea is running and there's a great deal of wind, the helmsman will have to power ahead slowly, no faster than the chain is coming aboard, which often means interspersing short periods of power with neutral. He or she will have to follow the lead of the rode, that is, keep the bow lined up with the direction of the pull. Since the wind and waves will be trying to push the bow one way or the other, the utmost concentration is mandatory.

Meanwhile, the bowman winches the rode home when the bow drops on the waves. When the boat is lifting, you want to dog off the clutch. As the anchor is close to being broken out, you must be careful not to overload the system as the bow lifts to waves. If you are concerned with a fouled or an extremely well dug in anchor, you may want to ease out a little as the bow lifts, to reduce shock loading. (Most anchor chain failures occur when the chain is almost vertical, with the bow trying to lift to a swell. The load at this point will be much greater than with an angled pull. Be careful of this possibility in a foul anchorage, where your chain may catch on a rock or coral head and snub you up short.

Once the anchor is aboard be sure to lash it in place. Don't

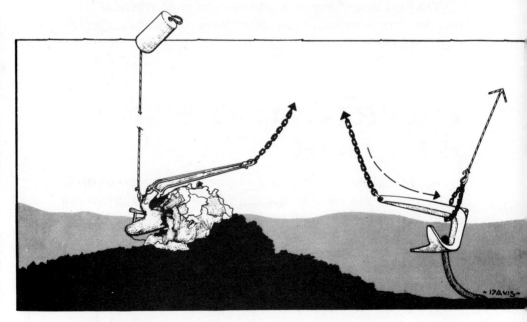

A trip line should be rigged anytime you are anchoring on a foul bottom. A jammed Bruce anchor can sometimes be worked free by sliding a rope loop down the rode and reversing your angle of pull. The best system for retrieving fouled anchors, though, is to carry SCUBA gear.

rely on the chain gypsy or primary rode to hold it. At sea over a period of time the anchor can loosen itself, and if it does, it can do an enormous amount of damage very quickly.

Retrieving an anchor that has fouled is a special art. You first have to determine if the problem is with a fouled chain or a stuck anchor. On coral bottoms you can frequently bring the chain up short and allow the sawing action of the chain on the coral to break off the obstruction, assuming not much of a sea is running. On the other hand, if the rode is caught on a really large head or rock, you may have to unwind yourself. This procedure usually requires a methodical series of attempts. Keep a close eye on the manner in which you approach the situation because your first attempts may make the situation worse, and you will have to unwind these before you can deal with the real culprit.

Anchors that are hooked onto obstructions, such as pipes or wire, can often be freed by sliding the weighted loop of another rope down the rode and onto the shank of the anchor. This loop is then pulled tight about the head of the anchor and the rope is winched home. By easing off the rode the anchor is upset, and the tripping rope wrenches the anchor free of the offending obstruction. CQRs and Bruces are particularly amenable to being freed by this procedure.

Diving is the best means of clearing fouled anchors and chains if the water temperature and clarity allow. Even if the hook is too deep for you to dive to it, diving may enable you to see the cause of the problem. We feel scuba gear and the knowledge of its safe use are essential ingredients of seamanlike anchoring.

If you are in doubt about the condition of the bottom, use an anchor buoy. This line is attached to the head of the anchor and can be used as a trip line if the anchor fouls.

We don't advise that you use a rope rode when anchoring in coral. Rope cuts too easily, and coral presents far too many hazards. But if you are caught in coral without choice, or on some other foul bottom, putting a float on the end of the chain and then attaching it to a floating sized rode will reduce the chances of a bottom foul. The float should be sized so just a few feet of chain floats clear of the seabed. Initial holding will be reduced if the chain is too far off the bed, though. Beware of floating anchor lines in crowded anchorages. They snag keels and propellers.

EXPOSED ANCHORAGES

An enormous seal rookery erupts in welcome as our anchor and chain make their noisy escape from the forepeak. *Intermezzo* is once again enjoying a new anchorage. Linda and I stow sails and coil sheets, while Sarah and Elyse look with wonder at the seal pups swimming around our hull.

The steeply shelving bottom and rocky beach of Cedros Island make a fine habitat for our mammalian cousins and for us a weather shore protected from the prevailing mid-winter westerlies.

We are heading north along Mexico's Baja peninsula, not a pleasant prospect at this time of year, but business commitments make the trip necessary. There is still time, though to give the children (and their parents!) a chance to watch the daily patterns of a seal population without the hindrance of concrete or wire barriers.

In both directions ashore beached hulls give warning of changeable weather. But for now, with commercial fishermen anchored close by, we feel comparatively safe.

If this book had been written a few years ago, the subject of anchoring in exposed locations would never have come up. To a semiexperienced sailor, it is axiomatic that one takes the greatest of precautions when anchored with a lee shore at your back. But today more and more sailors are going cruising without benefit of experience. And to those that have not felt the dread of a lee shore close by in a strong wind the temptation to use less than the greatest degree of caution may be great.

From time to time most cruisers will be faced with a similar situation—an anchorage partially open to some segment of the

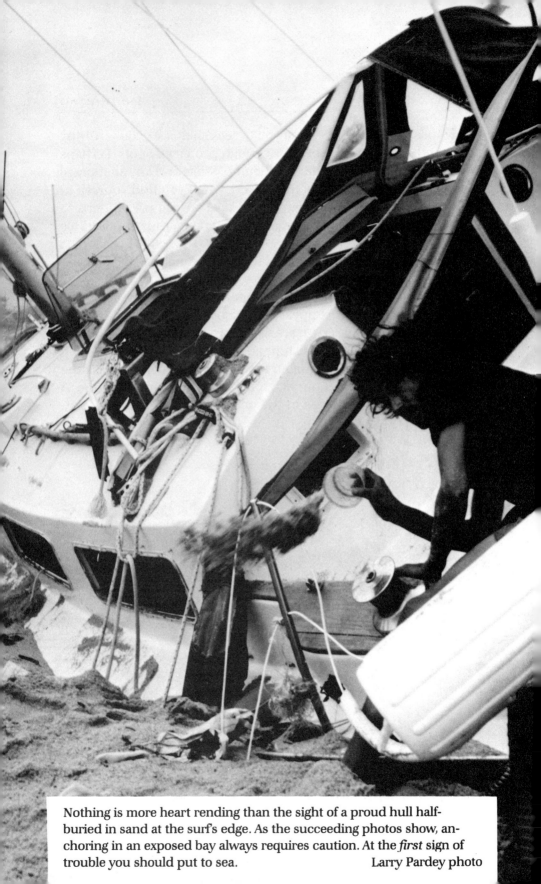

Nothing is more heart rending than the sight of a proud hull half-buried in sand at the surf's edge. As the succeeding photos show, anchoring in an exposed bay always requires caution. At the *first* sign of trouble you should put to sea.

Larry Pardey photo

compass. Weather may force you to seek shelter, or your cruising grounds may simply not offer enough protected spots. Perhaps the crew is overtired from a difficult passage and any anchorage looks good. Regardless of the reason, when you find yourself in an exposed anchorage, you should take special precautions to protect yourself against the potentially dangerous exposed lee shore.

With *Intermezzo* quiet we launch the dinghy to get a closer look at the seal families. A noisy chorus of inquisitive black heads and whiskers circle within petting distance. Every so often a stern older face appears and shoos the friendly pups to a safer distance from us. We are treated to a riotous display of diving, leaping, rolling, and clapping.

That evening, out of habit, I tap the barometer as I pass the navigation station. A jump of 2 millibars catches my attention. A change in the weather is in the offing. An exquisite winter sky,

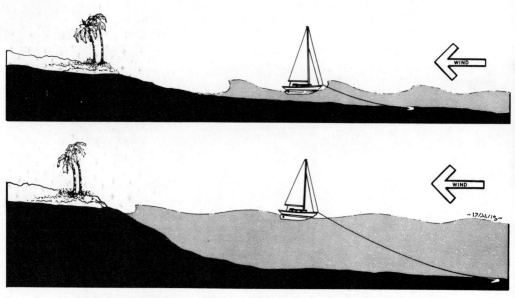

A gently sloping bottom allows surf to form farther offshore, trapping boats anchored in shallow water. With a steeper bottom, surf forms closer to shore, giving you more warning to get out.

clear of all cloud and thick with brilliant stars, portends a high-pressure system. If it moves over the Sea of Cortez and combines with a low that has been kicking around, it could generate a northeaster that will leave us on an exposed lee shore instead of a protected weather one. Even though the wind stays gentle in the west, I bring the dink aboard, remove sail covers, and attach halyards, just in case.

Being prepared for a hasty exit is of paramount importance when you're in an exposed anchorage. The final decision to stay or to put to sea will depend on how good the holding ground is, the distance offshore at which you are anchored, and what you feel the sea or weather may dish up. The key lies in timing. At what point do you make the decision to go? Obviously it is before the situation deteriorates to a dangerous state. But knowing when to draw the line, being able to gauge accurately the difference between comfort and convenience and prudent seamanship, is critical. When in doubt it is always best to put to sea.

While Linda gets dinner ready I review our situation. If our holding was better and there was room to drag, wind might not pose a major problem. Our ground tackle and attachment points aboard are enormously strong and will take substantial loads without failure. Lying-to a nylon rode will offer the best shock-absorbing qualities, reducing the loads on both the anchor and whatever the rode is attached to at the bow. If we are faced with a lee shore and good holding, I set our second anchor on nylon rode and take the initial load on it. But for now, lying-to our chain, I use a nylon shock-absorber.

Getting the anchor back aboard under stress of wind and wave may be a problem. The loads on the windlass will make it necessary to use power to bring the vessel forward. Careful coordination of engine rpm and helm will be required. It sounds simple in a protected spot, but we know from experience that when things get bad, it is a very difficult operation.

Once the hook is aboard, actually leaving the anchorage itself may be a chore. If the bow isn't heading directly into the seas, we will experience a violent corkscrew motion until steadying sail is raised. At least here we have a straight shot to sea with no off-lying dangers or obstructions with which to contend.

In a crowded anchorage we would have to be wary of the other vessels in the anchorage. There may be mass confusion if the spot is crowded. That's definitely not a problem here. But if it were, I would be concerned about the swinging radius of our neighbors and if they had room to drag a bit. Situations that look good initially may become a tangle with a windshift.

The sea poses our biggest danger. If trouble comes from a local wind system, there is time to watch the waves develop. In shallow water the most important factor is the shape of the sea bottom. Anchorages with a long gentle slope towards the shore provide an excellent chance for surf to build. Breaking seas gen-

Where deep water surrounds an island it is sometimes possible to row an anchor to land, if there is a steady breeze to hold you off. A bow anchor is then dropped to (hopefully) snag something if the wind should shift and blow you towards shore. Although we have used this system in the past we don't recommend it except in extreme cases.

erate enormous anchor loads, and it is a rare yacht that has the gear to withstand these forces. When you are unavoidably caught in such conditions, moving into deeper water will reduce the risk of being caught in surf. We won't have to worry about that here because the bottom is steeply shelving and there isn't a great deal of fetch between us and the mainland.

More dangerous can be seas generated in a far-off storm. Their arrival may remain unheralded until the last moment. With a potentially long fetch we pay special attention to any unusual swells. A few small undulations from seaward may be all the warning given before breakers start.

A turn around the decks at midnight reveals that our neighbors have departed. The wind is still light in the northwest; the

sea, calm. Are they off for a night of fishing or do they know something we don't? At 0200 a slight swell starts to sweep into our anchorage from the northeast. Asleep below, we are immediately roused by the change in *Intermezzo*'s motion. In a warm, snug bunk the idea of getting dressed and going topside meets with little enthusiasm. Still the sea has given us fair warning. Should we heed it? After all, the wind is still light in the west.

With a longing glance at the snug bunk, I get dressed and start the engine. In less than 6 minutes the hook is winched home, and we have put sea room between ourselves and the rocky shore. Now, 2 miles offshore, there is no sign of a northeaster, just a light swell. The desire for comfort wins out, and we head *Intermezzo* back to anchor, this time farther off the beach. But peaceful reverie eludes Linda and me. Finally we put to sea

Larry Pardey photo

Despite taking precautions, mistakes are made. Having a yacht that will stand up to the punishment of a grounding is a prerequisite for serious cruising.   Larry Pardey photo

again, this time for good. Fifteen minutes later it is blowing 50 knots. As *Intermezzo* staggers to windward, I hurriedly shorten sail. The wind continues to increase until we are forced to run before it. As we head south past our late anchorage, the wind is gusting in the seventies and the sea is a welter of breakers ashore.

Anchor watch is a chore in which shorthanded cruisers rarely indulge. The prudent skipper will sleep with one ear alert to changes in motion or sound: chain growling as it moves over the bottom (except in soft mud), a halyard slapping as the wind increases. Sleeping forward, however, will ensure that you get the loudest possible message from any changes in motion or sound. Then you can decide if a fast exit is necessary.

Of course, being ready to exit quickly involves more than preparing just the vessel. Navigational problems need to be worked out beforehand. It has become my habit to have the exit course and distance written into the logbook.

Should you use more than one anchor in an exposed an-

In this peaceful anchorage on St. Helena Island in the South Atlantic 20-foot rollers could appear in a matter of minutes. You can still visit such places, but you must be ready at all times to put to sea.

chorage? It is not unusual for a swell from prevailing winds to sweep around a headland. It may run at a different angle to wave action set up by a local breeze, resulting in a very uncomfortable, rolling motion. Setting a stern hook to hold the bow into the sea alleviates the problem but creates a new one if you want to exit hurriedly. You could waste valuable time getting the hook back aboard. Worse, however, is the possibility of fouling the stern rode in the prop. If this happens, and it has to more than one cruising boat, you had better be prepared to sail your way out.

Consideration also has to be given to fouling the rodes of other boats in your prop. The solution is to stay away from double-anchor setups in exposed anchorages. If their use is unavoidable, be prepared to bring the second anchor aboard at the first sign of trouble. Or, buoy the anchor when it is first set so it can be cut loose and recovered at some later date.

If you are caught out unexpectedly you may have no choice but to slip the main anchor. If chain is being used, is the bitter end easy to cast free?

Being alert to the wind and sea in exposed anchorages, even when it means giving up a warm bunk, is a tenet of cruising seamanship that cannot be ignored. It is imperative to get out *before* conditions deteriorate to a dangerous state. Making preparations in advance means the actual decision to put to sea can be quickly executed, with less reluctance.

MOORING MEDITERRANEAN STYLE

Another, more esoteric, aspect of anchoring comes into play with a "Med moor." Mooring Mediterranean-style, in which the boat's stern is tied to the dock or quay while her bow is held by an anchor, is becoming more common in many parts of the

cruising world. Mooring Med-style creates two sets of problems. The first are mechanical. Your boat must do something few boats do well: back down in tight quarters. To compound the situation, precise anchoring is required.

The second set of problems stem from the nature of the moorage. Gunwale-to-gunwale boats mean a large critical audience is in attendance. The slightest faux pas is eagerly awaited, while the participants' urge to yell, scream, wave, jump, or simply sit down and cry must be controlled. The skipper has to stand at ease, head erect, stomach flat, chest out, and direct the foredeck crew with but a nonchalant comment or two. An occasional burst of power or turn of the helm should be all that is required to control the boat.

First light has *Intermezzo* and her crew lined up on the range outside Papeete harbor. For years this place has been our goal. Visions of Quinn's Bar, Tahitian maidens, and tropical paradise are filling my head. Linda is fantasizing, too, about a night on the town. After all, it has been five months since we've been in civilization. Elyse's and Sarah's main concern seems to be the availability of ice cream.

We are about to confront mooring Med-style for the first time. Papeete harbor serves both commercial and pleasure vessels. The yachts get the quay alongside the front of town. The first 60 can tie stern-to the sidewalk. After that it is coconut trees and light poles behind the beach. As we power around looking over the situation, we spot *Wind'Son* and Jim and Cheryl Schmidt, whom we last saw in Fatu Hiva, in the Marquesas.

"Bring her alongside us!" Jim shouts.

Heads start popping out of companionway hatches. A new arrival has been spotted, and the already settled sit down in their cockpits to watch the fun. It is obvious we are the morning attraction.

The space Jim wants us to use can not be more than 14 feet wide. Given *Intermezzo*'s 12-foot 6-inch beam, it leaves 9 inches on each side, just enough for fenders.

To make a clean Med moor a certain amount of preparation is necessary. Ground tackle is a good place to begin. "What kind of holding do you have?" I yell across the water.

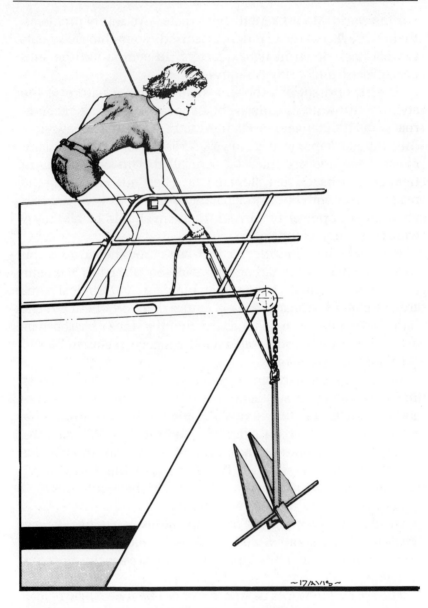

With larger anchors a trip line will make releasing the hook on a timely
basis an easy chore. Secure one end of the trip line to the bow, pass the
end through the shank of the anchor, and hold onto the free end. With
really heavy anchors, taking a half-turn around a cleat can ease the
load.

"Got a good bite the first time," comes Jim's reply. Knowing that Jim is among the onlookers just waiting for a mistake, I have to decide if this is straight data or perhaps a bit shaded—just enough for us to make fools of ourselves.

Anchor selection is important. Once again, a CQR or Bruce-style anchor will work well in a hard bottom, but thin sand over rock or soft mud will make the use of a Danforth type advisable.

Next, there must be substantial rode available. The anchor may have to be dropped farther out than scope alone dictates. Generally speaking, the farther out the anchor is set, the better maneuverability you will have backing down into the dock.

If chain is being used, the operation of the windlass clutch will be critical. Does it release and brake the chain gypsy evenly?

Deciding that discretion is best in this case, I break loose our 35-pound Danforth. It is sufficient to restrain our boat in a beam wind, when the loads on the anchor will be susbstantially greater than when the boat is allowed to weathercock. The Danforth will also bite in more quickly than the CQR, and if the mud bottom is soft rather than hard, it will do a much better job of holding.

To make the anchor easy for Linda to drop, I tie a ⅜-inch line, doubled up, to the end of the shank. She can simply let one end go when I give the signal, dropping the Danforth exactly where I want it. We also flake 250 feet of nylon rode down the deck to ensure a smooth run. I don't want to chance a foul-up in front of this audience.

In a tight harbor the anchor must be dropped in precisely the right spot, so if you waste a few seconds, you are out of position. When we use an anchor on chain, we drop the anchor over the bow roller, ready to go. With heavy anchors, those over 75 pounds, we also rig a trip line, which we cut at the precise moment the anchor is to be dropped, as I have been stymied by a balky windlass clutches more than once.

When we have the ground tackle squared away, we hang fenders on both sides to appease the concern of our about-to-be new neighbors. Image is not a question here, so we have the kids hang two fenders over the transom as well. Finally, we feed our stern lines through their chocks and out over the top of the

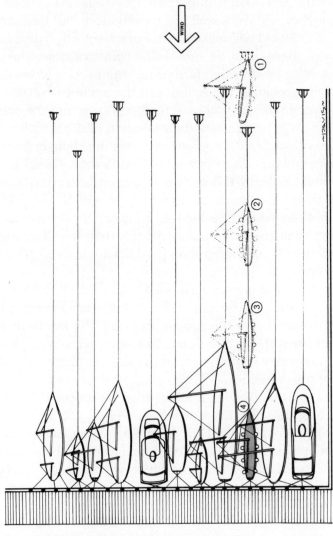

When you moor Med. style you want to have the fenders and stern line
ready before you start backing down. The anchor line should also be
flaked and ready to run cleanly. Be sure you allow plenty of room for
the hook to drag before it gets a good bite.

pushpit and coil them down, ready to throw.

The particular tactics you employ to position yourself depends on the backing characteristics of your sailboat and the relative direction of the wind and current and position of those already moored.

Wind is the most critical consideration. If it is light and on the nose, life is simple. Starting dead upwind of your chosen space, begin to back down; when the bow passes the exact spot for the hook, the foredeck hand lets the ground tackle go. Be sure to allow distance for the anchor to drag a bit before it sets; with burying anchors this distance can be substantial, especially if the bottom tends towards soft. Pay out the rode, without strain, until there is sufficient scope for the anchor to start digging in. Then apply some friction so the bow stays head-to-wind. If your boat tends to back in a circle, you will want to start this procedure at a compensating angle, so she is backing straight when you reach the spot you want to drop the anchor. Then the friction of the rode can be used to help her stay in a straight line.

Accomplishing the same task with a cross wind is more difficult and demands flawless timing. If your vessel will back down with control, you can position her well out from the desired spot to build up enough way to back her up straight despite the wind.

If your boat is contumacious in reverse and the wind is blowing opposite the direction her stern wants to turn, the wind can actually be used to compensate for prop torque.

When it is impossible to power the stern to the appropriate spot, good seamen employ an alternate system. Set the bow hook conventionally and then row a long stern line ashore. Once the stern line is secured, a winch can be used to crank you home.

In our case, boats and anchor lines are chock-a-block about us, and the only thing we have going for us is a light breeze on the starboard beam—it might be enough to check *Intermezzo's* tendency to circle counterclockwise in reverse.

Linda and I run through the procedure with the anchor and rode again, and Sarah is stationed near her mom to relay mes-

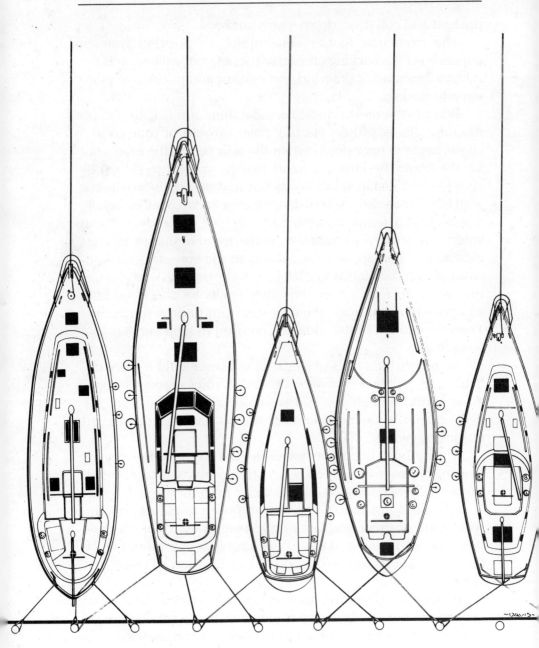

There are many ways to rig stern lines with a Med. moor; which you
choose depends on surge, how tightly packed you are, and the shape
of your stern.

sages from me at the helm in case Linda has to watch the rode. Elyse is ready with a stern line.

The bow hand must keep one eye on the skipper and dock. As the stern closes the dock, the rode must be tightened up, setting the hook and stopping the boat. At the appropriate moment the stern line is tossed, or better handed, across. It is important at this point to appear cool and in control of the situation, even if your heart is pumping madly.

Finally all is set, and I nudge *Intermezzo* into gear. We head up harbor and stop with the stern at a 45-degree angle to our final course. As the wind starts to blow the bow off, I put her into reverse and then signal to Linda.

"Mommy, Daddy is waving!" announces our intermediary.

The anchor splashes down, and I put the helm over and move slowly astern. This is the critical point. If we are lucky, and if there is enough drag on the bow rode, *Intermezzo* just might put her stern alongside *Wind'son*. If the hook doesn't bite properly, I may need to use a sudden burst of power to push the boat back into clear water. I won't have much time to decide if I want to avoid blowing into my neighbors.

As the 20-fathom mark flashes by, Linda starts taking load on the warping drum. Our circling motion is checked, and we begin to back in a straight line. Thirty seconds later Elyse is handing stern lines to our neighbors.

There are several choices for how the stern lines should be tied. One approach used in tight anchorages such as Papeete is to cross the lines to keep the stern from swinging and to avoid running a line across a neighbor's lines or transom. Splaying the lines outwards from the stern avoids chafe on your own lines but may annoy your neighbors. If you've plenty of space between boats, a set of lines can be run out from the quarters to control side-to-side movement while a single line from the stern adjusts distance from the dock.

"Why don't you all join us for breakfast after you're secure!" calls Jim. At least we have one friend in the anchorage. We may need time to break the ice with the other cruisers. After all, our flawless mooring procedure had just deprived them of the day's laughs.

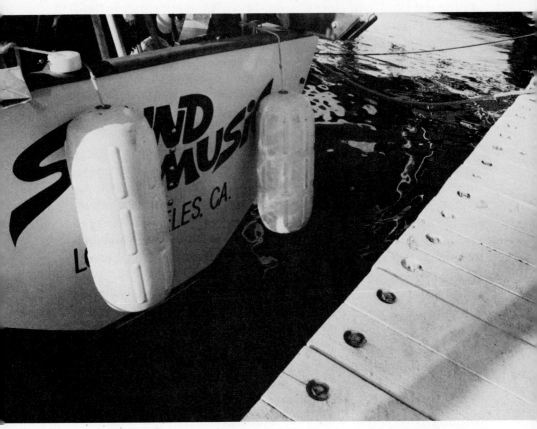

In a Med. moor fenders over the transom are a good idea, just in case!

Tension on the rode and docklines from wind, tide, and current may require us to readjust them later—or even reassess whether we need a second anchor. We double check our distance from the quay; even in quiet harbors we make it a habit to put some distance between ourselves and the dock and then winch ourselves in when we want to leave or board the boat. When moored with surge it may be best to leave the stern some distance out and use the dinghy to get back and forth.

The key to success in anchoring stern-to is being prepared. With the right ground tackle at the ready, knowledge of your boat's backing characteristics, and two or three practice runs, you should handle the Med moor with ease.

Stanley Dashew photo

ACCOUNTING FOR TIDES

In most of the world most of the time tides are something cruisers make note of in case they need an extra foot or so of water to get into or out of a favorite anchorage. Tides normally range from 2 to 6 feet. This range, and the current that accompanies the water's ebb and flow, will usually not have a major effect on your plans.

But when conditions are right geographically, substantially higher tides and stronger tidal currents can result. When these occur, you need to take special precautions in a number of areas.

Intermezzo is gliding along under #1 jib topsail, staysail, main, and mizzen as we pick up the light on the eastern corner of the Dundas Straits, the gateway to northwestern Australia. An undercurrent of excitement runs through the crew. Civilization is but a day's sail to the south. Shopping centers, ice cream stands, movies, and supermarkets all await us after a year in the Melanesian wilds. But first we must thread our way through the shoals and islands of the Van Diemen Gulf and Clarence Straits. By watching for the munificent array of navigation lights (supposedly working) and using our radar, there shouldn't be a problem. But there is a catch: tides and currents. Even though we have planned our arrival to coincide with the neap tide, when the moon is exerting the smallest force on the ocean's waters, we are still looking at 16 to 18 feet of change and 3- to 5-knot currents.

Diagrams in the *Admiralty Pilot* show the points of maxi-

Where the tidal range is substantial, the longer your dock lines, the better. More length means flatter angles, which can tolerate greater tidal range without adjustment. But in some locations dock lines will have to be tended throughout each tidal cycle.

mum ebb and flow for various periods in the tidal cycle. We will have to kill time once we each the middle of the gulf to wait for the tides to switch. Better to sit and wait a bit than buck the flow.

Even with this amount of data we keep a close eye on our running fixes, radar bearings, and plotting to make sure we are on the right track.

With the Clarence Straits now behind us and the lights of Darwin twinkling in the distance, we begin to clean ship in preparation for our arrival. The anchorage in front of the Darwin Yacht Club is filled with cruising yachts, many of them carrying old friends from New Zealand and Polynesia. But first we must find a good spot to anchor.

The bay is wide and gently shoaling, and at high tide there is water right up to the front of the yacht club. At low tide we need to be a mile from shore. The outboard will see service here!

A week later, the entire fleet moves another ¼ mile offshore. With the moon and sun beginning to pull together on the earth's oceans, the tidal range increases up to 24 feet.

At low water there is ½ mile of beach exposed in front of the yacht club. Trips ashore with the dinghy have to be planned carefully. If we go in at high water and pull the dink up on the beach and then return at low water, we'll have a long haul through the sticky sand before we get the dinghy floating again. Conversely, if we're ashore at low water and anchor the dink, there could well be a long swim in store for one crewmember. Most of the cruisers in Darwin solved the problem by coming ashore in pairs. That way one dinghy could be left anchored offshore and another on the beach close at hand.

Tying up to a fixed pier in an area of great tides means using extra-long docklines, which must be tended as the vessel lifts and falls with the tide. However, the flatter the angle fore and aft, the less tending that will be required. The ideal situation is to lie alongside a commercial vessel or another yacht and let it do the work for you! Don't forget to take into account how you will get on and off your yacht as well. We tied up at Marsden Wharf in Auckland, New Zealand, at low water and were trapped. With a 14-foot tidal range, there simply was no way for us to climb ashore.

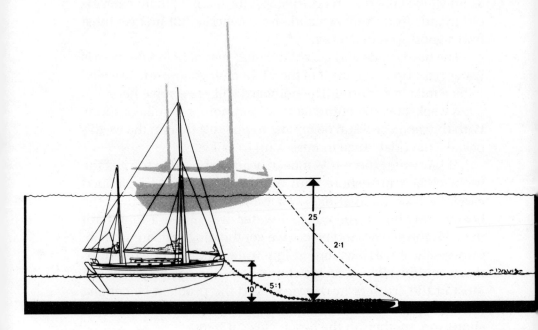

With large tidal ranges assume the highest tide when figuring scope.
Otherwise you will find yourself with limited holding power!

There's one more reason why cruisers should pay attention to tidal heights and cycles. Move with us now to Taboga Island off the coast of Panama.

Intermezzo II has just finished her first transit of the Panama Canal and rests quietly with a fleet of other cruising yachts in a large semicircular bay, fronting an enormous expanse of ocean. Here, with all that ocean water piling up against the Panamanian shore, 10- to 15-foot tides are the rule. Space is tight and after setting our big Bruce anchor in full reverse, we shorten up the chain to three-to-one scope.

The next morning we walk ashore to find the bakery. On our way down the beach we see a large modern schooner careened. Closer inspection shows she is on the rocks. There's a hole punched into her side, and the decks are slowly being inundated by the incoming tide. It is a sad sight, and I can't bring myself to photograph her.

We find the bakery and after a brief exploration we begin rowing back to *Intermezzo II*. The tide is now reaching its maximum height, and the quiet beach on our port side is disappearing. At high water we discover we are anchored in 22 feet, and have less than two-to-one scope on the anchor. A gentle wave is all that is required to lift our giant Bruce right out of the seabed. Had we stopped for some more postcards...

Stanley Dashew photo

NAVIGATING THROUGH CORAL

The rumble of anchor chain on coral wakens me. Lying groggily in our forward double bunk, I try clearing away the cobwebs of sleep. Awkwardly, so as not to wake Linda beside me, I fumble for my watch. 0445. The tide has started its ebb, and *Intermezzo* has swung around. I head topside to check the weather. The morning stars are brilliant, and the sky looks clear in all directions. Hope it stays that way, I mumble to myself as I head below for a last few winks.

Intermezzo and her crew have been temporarily trapped inside a maze of coral-infested waterways at the north end of Malaita Island in the Solomons. We had been lured to Lau Lagoon with tales of ancient man-made coral islands, the best barter market in Melanesia, and the hope of acquiring artifacts. Now the forepeak is jammed with our successes, and we're ready to exchange this labyrinth for the safety of the open sea. With charts and other aids to navigation marginal at best, making our way to deep water safely will require eyeball navigation.

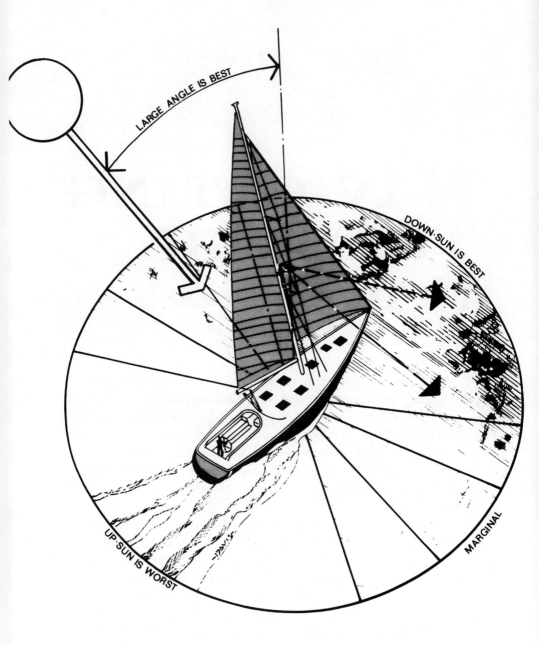

The further behind you the sun is and the higher you are off the water,
the better will be your viewing angle.

Several factors must work in our favor. First is sun angle. The lower and the more directly behind us the sun is, the easier we will find it to see underwater obstructions. As the sun climbs during the day, our viewing range will become more limited down-sun, but we will have marginally better viewing to the sides. When the sun goes directly overhead or forward of our path it will be impossible for us to see through the water except dead astern.

Because it is October, the sun is just below our latitude (11 degrees S.). Visibility will be best in a west to northwesterly direction early in the day and in an east to northeasterly direction in the afternoon. We will have some viewing range directly to the north except for an hour on either side of local noon. I silently wish it were later in the year. If the the sun were lower I would have a good range of visibility to the north for most of the day, and that is the general direction we will be heading.

The weather will also have to work for us, and it is the weather I am most worried about. A beautiful clear sky allowed us to enter the lagoon without difficulty. But for the last five days we have had periods of intermittent overcast and showers. To exit safely we need at least 4 hours of clear sky. An overcast sky produces no shadows beneath the water surface, making it next to impossible to discern what lurks below. A few clouds can be dealt with and will have to be interpreted. The dark spots they cast on the bottom resemble coral heads.

When morning does arrive I am pleased to see blue sky. The current is running swiftly, dropping the water level several feet. Good. The lower the tide, the easier it will be to make out the edges of reef and free-standing heads. Most of our trip will be made at low or slack low water. That is ideal.

Our ship's clock sings out 0800. It's time to get ready. In another half-hour the sun will be high enough in the east to allow us to start in a northwesterly direction. I check the engine V-belts and the water and oil levels and have a look around for electrical or hose chafe. Nothing is amiss. Elyse hands me a flashlight, and I crawl under the companionway for an inspection of steering cables and quadrant. Under the conditions in which we will be piloting, I want to be certain everything is going to work! On deck sail covers are removed and halyards attached. I don't expect to sail, but if the engine develops a problem, we need to be ready to set canvas instantly.

A light trade wind ruffles the water surface. Down-sun I can see the coral 30 feet below us. One hundred yards away the irregular edge of the reef is clearly outlined. Up-sun, to the east, there is a blank: no visibility.

The best viewing comes where there is some texture to the water surface. A smooth surface reflects sunlight and clouds, making it difficult, even impossible, to penetrate visually. Big waves are better than a flat surface, but the wavelets we now have, kicked up by an 8-knot southeaster, are ideal.

Water clarity is also very important to being able to navigate through coral-strung passages. Lau Lagoon has a good tidal flushing action and almost no man-made pollution. The closest island mass is several miles away and mainly volcanic so the likelihood of suspended sediments clouding our viewing is minimal. There is little runoff anyway. The sediment that rivers deposit at their mouths and for some distance out to sea can cut visibility substantially. Rain creates two problems. One is direct visibility. A light shower will cut viewing by 80 percent or more. If there is a runoff from the land that carries mud or debris, the effects of the shower will be long lived.

We're nearly ready now. I go forward to check our second anchor. It is unlashed and ready to go, just in case. So is our stern hook. I bring our little diesel to life, and Linda comes on deck. "Here are your hat and glasses," she says. "I brought up the dark ones."

We carry two densities of polarized sunglasses aboard, a very dark pair for clear, bright days and a medium pair for slightly overcast periods.

I slip on the hat and glasses, and Linda and I repair to our respective stations: Linda at the helm and, once the anchor's raised, I to the rigging. I climb the teak ratlines until I am 15 feet above the water, halfway to *Intermezzo*'s lower spreaders. I can now see down-sun several hundred yards. The higher I climb, the better my vision will be underwater. But for now, with clear water and the sun at a good angle 15 feet is fine.

"Head for the first triangular marker to port," I yell aft.

This is marker #19 on the chart I have fastened to the clipboard I carry up the rigging with me. As we pick up speed the coral heads flash by 20 feet below our keel. The water is a light blue right up to the steep sides of the coral canal we are traversing.

"Hold her at 3.5 knots." Because *Intermezzo* has a folding propeller, that is as fast as we dare go in case we need to stop suddenly.

As marker #19 comes abeam we swing 15 degrees to starboard to follow the channel due north. The sun's glare blanks out the coral directly on our starboard beam, but ahead and slightly to starboard I have some degree of visibility.

"Move over toward the port side of the channel," I tell Linda. "Keep about fifty feet off the coral edge."

Looking to port, down-sun, I have an excellent view of the coral. For now, hugging this side of the channel keeps us clear of any dangers that we can not readily identify. Then ahead I see the water turn a pale green. That will be about 10 feet deep. Getting tight on this side, I say to myself as I signal Linda to move toward the center of the channel.

Over the next 2 hours, keeping a wary eye on the climbing sun and on the sky to windward for any cloud masses, we wend our way through the coral maze. Then there's just a short way to go—one shallow spot to cross and we will be in deep water again.

Ahead and to starboard I can see coral fully exposed by the low tide. And although I can't see below the surface because of the sun's angle, I know there's more coral close by underneath as well. The boiling, turbulent wave action in the top 6 to 12 inches outlines their position clearly.

Directly ahead, in the northwest, the water changes from light blue to light green to white. That will be the 7-foot spot shown on the chart. Since coral grows at a rapid rate it may be shallower, and Linda moves *Intermezzo* to starboard a bit in the darker water; there's no sense in scraping bottom paint off the keel.

With the sun now overhead, I can see well to port and star-

board and out quite aways. But directly under our bow definition is lacking. Here I have to rely on the depthfinder. "Slow
down to two knots. Steer singing out the depth, please."

"Fourteen, fourteen, twelve feet," comes Linda's reply.

"Cut her back to seven hundred rpm, just enough for
steerage."

Intermezzo's prop slows its vibration in response. We are
crawling forward at barely a knot. "Ten feet, nine, eight. Are you
sure we're in the right spot?" Linda questions.

"We'll be free in a few more minutes," I answer, evading the
issue.

A sudden thump and crunch indicates that Linda may have
had a point. I grab cap and lower shrouds to hold my place as
Intermezzo comes to an abrupt stop. Linda has the engine in
reverse before I can speak, and we slide backwards off the coral
head.

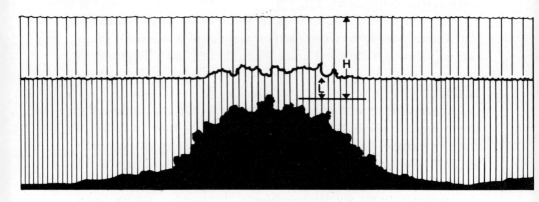

Tidal state has a large impact on the surface visibility of obstructions
below the surface. With calm water, at high tide (H) the surface may be
smooth, leaving no hint of dangers lurking below, while at low tide (L)
the surface undulations may give you warning.

"Missed one," comes my sheepish reply. With the sun over-head, it is very difficult to see directly beneath the bow. At a slow speed with a stout fiberglass hull, we can take an occasional bump, which in this type of piloting is to be expected.

Once more we proceed slightly to starboard. I can see the head, really more of a cluster of heads, as it glides by. "Okay, we're clear now; swing back to three hundred fifteen degrees, and head for that patch of dark blue water!" We are back in open ocean.

Most eyeball navigation takes place in tropical waters. How-ever, it is not unusual to use the same techniques in colder climes if the water is clear. Sun angle will always be lower because of the higher latitude, and the viewing range will be more limited but the principles are the same. Where water tends to be obscured with marine life or mud, surface turbulence of-ten gives warning of underwater obstructions. You must know the state of tide to judge how much faith to put in this form of intelligence; high water yields the least evidence of danger.

Where mistakes in eyeball navigation can be dangerous, pa-tience is a necessary virtue. Waiting for the right conditions is the secret to success. Clear, slightly ruffled water and a bright sun behind you are the keys. Height and good-quality polarized glasses are the tools. The rest depends on judgment.

Stanley Dashew photo

CROSSING A HARBOR BAR

Running through breaking waves across the entrance to a snug inlet or river mouth harbor is certainly one of the most hazardous tests of seamanship a cruising yachtsman can face. A collision of short- and long-term forces of nature creates the problem. The need to seek shelter exacerbates it. Time, patience, and a well-thought-out plan are the ingredients from which success is forged, *and this includes having an alternative to running the entrance.*

An ebbing current opposing either locally or offshore-generated wave systems can create unstable, often dangerous seas. The more the current or the larger the sea, the greater the chance the sea will crest and break. When this situation occurs over a rapidly shoaling bottom or the sandbars that often exist at river mouths and inlets through barrier islands, breaking waves are a certainty. These rapidly moving cresting seas make it difficult to maneuver most small yachts, and if you are caught in the wrong part of the wave at the wrong time, substanial damage to yacht and crew can result.

Where and when a breaking sea develops over an entrance bar is influenced by the height of the tide. When the current reverses and begins to flood back in, water depth increases, and the tendency of the shallow water to cause the waves to break will be reduced. Current flow in the same direction as the waves smooths out the seas as well. Many bars that develop dangerous breaking waves at low water or half-tide are stable at slack water

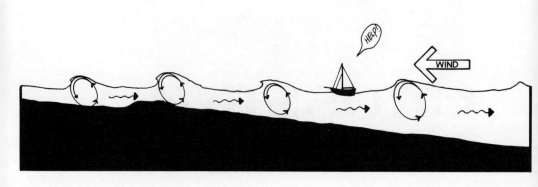

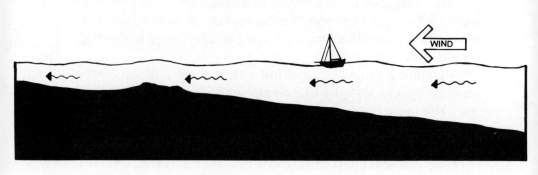

When the current runs against the seas, it stacks them up, causing the waves to become unstable and to break. A current that flows with the seas calms them. The best time to cross a bar is usually just *before* high water. That way you have the current and maximum depth going for you.

or when the current has started to flood back. In some entrances tidal height is even more critical a factor than the direction of the flow.

You must consider the state of the tidal cycle. At springs, when the moon and sun are working together to exert the most force on the oceans' tides, the effects on the bar will be the greatest. At neaps they will be minimized.

The state of the sea is another factor to consider in assessing the safety of crossing a bar. Locally generated wind waves with short lifespans are apt to be predictable. But waves generated by a distant storm change size very quickly and may arrive unannounced and be inconsistent, washing through only now and then.

One of the most illusive bits of data is bottom condition. Many bars have constantly changing contours. Local buoys cannot be relied upon unless verification of their accuracy is made with harbor or Coast Guard authorities.

In spite of these uncertainties bars can be used, even in potentially hazardous conditions by people familiar with crossing procedures in general and the *bar in question* in particular.

You must first evaluate how your vessel will react in the crossing situations. The condition is analogous to heavy downwind surfing. Just as you need good steering control to keep your vessel from broaching when running free in big seas, so you need ultimate steering control when riding a breaking wave across a bar.

Light-displacement, long waterline vessels with large detached rudders will handle the best. At the other end of the spectrum are heavy-displacement, long-ended, full-keel sail or motor yachts. Vessels of this type can be coaxed safely across, but they will need milder conditions and will go with less of a safety margin.

Reliability of power is critical. It behooves the cautious seaman to check his machinery and steering systems in advance.

The technique for crossing bars will vary with type of craft and conditions. On the outside, looking in, you must remember that seas always look smaller from their backs. Height from which to judge the waves is a help. Try for a perch on the spread-

Betsy Clapp and Bob Wake photos

Timing is critical when you run a breaking bar. This series of photos was taken off Ventura, California, during the winter of 1983, over a period of 10 minutes. The crewboat in the first shot waited until a large set of waves had passed and powered out through a small sea. The fishing boat, a converted 42-foot Coast Guard patrol vessel, just charged ahead 2 minutes later. She was caught by the first wave and spun broadside; then partially swamped, she tried again. Somehow she made it back against the breakwater. The crew was unhurt, and thanks to sturdy steel construction the boat was fishing again after some major repairs.

ers or the fly bridge. Then give yourself plenty of time to study the pattern of the seas, and where they are breaking, keeping an eye out for any unusual arrivals from a distant blow.

If you are not certain of the bottom contour and depth, the pattern to the sea's break will give some indication of where the channel runs deepest. If the current is modest, the seas will steepen more quickly where the water shoals. If there is a strong ebbing flow, the breaking seas will be greatest in the deeper parts of the channel. To be able to use this form of analysis, some local knowledge is necessary.

You must wait until the tide has turned in your favor and is flooding back to have the safest shot at crossing a bar with breaking waves. In most cases the ideal time will be just *before* the beginning of slack high water. Running bars with an ebbing tide reduces the odds of success.

In many parts of the world ports with bars have Coast Guard or lifesaving teams on duty who can be called on VHF for information. In passable but potentially dangerous conditions they will often assist you via radio or a patrol boat to pick the right moment.

If other vessels are running the bar, don't follow the first one you see. Try to watch a series of boats, noting when, how, and where they go. Be sure to factor in apparent draft. A moderate-displacement fishing vessel will frequently draw only half the water of a comparably sized sailboat. Be wary of advice given by amateurs.

Before making the final approach be sure all crewmembers don their lifejackets. If you are in cold waters survival suits should be worn. There is debate about safety harnesses. Some feel one you are better away from the boat if she rolls over. Others feel staying with the vessel is important. There is more immediate danger to you from contact with the vessel, but if your vessel is closed up and watertight and has a low center of gravity, you'll be floating right-side up in a matter of seconds. Being thrown clear avoids contact with the boat, but leaves you at the mercy of the surf in conditions that may make it difficult to find a man overboard.

On deck, all hatches must be dogged, dorades plugged, and

companionway hatch slides inserted and locked. Loose gear should be stowed below. Anything tied on deck should have double lashings. Crewmembers should be positioned so they are securely braced.

Once you are committed to the entrance, it is critical to keep your stern square to the waves. Try to ride on the *back* of a sea. The minute a crest starts to lift the stern you quickly lose steering control, and if your stern should get pushed aside a broach is possible. Very few sailboats or displacement powerboats will have the power necessary to stay with a wave for much distance. If you will have to ride more than one wave, the boat must have good surfing qualities. Otherwise, stay offshore until the bar is quiet or seek an alternate harbor.

From the inside looking out, a better evaluation of the conditions both as to wave size and timing is possible. You want to pick a smooth patch of water and then go as fast as possible to get beyond the breaker line. Remember that the waves generally come in sets of increasing size, and if you spend enough time watching them, a clear spot will usually appear. If you make a mistake, and it appears that a sea will break aboard, it is critical to get the bow straight through the crest. If the crest can be penetrated before it breaks you may be rocked at a severe angle, but damage is unlikely. If you are caught remember that another sea is following. You must push on before the next one catches you. Getting out beyond the breaker line is critical.

Anytime you're approaching a potentially breaking bar, whether from the inside heading out or outside in, all aspects must be considered: tidal state, amount of current, period of slack high water, forecast of local weather, and long-range wave systems. Even if the bar looks safe you must still take a moment to think through all the possibilities before crossing. If the bar isn't calm, evaluate other avenues before deciding to try your skill. Remember that every breaking bar is different and rarely will the conditions be the same on any bar two days in a row.

GETTING THE DINGHY THROUGH SURF AND ASHORE

The gleaming white beach is a few yards ahead. I am study-ing the rise and fall of the sea from just outside the surf line, where the great swell of the ocean feels the bottom and begins to break on the beach. Linda, seated in the stern of our 9-foot Dyer fiberglass dinghy, is relaxed, anticipating the childrens' joy. Elyse and Sarah, ages two and five, sit in the forward seat in their lifejackets, gripping the gunwale with one hand and their buck-ets and shovels with the other. Just offshore, *Intermezzo* stands quietly at anchor, a gentle swell occasionally lifting her stern.

Our situation is one in which most cruisers find themselves at one time or another: an inviting shore beckons just beyond a "beach break" or surf line, and there's no protected way from boat to land. The basic approach to getting through the surf line is similar in many respects to that necessary to coax a yacht across a breaking bar. The first rule in such a situation is to study carefully, from the outer edge of the break, the rhythm of the surf, counting the wave sequences and noting their size and where and how they break.

Two sets of waves pass under our little dink. "No problem," I say to the ladies seated around me. "I shall deposit you ashore in style."

I give a light heave on the oars, and we coast forward. Now, eyes glued on the sea before me, I jockey the oars to keep our bow straight and the broad stern of the dinghy square to the oncoming wave. Too late I realize I've made a mistake. I have forgotten that a beach break looks much smaller from seaward, from the back side of the wave, than it actually is.

With a rush, the surf has us in its grip. The bow starts to crab sideways. I am unable to straighten out our trajectory. The rail starts to tip while the stern lifts crazily. Instantly we're over, the wave crest depositing the four of us, dinghy, seat cushions, and one oar at the edge of the steep beach. Linda and I grab the kids

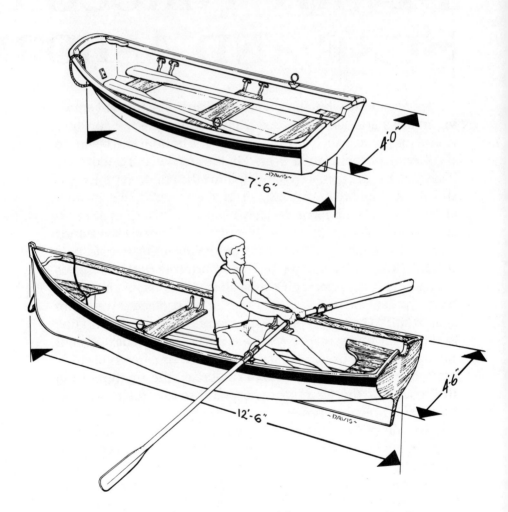

A long skinny dinghy does better in surf than a pram type. It gives you better boatspeed and directional control.

out of the surf first and then the dink. We pull the oars from the next wave. The boat is intact, and except for a superficial cut on Sarah's head, we are physically unscarred. Mentally it's a different story. It will be three years before Sarah voluntarily rides a dinghy to shore again unless a dock is present to ease the transition to land.

Rowing into that beach, I made several major errors. The first was in timing. I should have studied the wave pattern for at least 15 minutes. Beach surf generally arrives in sets of seven to nine waves. Between sets there can be a variance of as much as 100 percent in wave size. The waves within a sequence also vary greatly in size. I hadn't waited for the smallest wave in the set. Next, I had forgotten that waves look much smaller from their backs. I thought I was dealing with a 2-foot break that in reality was closer to 5. Twice outside visual height is the forecasting rule we now employ. Last, this surf was no place for our squat, directionally unstable dinghy powered by short oars.

This last problem is one most cruisers face. The dinghy, designed to ferry passengers to a dock or from boat to boat, is short for ease of stowage and beamy for stability. Since the oars have to stow inside the dink, they are short as well. All these factors deprive you of the necessary control in the surf line. In reality what is needed in surf is a long, moderate-beam boat with a narrow stern and long, powerful oars. These design characteristics promote boatspeed and directional stability.

There are two broad types of beach surf, each of which creates different problems for someone trying to shoot through it. A rapidly shelving bottom generates a short, steep wave that forms and breaks close to shore in a few seconds. This type of wave is the most difficult to ride in. Conversely, because it forms so close to shore, it's easier to get off the beach and back out through the surf line. A slowly shoaling seabed, on the other hand, promotes a more gentle wave that begins to form well offshore and has a breaking crest that can be ridden a long way. It is easier to get in with this type wave, but because the break starts well offshore you have a long way to go before you are clear when you try to head back out.

Regardless of the type of dinghy, once it reaches shore, the

passengers must disembark quickly and drag the boat out of
reach of the sea before the next wave hits the beach.

No matter what type of wave there is, one of your most
important observational tools is height. Standing up in the dink
will give you a better view of conditions. By watching the incoming swells you can learn much about the size and timing of what
is about to form into surf. Correlating what you see offshore with
what happens a short time later in the surf line helps you predict the right moment for your own ride to the beach. When
you're ashore, climb a tree, sand dune, or rock pile to get a better
view of the swells and the surf development.

We solved some of our surf problems by trading the Dyer for
a 12-foot Wherry; over the years this lean, quick, small boat has

With a high-powered inflatable, it is much easier to pick the right spot
on a wave and to stay there as you head for the beach.

served us well. Experience eventually lead us to buy a special pair of "surf" oars, as well. These 8-footers were extra heavy, and I could lay on them with full power to brake our progress or change direction surfing into shore.

The technique I use depends upon the speed of the breaking waves. If they are slow, and I feel I can keep up by rowing, I follow the wave in just *behind* the crest. This means the dink must stay ahead of the next wave, or it will broach. If the waves are moving quickly, beyond my capacity to stay with one, I try to position us in the top of a crest. The oars are then used to brake our forward speed and to keep the bow headed straight. It is essential here to prevent the boat from surfing down the wave face; that is an invitation to disaster. The loads on the oars are enormous during the braking process; the ones we used were twice as strong (and heavy) as those used for normal rowing.

To ease our passage from shore back out to the boat we added a second pair of rowlocks for the aft seat. With Linda at the main oars and the kids in the bow, I would stand in the water at the beach's edge, holding the stern and watching the wave sets roll in. When the waves had temporarily died down, I would shove out, jump into the stern, and push on the after set of oars while Linda leaned to hers. Our *combined* power would speed us beyond the surf line before the next wave could form.

Our first chance to put this system to the test came in Jalapa, just south of Puerto Vallarta on the west coast of Mexico. *Intermezzo* was anchored in the open bay of this picturesque, isolated resort. We had come ashore for a walk on *terra firma* before setting off across the Pacific. As the afternoon wore on, I failed to notice the slight increase in swell sweeping into the bay. Just before dusk, and as we were about to dine out for the last time in weeks, waves began to break on the beach with real force. There was no choice; we had to get back to *Intermezzo* quickly. For half an hour we waited at the beach's edge for a small set of waves that would allow us to get offshore safely. In the last rays of daylight we launched, and with the help of a substantial flow of adrenaline, Linda and I used our combined power to blast through the break. Our dinner out would have to wait for the Marquesas Islands, 2,800 miles to the southeast.

Stanley Dashew photo

This type of powerful (and heavy) surfboat with a trained crew can
negotiate 6 foot or larger breakers.

What if you can't find the room or don't want to put up with the inconvenient stowage of such a dink? A powered inflatable is the answer. The emphasis here is on speed. Planing speed of around 13 knots is the minimum you need. A 10-foot inflatable keel model with a 7.5-horsepower outboard should just reach this speed to ride the back of most waves safely with a load of two adults. The important thing is to stay ahead of the next wave while not powering ahead onto the face of the wave you are riding. Coming back off the beach, the speed will move you out through the surf line before the big waves hit.

Move with us now to the magic of Taieohai Bay in the Marquesas Islands. Linda and I walk to the beach carrying our new, custom-made Marquesan ukelele, a marvelous four-string cross between a banjo and guitar, carved from a solid chunk of hardwood. Even though the beach break is miniscule I wrap the

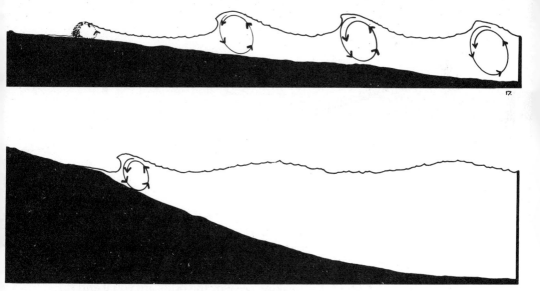

Bottom contour plays the major role in how surf develops as it hits a beach. A steep bottom has faster-moving waves breaking very close to shore, while a gentler slope causes the waves to break farther out.

uke in plastic. Without watching the waves we launch. We're clear at first, but then a breaking wave farther out from the beach than we expect invites itself into our dinghy, half swamping us. With our buoyancy tanks keeping us afloat, I pull at the oars to get us past the next wave while Linda frantically bails.

The size of buoyancy tanks contribute directly to your safety in a swamping. Bigger is always better. If you can fill your dink with water, continue to row, and bail at the same time, the tanks are large enough.

On to Fatu Hiva, perhaps the most beautiful island in the world. We have come ashore with friends Jim and Cheryl Schmidt for a day of exploring at Hanavave. The afternoon ends with the discovery of a local tapa collection, and we excitedly buy several of the beautiful handmade bark-cloth paintings. Escorted to the beach by a group of our new Polynesian friends, we are dismayed to find a large surf breaking just 100 yards offshore. I look at the four adults and two children and then the 6-horsepower motor that will have to power us and shake my head. Even with Jim's buoyant Zodiac, it looks like a tight squeeze.

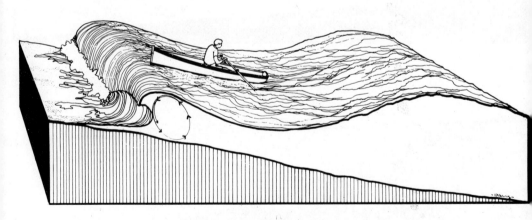

The ideal position is just behind the crest as the sea breaks on the beach. You must avoid the breaking crest or the odds are you'll end up swimming. If you do go "over the falls," boatspeed, if you have enough, may give you the directional stability to stay in line with the wave and thus avoid swamping.

At the other end of the beach, where the waves break first, we see a group of islanders clustered around an outboard-powered outrigger canoe. The district priest has come to visit and is waiting offshore in his small motor yacht for the islanders to ferry him to dry land.

Aha, I think. Now we will see a true example of Polynesian seamanship.

There is lighthearted banter up and down the beach as our group argues with the other about the best time to head out. The six of us sit in the Zodiac, held by our friends, in the turbulent water just off the beach, watchful, waiting. At what looks to me like an inopportune moment, the outrigger heads to sea. It makes the first wave but is caught by the second. The bow rears up, up, and then flips over, swamping the motor. So much for local seamanship.

It is all a great joke to our handlers. But now I am concerned and with Jim begin to watch the wave sets in earnest. Our first attempt ends with a breaking wave in the bow. Thankful for the buoyancy of the Zodiac, we pull back to the beach and bail. On our second attempt the overloaded engine tries mightily to gain offing before the next sea forms. We lumber forward, racing the oncoming swell. Our bow begins to lift just as the crest forms, ready to break. With a lunge we are through the crest, intact, and with tapas dry. Had we used Jim's larger engine, we could have made it with ease the first time.

The key to negotiating a beach break successfully is watchfulness and patience. Study the wave patterns, their timing, and how and where they break. Decide if you have the right equipment for the conditions. If you do decide to go ahead, always bear in mind the point of no return. If you err in your timing, don't be afraid to reverse course and wait for another wave set. But once you are fully committed to the surf, keep fighting, regardless of what happens. Although disaster appears imminent, it may still be possible to save the situation by strenuous exertion or a timely maneuver.

Stanley Dashew photo

LEAVING THE BOAT UNATTENDED

One disadvantage of the sea life becomes apparent when the time comes for a visit ashore. What do you do about your boat? It's your floating home and is probably underinsured, if not uninsured.

Even though our boats have been well constructed, with lots of built-in safety factors, big pumps, and heavy ground tackle, I never liked the feeling I got when we left them. In the back of my mind that nagging question always lurked: "What if something goes wrong?"

Most cruisers and liveaboards learn to live with the problem, and the doubts are partially counterbalanced by the joy of seeing the boat serenely afloat upon their return. Over the years Linda and I have adopted certain procedures and equipment to minimize risk and maximize protection. Which precautions we took varied with the length of our anticipated absence and the potential risks in the anchorage or marina.

My first concern is always with leaks. To allay this worry we installed an automatic bilgepump in each watertight compartment. The bilgepumps did not go through the master circuits but rather had their own breakers. Each pump had a large-capacity strainer, which we made sure was clean before we left. One friend hooked up his bilge alarm to the masthead strobe light and a loud, external bell. It is an excellent warning system for times you are visiting close by or having a friend look after the boat.

Ground tackle is my next consideration. If the anchorage was fully protected, the weather settled, and the holding good, we might sit with a single anchor. But if there was any question and we were going to be away for more than a half a day, we set a second hook. If we planned a long visit ashore—perhaps several days—we usually shackled a second anchor onto our main chain, behind the first, to give extra holding power.

We never left a boat unattended for more than a few hours if the anchorage was not *fully* protected. Where a single quadrant was exposed and the weather was normally okay from that direction, we all might go ashore briefly, but even then we preferred to leave one adult aboard.

As we prepared to go ashore I made it a routine to check the bilges, keelbolts, and shaft packing gland (you should check the rudder, too, if the gland is below the waterline) to make sure we were watertight and there was no sign of leakage. This inspection could be made in 2 minutes and was faithfully adhered to. If we were going to be ashore for more than a few hours, say half a day, then I closed the through-hulls, except for the bilgepump exhausts. However, yachts plumbed so the galley sink drain shares the cockpit drain should have a separate shut-off on the sink, leaving the cockpit drain itself open. If the seacocks in this system are shut off and a severe rainstorm develops, the cockpit will empty through the sink into the boat, flooding it. I shut down electrical circuits and opened the master battery switch (the pumps had their own circuit direct to the batteries). If we were not on chain, I checked the anchor rode chafing gear.

I always notified a nearby yacht that we would be ashore and asked the crew to keep an eye on our boat, even when we thought we would just be away a few hours. If we were going to be gone more than a day, I tried to find someone to come aboard once or twice a day and check things. To make their job easier, I pulled up the floorboards over the sumps, exposed the through-hulls, and left a written list of instructions on what to expect and do in any conceivable situation.

If your boat has a freezer or batteries that need to be charged, leaving a boat for any length of time is a bit more complicated. With an absence of a month of two, you may want to have machinery run once a week. Your list of instructions will, of course, have to be more detailed. In fact, we liked to leave signs with information taped to various valves and switches just to be sure nothing was forgotten.

For most cruisers the refrigeration system presents the biggest problem to leaving a boat. Even though the fridge or freezer isn't being opened daily, the compressor must still be run every so often. A system with large holding plates and heavy insulation can hold cold for several days, but then the engine or generator must come into play. If possible, we try to find a home for our refrigerated foods in a cooler ashore or on another yacht while we are gone, which eliminates the problem of running the engine.

In some parts of the world cruisers tend to go ashore for extended periods of sightseeing, and it is not unusual to see their yachts hauled out in dry storage. If it is economical, and in many places it is, this is the safest way to go.

Leaving a boat for an extended period tied to a dock involves other questions. Docklines must be checked for chafe and doubled up. I like to disconnect shore power cords so there is no chance of an electrical problem. We make sure the fenders are properly placed and their lines secured.

PREPARING FOR A HURRICANE

"Starboard ten degrees," comes the call from Linda, standing on *Intermezzo*'s lower spreaders. "Hold her steady right there. It looks like we'll have room to swing just around the point off to port." We are threading our way through one of the fjordlike channels of Papua New Guinea's Cape Nelson region.

For the past six weeks in company with the Schmidts aboard *Wind'son* we have been exploring this rarely visited part of the world. We have been rewarded with both beautiful deserted anchorages and visits from primitive but friendly villagers. But now both crews are restless and looking forward to the big city, Port Moresby, a few hundred miles away, just around the corner. It is the end of April, the "official" hurricane season is about to close, and we are ready to move out of the "safe" area towards one frequented by typhoons in the Southern Hemisphere summer.

Although our cruising ground was exotic, the seasonal migration we were effecting was typical of that of cruising yachts all over the world. Most choose to travel to new areas outside of the hurricane belts during the summer. In the West Indies, people head for the Mediterranean or the eastern seaboard of the United States. South Pacific cruisers usually head for New Zealand. A few hardy souls stay in the tropics but spend much of their time anxiously listening to forecasts and keeping a weather

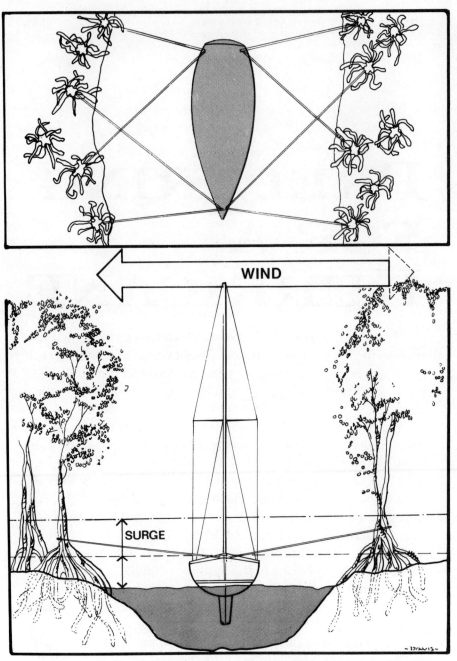

WIND

SURGE

The best protection in a hurricane is in a mangrove swamp, a common feature in most of the tropical rivers of the world. The exposed roots provide lots of firm tie-up spots, while the foliage is an excellent windbreak.

eye on the local hurricane hole as they enjoy deserted anchorages.

As we make our turn to port a large cul-de-sac opens ahead; several deep-water streams emptying into the anchorage give promise of tasty mangrove oysters. We might even see one of the saltwater crocodiles for which this part of Papua New Guinea is famous.

The steep-sided channel is flanked by craggy cliffs and steep hills. Once inside we are confronted by a vast flat bowl with the cliffs receding into the background. As we look around, an eerie feeling overtakes us all. Something isn't right.

The lush jungle foliage of the entrance channel has given way to a semibarren, contorted landscape. Instead of huge, brilliantly green trees draped with vines, we see broken and twisted stumps, uprooted giants thrown about at crazy angles. It looks like the set for a Grade B jungle horror movie.

We drop the hook, get a good bite under power, and launch the dinghy. A short ride brings us to a landing, where we can scramble ashore and head for the local trading post. Linda is after some fresh bread, and I am hoping for a few tall tales. We are frankly curious. What we learn generates more unease than any horror story.

Two years previously there had been a 180-knot blow through the anchorage. Not only is this area outside the hurricane belt but that storm had occurred in June, well outside the Southern Hemisphere summer season. The storm had devastated the local crops, forests, and villages. The tale brings home most forcefully the fact that *hurricanes can happen almost anywhere, at any time of year*.

The message is clear: never take for granted that you are fully safe from a major tropical storm. Of course, properly prepared, with a well-found yacht, in a secure anchorage, you can ride out a revolving storm with a minimum of trauma. The key is preparation and having the right gear aboard.

If a tropical storm is imminent, your first decision is where to shelter. Consider the expected direction of the wind and any shifts, the height of water from flooding or storm surge, damage from flying debris, the number of other vessels in your an-

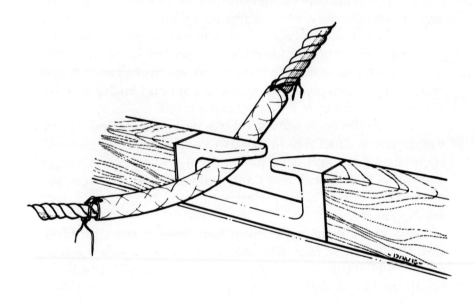

Chafe gear must be in place on all lines and be monitered constantly. Under hurricane strains even a mild burr on a fairlead, chock, or cleat will make short work of your lines.

chorage, and the protection from wind and sea afforded by the surroundings.

When summer cruising where the possibility of a storm is present, it is always best to stay close to a "hurricane hole" and to have alternative harbors in mind in case traffic or weather makes getting to your first choice impractical.

Your best bet is to go up a river or creek or into a mangrove swamp. The close foliage will act as a wind break and in many cases cause the worst of the storm to pass overhead. Second, there will be plenty of ways to tie the boat. Mangrove swamp streams are usually narrow enough for you to center the boat between the banks, tying off to the mangrove roots.

Where each line you put out passes around a tree, lamppost, or even cleat (be sure the cleat is well secured), chafing gear must be employed. We find that nylon reinforced vinyl hose is ideal. On board chafe must be watched as well. Chafe is more severe in one of these blows because the wind is unsteady, causing the nylon to stretch and contract. Any corners or rough surfaces will abraid it rapidly.

If your only options are anchorages, look first at the amount of protection from the expected direction of the storm winds. Secondly, consider what you will do once the eye passes and the wind goes through its major shift. Normally you move to the next windward shore during the lull before the storm resumes. Is there sufficient protection there? (It is also important to know the lay of the anchorage so you can make the change in less than ideal light if necessary.)

Think about the bottom characteristics. Only the best holding will suffice in a true storm: hard mud or deep sand. We always checked holding by reversing at full throttle against a medium-sized anchor. If it held, I was sure our big hooks will do well in the blow.

If it's likely that you'll have to share the anchorage with other boats, commercial or pleasure, it is important that you be in the best spot early. That may mean moving before an actual alert is given that danger is imminent. In many parts of the world the biggest risk in a blow is from other boats dragging or breaking free in crowded anchorages.

Many times a storm will be in your general region but too far away to cause damage. It may even be heading away from you. This can create a false sense of security. If it changes direction suddenly, within hours the clouds and rain that are usually on the fringes of a storm may make it impossible for you to move to your protected spot.

In storm conditions you should lay out two or three hooks, preferably on nylon for shock-absorbing qualities. The main hook on chain should be left slack so that it only takes load when the nylon rodes have stretched to their limit. Chafe at the stemhead must be watched carefully.

If the option exists, try to orient your boat's bow towards the expected worst direction of wind. Remember that in gusts she may be heeling, perhaps almost on her beam ends. Is there room for your mast to clear other vessels or trees?

It takes lots of line to do a good job. Most experienced cruisers carry enormous quantities in the unlikely event they will need it. Aboard *Intermezzo II* we had a total of 1,200 feet of 3/4-inch nylon and 800 feet of 5/8-inch nylon for use as either rodes or securing lines. If we had been caught in a hurricane, you can bet every foot would have been used.

Obviously anchors must be substantial. Our primary, every-day anchor was storm-sized anyway, a good rule for any cruiser to follow. On deck, or in the bilge, you should stow at least two and preferably more, full-sized hooks for just such an occasion. Each should have a short length of chain for bottom chafe.

The boat takes a bit of preparation for a hurricane, too. Sails on booms, roller-furled canvas, even halyards, should be brought belowdecks to reduce windage and the chance of something getting free and causing damage. All hatches should be dogged and storm covers fitted. Dorades should be removed, and cockpit lockers sealed shut. Deck and cockpit drains must be clear and free running. More than one yacht has been sunk by *rain* in a tropical storm. If you expect flying debris, your storm shutters should be rigged.

After the storm hits, take bearings to ensure that you aren't dragging, and maintain a careful eye on the storm surge and flooding. If you are tied close to a dock or trees, the water's rise and fall will make line adjustment necessary.

Yachts in cyclone-prone areas such as Fiji and Guam have ridden out 200-plus-knot storms. The key is being prepared in advance and taking action to find shelter while your choice of adequate hurricane holes is best.

Larry Pardey photo

Never give up hope. Work as fast and as hard as you can. Somehow, in some way, you'll get your boat afloat. This fine yacht is still cruising, thanks to the efforts of her owners.

SALVAGING A MISTAKE

Salvage is one aspect of yachting most of us would rather forget. But preparing your crew to deal with seagoing emergencies and making a modest investment in damage control gear can go a long way towards reducing the risk to life, limb, and boat in a salvage emergency.

Common sense and the fine print in marine insurance policies dictate that the master of a yacht in distress take every reasonable precaution to protect his vessel and crew. The insurance company expects you to deal with emergency situations as if you were uninsured. Walk away from a mistake, and you may have a carrier who feels he doesn't have to pay.

If you do find yourself in trouble, there are two basic avenues you will have to consider. The first is accepting help from others, and the second is dealing with the situation yourself.

Unfortunately, even in a book on seamanship we also have to look at the legal aspects of this subject as well.

Some of the oldest federal laws deal with just this subject. If another vessel or individual renders you aid, he is entitled to fair compensation for that assistance. Anthony Mohr, a Beverly Hills, California, attorney, states that "Federal law *requires* that the master of a vessel render assistance to a person found at sea in danger of being lost. Compensation is intended to offset this requirement. There are even penalties in the federal statutes to be assessed if aid can be given but is not."

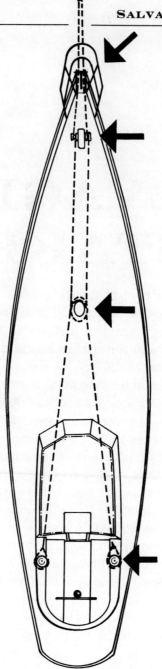

A towing bridle should be rigged so the loads are distributed into the strongest parts of the boat. Windlass, mainmast, and primary winches are the best connection points.

If you must call for help from outsiders, it is best to make an arrangement in advance over the fee to be paid. If you don't you may find your vessel impounded by a salvor's lien while you await the ponderous course of justice in the Admiralty court system.

Ben Weaver, a Fort Lauderdale, Florida, attorney specializing in Admiralty law, told me, "The claim a salvor is likely to make will depend upon the weather conditions at the time, condition of the vessel, danger to her crew, value of vessel and cargo, and danger to the salvor's crew. If you run out of fuel on Sunday afternoon and accept a tow to the local fuel dock, the award is likely to be minimal. But if you are caught on a lee shore, with a dangerous sea running, the Admiralty court is likely to hold that a good percentage of the value of vessel and cargo be paid to the salvor."

Obviously a small runabout will have to pay less than a large motor yacht. It is not unusual, however, with smaller or older vessels to find the salvage claim more than the boat itself is worth.

"On the other hand," Weaver points out, "the salvor must act in good faith, or the court may disallow his claim."

One of the best ways to avoid such legal entanglements is by looking at the various things that can go wrong and then planning how you will combat a potential crisis *before* you leave the dock.

A towing bridle is the first thing to consider. The loads on this gear will be substantial. The bridle must be attached to very strong fittings aboard in order to take the strain. Proper towing bits are rarely found on most yachts. Powerboats can rig a bridle clear around the hull, making ties to lifeline stanchions or through the bulworks to hold the bridle up and in place while the towing load is distributed into the stern quarters of the hull, one of the strongest parts of the boat.

Sailboats have masts and heavy sheet winches, which make excellent attachment points for towing. Making up a bridle that uses a series of these "hard spots" will distribute the load throughout the hull and deck structure. Remember to have the bridle secured close to the centerline at the bow. This will help keep your yacht straight as she is pulled.

Having aboard a large inventory of heavy nylon line eases the task of rigging a bridle. You will need enough to make several passes around the hull, with enough left over for the actual tow line. Sailors have a ready inventory of sheets that will work in a pinch, although the Dacron used in these lines isn't as chafe resistant or shock absorbent as nylon. Motor yachts can call upon their nylon anchor lines. If you have three heavy rodes aboard, they will probably take care of most situations. A substantial supply of chafing gear is also important: nylon reinforced vinyl or heavy rubber hose works the best. If you don't have extra it can always be scavenged from the plumbing system.

Dealing with severe leaks is another area where preparation will pay dividends. Most important is to be sure your bilges are clean and that nothing is stored in or near the bilges that could decompose if wet and clog your pumps. Paper products such as the labels on cans are the worst offenders. Then be sure every pump aboard is fitted with a *high-capacity* strainer. There should be a series of independent pumps. The everyday submersible bilgepump is okay for normal leaks, but a high-capacity damage-control pump, engine- or generator-driven,

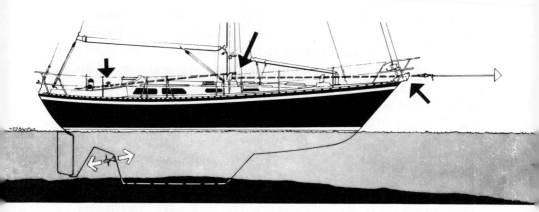

Another view of rigging a tow line to spars and winches. The bridle must be securely fastened at the bow roller to insure the pull is straight on the bow.

will be essential if a gusher starts. Even better is a separate industrial type centrifugal pump. These are available with noncorrosive bodies and impellers, powered by small gas or diesel engines, and will remove as much as 200 gallons per minute. A pump of this nature with a single cylinder gas engine can be purchased for less than $400—a modest investment for the security it brings.

A majority of severe leaks start with through-hull fittings or their attendant plumbing; know where every through-hull is located, make certain there is good inspection access, and be sure the valves operate properly. Store tapered soft wood plugs near each valve for emergency use.

Be familiar with your saltwater plumbing system. Once a leak is discovered, speed in closing through-hulls and checking out the potential trouble spots will be critical.

The hull area around prop shaft supports, rudder stuffing boxes, and shaft packing glands are frequently sources of leaks. It is often possible to isolate these areas with a watertight bulkhead. This contains the source of trouble within a relatively small part of your hull.

A mask, snorkel, fins, wet suit, and weight belt stowed handily will help you deal with leaks from the outside and free propellers from entangling snarls. If you are drifting down on a lee shore you will want to be able to get at this gear in a hurry. We have always kept dive gear near the helm for just such emergencies and have used it on several occasions when this expert forgot to check for sheets over the side before engaging the prop.

If you have to tow another boat, or accept a tow yourself, it is best to establish communications early to plan how the rescuer will approach the helpless vessel and at what speed the tow will be affected. Be sure to detail a crewmember to keep an eye on the tow line to help the helmsman keep it clear of the prop. If a direct radio link isn't available, try working out a system of hand signaling on speed. Once the tow starts, engine noise will make voice communication impossible except by radio.

A towing bridle should have already been rigged so all that is required is to hook in the towing warp. A heaving line with a weight attached can be used to establish a link between the two

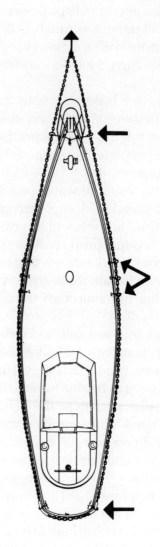

For more serious salvage tows a chain or rope bridle may have to be rigged around the hull itself. This puts the tow load into the stern quarters of the hull. The chain should be secured at various points around the hull to keep it in place.

vessels and then to pull the heavy towing bridle across. Start the
tow slowly, allowing the following vessel to align herself gradually with the direction of travel. It is best to steer as much in the
wake of the towing vessel as possible. Avoid getting out at an
angle, as this positioned increases loads dramatically. If steering
difficulty is encountered try dragging warps to keep you in line.

One of the most critical aspects of the tow is picking the right
speed. You want to move as fast as possible to get back to port,
but the loads on the towing gear increase with the square of
your speed, and a small yacht being towed by a large powerful
vessel can run into severe problems if towed too close to her hull
speed. A tow at 6 knots will create better than twice the strain as
one at 4. On the other hand, maneuverability also has to be
considered. Enough speed will be required so the tug has good
steering control.

The length of the tow line will vary with speed, sea conditions, and steerage. The rougher it is, the farther back the tow
will need to be. This leaves more line to absorb shocks.

As you get into crowded waters the tow length and speed
will have to be reduced. Depending upon current, wind, and the
berth, it may even be best to bring the two boats alongside for
the final approach.

If you are doing the towing, and you feel uncomfortable
bringing the two into the dock, it may be best to have the dis-
abled vessel drop her anchor once shelter is reached and wait
for professional help or calm conditions for the trip to the dock.

If you do decide to bring the towed vessel into the dock
remember that she has no reverse gear. She must be brought to
the dock very slowly. When a cross wind is present, the slow
speed will cause her—and you—to drift downwind, perhaps at
a rapid rate.

When the problem is a severe leak, there are two considerations. The first is the possibility you might need to abandon
ship. While the source and magnitude of the leak are being
determined, preparations should also be under way in case this
drastic step is necessary. The second is fixing the leak. In most
cases leaks can be brought under control to the point were a
good damage-control pumping system can cope. If a plank has

sprung, or there is a crack in the hull, try stuffing towels and other dunnage into the opening. If this is braced in place, perhaps with a piece of furniture, the extra pressure will help keep water at bay. Working from the outside is a better bet if sea conditions allow. This way the water pressure will hold the caulking in place.

If the leak is of less than epic proportions some sleuthing may be in order to find the cause. The first thing to do is check the taste. Fresh water indicates the problem isn't life threatening

Francis Breidenbache photo

This small sloop found itself in the surf line, stuck on the beach just outside of Marina del Rey on the southern California coast. Between hauling her down by the masthead and the efforts of a small harbor patrol vessel, she was pulled free.

Francis Breidenbache photo

(unless you are cruising in fresh water). With salt look first to the ends of your boat for a sign of running water that will lead you to the source. In the engine room leaks are sometimes harder to find. When water hits moving V-belts it sprays, making leak detection difficult. If the engine plumbing is suspect, shut down machinery, and close the incoming saltwater valve. Remember to check the shaft log. It is not unknown for a prop shaft to work loose from its coupling and drop aft through the stuffing box.

One valuable element in your leak containment arsenal should be underwater curing epoxy. This two-component material is available in most marine stores and will actually harden, within a day's time, when used underwater.

Our first emergency experience with this remarkable material came about in the Solomon Islands. *Intermezzo* had developed a substantial leak in the bronze tube that surrounded her prop shaft. It appeared to be due to electrolysis and was in danger of spreading. Since her engine was located low in the bilge, the shaft exited through the keel, and the leak was in the aft, narrowest part of the fin.

Ideally we would have hauled *Intermezzo*, cut open the fin, replaced the tube, and been on our way. But a lack of haulout facilities made that impractical.

To make a repair that would last for some time we first had to stem the flow of seawater. This was accomplished by using the underwater epoxy to pack the area around the shaft outside the hull. The seawater pressure helped keep the epoxy in place. With the inside pressure eliminated, we were then able to smear the epoxy over most of the tube inside the hull, after which we wrapped the entire affair in cheesecloth to help hold the epoxy in place and provide reinforcement.

Loss of mobility is probably the most common form of difficulty in which yachtsmen find themselves. In the absence of a lee shore, there is time to deal with the cause and correct it, but if you are drifting downwind and onto a shore, you must move quickly to stop the drift, or failing that, control the direction.

Assuming the water is too deep to anchor, if the bow is turned downwind it may be possible to direct your course either side of dead to leeward. Sailors, even if steering is broken, can direct themselves by balancing fore-and-aft sails. If you need to head downwind, ease the main or mizzen and overtrim the jib. Heading upwind is just the opposite; trim aft sails and ease the foresails.

If drifting ashore seems inevitable, aim for a spot that looks the "softest." A gentle shelving sea bottom made up of mud or sand is preferable to a steep, rocky beach.

Have ground tackle ready to go when water depth will make it effective. You will first want to use your heaviest anchor with a chain lead and then a nylon rode. The nylon is better than chain at absorbing wave shock. Have your second and third anchors untied, with their rodes flaked out and ready run, too. If you're caught on a lee shore, with the wind and waves against you, loads will be enoromous, and you will want everything you have working towards holding the boat in deep water.

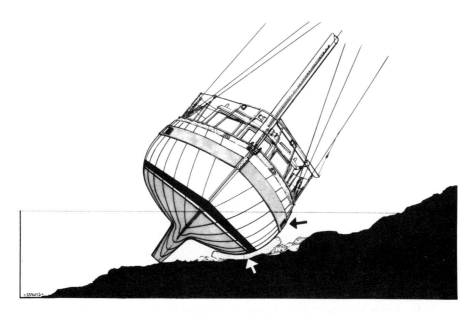

Try to protect the hull side and/or bottom with bunk cushions or even floorboards.

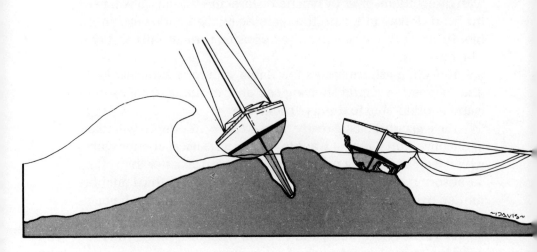

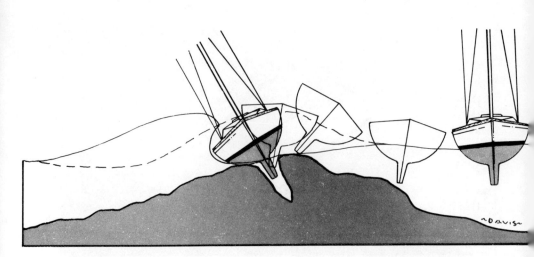

Yachts with deep keels are at greater risk in a severe grounding than shallow-draft vessels. Deeper keels have more propensity to become trapped in rock or coral pockets.

Be sure to keep a careful eye on chafe, and see that the mooring bitts or bow cleats are taking the wave surge loads. Backup bridles, such as those used when towing, may be necessary.

If you are assisting an anchored vessel, take care to keep your props clear of her anchor lines. As the anchored vessel surges back and forth, the increased strain on the rodes may cause them to pop to the surface. To minimize this risk, try floating a messenger line down on a cushion while stationing yourself well upwind. It can then be used to pull across the main towing hawser.

Aboard the stricken vessel preparation should be under way to minimize risk if the anchors fail to hold. This means donning lifejackets and garments to protect the body against abrasion on a rocky or coral shoreline. While it is almost always better to stay with an anchored vessel, if it is necessary to go ashore it will be best if a safety line can be established between shore and ship.

Throughout any emergency you must keep an eye on the elements. A minor problem in moderate weather can turn into a life-threatening disaster if weather deteriorates. Obviously the faster you can get back under way and in control of your destiny, the better; don't dally just because the weather at present looks good.

Using the radio under these circumstances requires the ability to stay calm and to transmit data in an orderly manner. You will first want to give your position, preferably latitude and then longitude, vessel name, description, and information on your predicament. It is best to designate one crewmember to stay on the radio in contact with rescuers or third parties who may be relaying the data.

The other side of the salvage question deals with the land and accidental encounter therewith. In many cases with modern, well-constructed yachts, a severe stranding need not mean the end of your dreams. Many amateurs have successfully rescued *themselves and their yachts* from the clutches of terra firma in situations that would seem to many to be hopeless.

The actions you take in the first few minutes of a stranding could make the difference between success and failure. The design and construction of your vessel will control, to some extent, the actions you take. Draft, keel type and reinforcement, hull material, freeboard, displacement—all play a part in how you maneuver and safeguard your boat.

Metal boats have the longest life span in a dangerous grounding. A moderately well-built aluminum or steel yacht can spend months or even years on a reef without sustaining major damage to the basic structure. Fiberglass is not as resilient, but a strong fiberglass hull can survive in salvageable condition a considerably longer period than one built of wood; ferrocement has little, if any, tolerance for withstanding impact.

The coefficient of friction of the hull material also figures in how you approach a salvage operation. Metal and fiberglass hulls slide easily over coral, small rocks, or rough sand. Ferrocement has some tolerance in this regard, while wood will abraid and develop a high degree of friction.

Keel shape is a critical factor in any grounding. Yachts with deep keels are more likely to become trapped in rock or in coral pockets. A beach, on the other hand, plays no favorites. Some

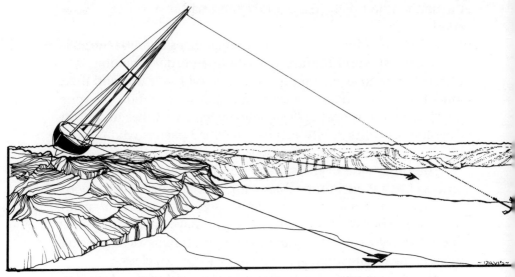

An anchor pulling from the masthead can be used to heave you down and reduce draft. That may just do the trick to get you across the reef or off a bar.

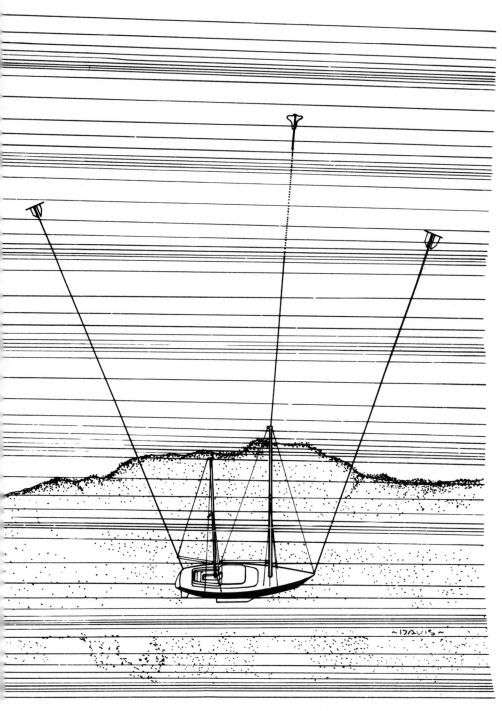

If you are stuck on a barrier reef, using a bridle of anchors from bow and stern you may be able to pull yourself across the reef to deep water inside of the lagoon.

deep-keel yachts have an advantage if their keel or ballast structures are removable. In a severe situation the removal of this weight will make refloating substantially easier.

If your boat has a deep fin keel and you think you might employ this approach should the boat become entrapped, have a good look at your keelbolts and be sure to carry onboard the right socket wrenches, extensions, and breaker bars to free them. And make sure they are not frozen.

The most powerful anchor windlasses are hydraulically powered. This one has a 5-horsepower motor and is capable of pulling this boat out of danger in most groundings.

The size and shape of the boat's deckhouse plays a part as well. If you have a lot of of superstructure, the boat is more likely to be damaged by breaking seas.

Displacement is one of the most important design factors to consider in attempting a salvage operation. Light-displacement vessels tend to be tossed out of the surf line, up and onto shore, out of harm's way. Heavy yachts will be get stuck in or near the surf line, where they are subject to more punishment. In the Cabo San Lucas disaster of late December 1982, in which 17 yachts were driven ashore by breaking seas, one 40-foot ultralight racing boat, whose scantlings were considered foolhardy by many, was thrown high up the beach and suffer less damage than any other vessel that found itself ashore. In the salvage operations, her keel was removed, after which she was towed back to San Diego.

The gear you carry will also greatly affect your options in attempting a salvage. If you are serious about having a good chance to rescue your own vessel, you will want to have aboard a modest inventory of specialized equipment. The first thing to look to is a method of working your way back to deep water. On your own, you will have to kedge off (unless you're lucky enough to ground on a rising tide). The friction loads between the hull and seabed will be substantial, and your gear will have to be powerful enough to overcome this resistance. I favor having the biggest anchor windlass possible for just this reason.

You should also have the means to assist the windlass manually; some types can be backed up with a hand crank to increase capacity when the electric or hydraulic motor starts to stall.

Many experienced cruisers carry extra-large snatchblocks as well. These can be attached to the end of a chain lead and create a two-to-one purchase between windlass and anchor.

You will also want to have aboard some means of coping with damage to the underbody. There is a chance that the boat's watertight integrity will be breached, and you have to be ready to deal with the water quickly. A collision patch, underwater epoxy, dunnage for bracing, and rags should be available.

If a leak does occur, one of your most important concerns

One of the victims of the 1982 Cabo San Lucas disaster was assisted in escape by a large backhoe. The backhoe was able to excavate around the hull while the tide was low until the sloop settled to an almost vertical position. A towing bridle was then rigged around the hull and keel.

As the tidal height increased to its maximum (it was just on springs) the sloop was pulled free by a powerful sportsfisherman. This same approach has been successful in other instances, using hand shovels and anchors.

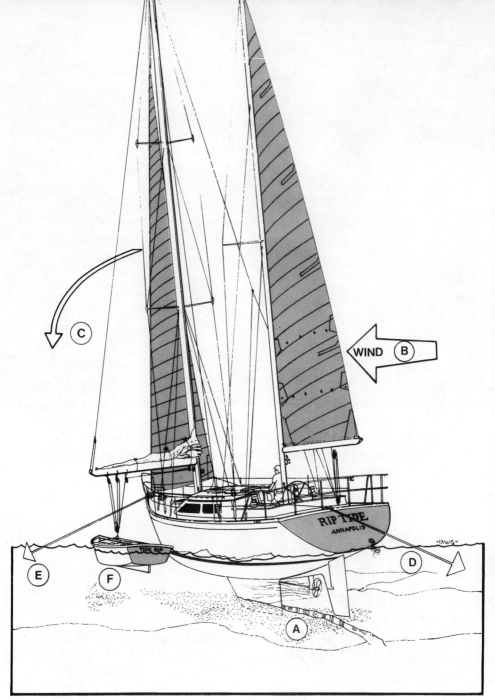

There are many ways to work yourself free from a grounding. The prop
wash (A) can be used to excavate debris from under the hull. You can
harness the wind to heel you over (B)—but be sure there are no rocks
in the direction of heel (C). An anchor (D) should be set in the direction
from which you took the ground. Sometimes an anchor from the bow
(E) will help to swing you around and out of the bottom suction.
Finally, hoisting the dink (F) full of water from the end of the main
boom can be used to heel you over reducing effective draft in the
process.

will be pumping the water back out. Once again the damage-control pumps we discussed earlier look awfully good.

If you plan to cruise where there are coral reefs, you will also want to have aboard the means of breaking a path through the coral to clear water. A pick ax is ideal; large angle iron stakes will also work. Coral is fairly easy to break away, and having the means to do so might make it possible to get your boat back to deep water or farther inshore, away from the dangerous surf line.

Preplanning is one thing, but what steps do you take once danger is imminent or suddenly a reality? There are two sets of decisions you have to make. The first concerns personal safety. You will want to don lifejackets, protective shoes, and clothing to shield you from cuts and abrasions; wet suits are ideal. You must of course, decide the best means of safeguarding the lives of you and your crew. Is it best to stay with the vessel, ride her into shore, take a small boat ashore, or as a last resort, swim for it? The major criteria will be your relationship to the surf.

Next, you must quickly decide a basic question of vessel survival. Is there a possibility you can get a hook set, hold the boat's head up into the surf, and kedge or power back into deep water? If it is not an immediate likelihood, what are the short-term prospects for holding your position and not sustaining damage? Or do you want to be driven ashore as quickly as possible, to get out of the surf line?

If you have hit an obstruction that is surrounded by deep water you also want to consider the consequences of freeing yourself if the underbody has been damaged severely. It may be that backing off into deep water will allow the boat to sink before the leaks can be stopped.

Obviously what you do depends on what it is you've hit and the type of shore line, if any, behind it. A gently shelving beach presents less trouble than a rocky coastline.

A main goal is to avoid being trapped at the surfline. If you are, work as fast as is safely possible to free the vessel to where she is in deep water again or where she can be washed farther up ashore. If you are on a coral reef but not yet trapped, be wary of your keel's grinding a hole in the softer corals.

Tidal factors play a big role in deciding a course of action. If you hit at low water and the tidal range is several feet, you stand a good chance of floating off quickly. In this case it may be wise to run out a kedge through the surf as soon as possible and then wait out the rising water.

After you assess your boat's chances of surviving, your next concern is her watertight integrity. As quickly as possible seal all dorades, engine room vents, and hatches. Remember the cockpit lockers, forward anchor hawse holes, and companionway slides. Keeping water and debris out of the boat is of paramount importance.

While most groundings, oddly enough, seem to occur during mild conditions, stop for a moment to evaluate the weather. What are the prospects for a swell moving in, or for a fast meteorological change?

If there is any single most important ingredient to success in rescuing a stranded boat it is speed. Once you recover from the initial psychological shock of that first series of impacts of hull and ground, formulate a plan and get right to work. Even if your vessel looks okay in its present predicament, don't waste time. A change in local conditions could put you at risk, or perhaps you can't see a rock grinding away under the hull.

Unless you have been fortunate enough to strike at the low end of a very high tidal range, you will probably find it necessary to remove as much weight from your boat as possible. Start by emptying watertanks, and then go for the canned goods, extra chain and anchors, and books. Removing sails, running rigging, locker doors and drawers, even floorboards can help reduce weight.

If you have emptied all the removables and find still more weight needs to come off, take a good long look at your keel. It is frequently easier than it appears to remove a ballast shoe or fin. If you have addressed this problem in advance, so much the better.

In some situations you may be able to float your boat on her side towards deep water. Being trapped on the seaward side of a lagoon or estuary will sometimes yield an easier escape across the shallows fronting the inland body of water. Heaving your boat down by the masthead will reduce her effective draft. A 40-foot sailboat that draws 6 feet on her feet may only draw 2½ at a 70-degree angle of heel. The mast head can be pulled down by attaching halyards to rocks ashore or by fanning out a series of anchors bridled together as a counterweight. As the mast comes closer to the water, less weight is required to hold the vessel. Winching from the masthead is also sometimes a means of both hauling down and moving a boat.

Powerboats that find a particular obstruction blocking their way may be able to heel a bit by using a small boat boom with a dinghy attached to exert side force. Filling the dink with water will increase its leverage tremendously.

You can accomplish kedging towards deep water by winching from one end only or from both bow and stern, pulling yourself along sideways.

Finally, outside help may offer to tow you. If this is the case and you have the time to do so, it is still important to lighten ship as much as possible to reduce the enormous loads on the towing bridle and vessel.

Be sure to discuss the direction of the tow carefully with the good Samaritan. You want to try to pick a path with minimum obstructions. It may even be possible to remove some of the obstructions if you have of our recommended tools aboard. Before towing begins, you want to have all your damage-control gear at the ready. Your pumps should be primed, with clean strainers. If an auxiliary bilgepump is aboard, make sure its tank is full and a secondary fuel supply is ready. Even though your vessel may be watertight on the reef, she may lose her integrity on the way clear.

Stanley Dashew photo

Choosing the Right Yacht

So far we have discussed many of the potential problem areas in cruising on a small yacht. Given respect for the sea and conservative seamanship, you will in all probability find that these problems stay in that "potential" category of thinking.

But mistakes are made by experienced, conservative seamen as well as by neophytes. Linda and I have had our share, as have most of our friends that have cruised. And the less experience you have and the more time you spend cruising building up that experience, the more mistakes you are going to make. That is inevitable.

In order to make sure you are able to learn from these practical lessons, you must have a forgiving vessel under your feet. It has to be designed and built to spend time aground, take knockdowns (or worse), and run into a dock or two, with no more than cosmetic damage.

Choosing the right yacht in which to cruise isn't easy. From all sides you are assailed by conflicting claims of seaworthiness as well as performance, of good looks and quality and comfort.

Yachting advertisements abound with references to "old world craftsmanship" and "unbelievable space." Boats with beamy hulls to accommodate the interior volume that is advertised are said to have raceboat performance to windward and maximum ease of handling as well as rocket acceleration off the wind. Obviously, no cruising boat can deliver it all.

A late Cruising Club of America design, like the Ericson 41
Windshadow, makes an excellent, strong, all-around cruising yacht.
The crew of *Intermezzo* were always happy to see our good friends the
Naranjos aboard their Bruce King-designed yacht.

Furthermore, the boatbuilder today is bombarded by competitive pressures that force him to cut corners. As a result, the average "sail-away" production yacht is no more ready for a sea voyage than a sailing dinghy is.

In order to survive, most builders manufacture what are euphemistically called "percentage boats." A very small percentage of boatowners ever use their yachts and of this group an even smaller percentage actually go to sea or will be exposed to heavy weather.

Thus, many production manufacturers gravitate towards the lowest common denominator. They build for the cruising owner who in reality is a daysailor. It is cheaper to fix the boat of a customer who happens to run into problems at sea (if he makes it back!) than it is to build all of them right in the beginning.

Larry Pardey photo

As we have said before, a yacht must be able to take her owner's occasional serious lapse of attention in stride. This Taiwanese fiberglass hull was obviously lacking in some areas of reinforcement.

I'm sure that many production builders think they are con-
structing seaworthy vessels. They point out the hard usage given
their models by various charter companies and how those
charterboats have been sailed from the plant to their chartering
destinations as proof of their seaworthiness. But, as we noted
earlier, truly bad weather is rare, and few of these vessels will
have really been tested.

Modern designs have also gone through a startling evolution
in the last decade. Under the influence of the early development
in the International Offshore Rule, common sense, and competitive pressure, cruising designs have trended away from heavy-

There are many versions of the lovely double ender Ingrid sailing the
world today. This 38-footer has been built in cold-molded wood,
fiberglass, steel, and as with *Eos* ferrocement. If the displacement is
kept to the original design, she is an excellent sea boat.

displacement, low-freeboard, full-keeled hulls to moderate-displacement high-volume designs. Some of these boats are drier, easier on the helm, and have far more interior living and storage space than "traditional" cruisers. The motion may sometimes be quicker, but so are the passages aboard them.

One problem faced by the recreational marine industry in general and by the serious, conservative buyer in particular is the lack of real seagoing experience at all levels.

In addition, while your local dealer, broker, or builder probably has some racing experience, and he or she can talk a good story, do you know how many *thousands* of bluewater miles he or she has accumulated? Over the years I have worked with topflight builders and designers all over the world; only a few of the individuals involved have been what I would term experienced seamen—not that most wouldn't love to have the time to pursue the pleasure of sailing and accumulate some bluewater miles. But economics usually dictate that aspiring designers keep their noses to the drafting board. Boatbuilders must stay on top of quality control and costs. The result is that they frequently operate in a virtual experience vacuum.

Take the chief executive of any boatbuilding corporation, place him in a small yacht off Cape Hatteras in a norther, and his entire outlook on the word "quality" will change.

Surprisingly, the cost difference between a boat properly set up for offshore work and the "percentage" boats needn't be that great. It is more a question of approach, of understanding what the sea can and may do, than of money. Sure, some extra expense is involved, but as a percentage of the vessel's total cost, it is insignificant.

Safety factors are the first area you should investigate. Most conservative naval architects specify that standing rigging and spars be able to carry 2.5 to 2.75 times the maximum working strains with the boat half loaded. This means if your cap shroud carries a 5,000 pound load when you are heeled at 30 degrees, the wire should be sized so that it won't break before receiving 12,500 pounds.

The wire is only the first link. Chainplates at the deck and tangs on the mast need additional safety factors, usually 1.5

Baruna, a beautiful yacht from a bygone era, is still turning heads wherever she sails. Conservatively designed and built yachts of this type can withstand far more punishment than their crews can take.

times wire size, as a minimum.

These safety factors are based on long-term experience, and the data base from which this information is derived includes a preponderance of weekend and daysailing boats. These vessels spend few hours at sea and are usually lightly loaded. If you are thinking about long offshore passages with a vessel fully loaded, the basis upon which you calculate the safety factor must be adjusted upward accordingly.

We always assume our boats will sail at full load and that they will be doing many thousands of miles a year. We have found that using the same safety factors and basing them on the righting moments at full load works well.

Beyond safety factors you must also look to the nature of risks you expect to face. The more cruising you do, the greater the odds that sooner or later you will end up on a reef or in a collision of some sort. Increasing your chances of escaping without major damage can be accomplished in the building stage without a great deal of effort or cost.

The key is to evaluate your hull shape and the keel and rudder configuration and how these will interact if the boat is stranded under various circumstances situations.

Not every condition can be allowed for, but in most cases the bottom section of the keel and the turn of the bilge will take the worst punishment. The area between these will normally be out of the way, unless there are protruding rocks or coral heads.

We addressed this problem in detail when working out a fiberglass production version of *Intermezzo II*. Having been used to the security of aluminum construction, we wanted to maintain as much of this as possible in switching to fiberglass. While a majority of the hull and deck structure was to be built to standard American Bureau of Shipping scantlings, we felt that she had to be more protected from reefs and collisions than is the normal production yacht.

To accomplish this we took several approaches. In the turn of the bilges, between the watertight bulkheads, ⅜-inch to ½-inch of fiberglass was added, solely for abrasion resistance. The bow was eliptically reinforced, from the stemhead fitting down to several feet aft of the waterline, with an additional 1½ inches of fiberglass. The keel, which really takes the punishment on a reef, is a steel weldment. The ¼-inch sides and ½-inch bottom make it highly unlikely that any collision or grounding would penetrate its plating.

The cost for all of this hull reinforcement and the higher rig safety factors worked out to less than 8 percent of the selling price. The fully loaded weight of the boat went up by 3.5 per-cent—an insignificant penalty to pay when everything is taken into account.

Another aspect to consider with any vessel is how she will behave in a severe knockdown or rollover. Every piece of gear

In most strandings the bottom of the keel and the topsides about the waterline take a majority of the punishment. The flat of the bilges is usually protected. If the keel and turn of the bilge is built with a severe grounding in mind your vessel will survive much longer without se-rious damage should she become stranded.

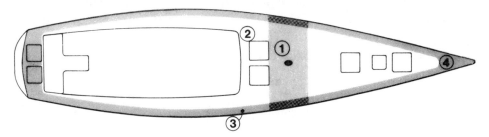

In this drawing of the production fiberglass version of *Intermezzo II* you can see how the highly stressed or risk-prone areas are heavily reinforced. These same principles apply to any type of yacht design.

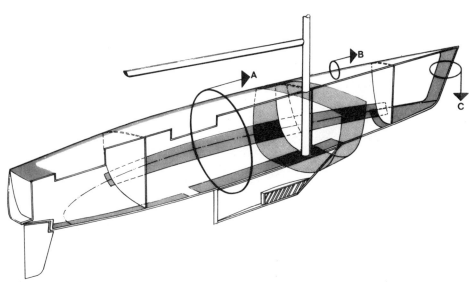

The area around the mast (1) needs extra reinforcement to take the chainplate and mast compression loads. A vessel strongly built in this area will be easier to keep dry inside. All hatch corners and combing corners (2) should have heavy reinforcements to prevent them from working and cracking under stress. The deck edge (3) and foredeck (4), especially where the windlass is secured, need beefing up, too.

must be secured so it stays put with the boat in an inverted position. This means batteries, stoves, floorboards, and everything stored under all the bunks and settees.

How do you assess a boat's ability to cope with these prob-

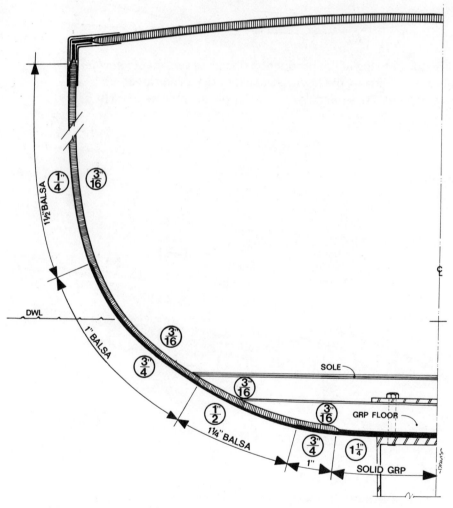

This cross section of a Deerfoot 2-62 shows how an American Bureau of Shipping laminate schedule in the topsides is beefed up for mistakes in the turn of the bilges and around the keel. Note that the *outside* laminate runs between ¾ inch and 1 ¼-inches in the high-risk areas, yet this boat is considered a *light-displacement* cruiser.

lems if you don't have bluewater experience yourself? The first step is to find someone to work with who has spent time at sea. A few professional yacht skippers work also as consultants. Some modern surveyors have had substantial sea time. These people can be invaluable *before* you purchase any boat. If you are building new, find a consultant, work up the added specifications you want, and then discuss your requirements with various manufacturers. Most will be glad to accommodate your desires, and in the end, will probably one day offer an "offshore" boat with the heavier scantlings you have requested.

Remember that in buying a used boat you must be sure she has the structure and inherent factors of safety to meet your requirements. Trying to beef up an existing boat is at best only partially effective and is enormously expensive.

Any new or used yacht should be purchased subject to survey and sea trials. If the boat is new and you have to put down money up front, specify that it be held in an escrow account subject to completion of sea trials.

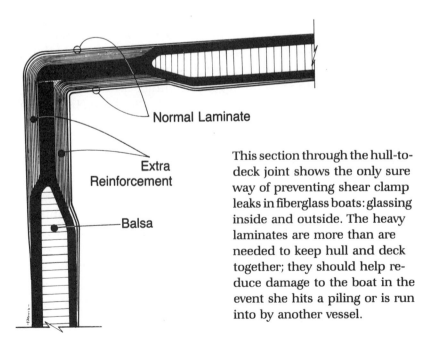

Normal Laminate

Extra Reinforcement

Balsa

This section through the hull-to-deck joint shows the only sure way of preventing shear clamp leaks in fiberglass boats: glassing inside and outside. The heavy laminates are more than are needed to keep hull and deck together; they should help reduce damage to the boat in the event she hits a piling or is run into by another vessel.

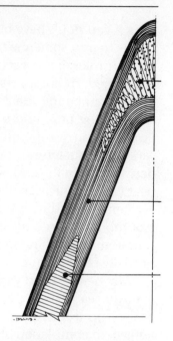

The bow areas must be reinforced to take the loads of a
collision with docks, floating
debris, or other vessels. On the
Deerfoot2-62 we have used a
combination of unidirectional
rovings and woven fabrics to
make a strong but light bow.
This laminate reaches a
maximum thickness of over
2½ inches.

Trials should be more than just an afternoon sail. All
machinery, electrical, plumbing, and sailhandling systems must
be used extensively. The engine should be run at different power
settings, right up to full throttle, for several hours to check for
vibration, noise, alignment, and hose and electrical connections.
The same goes for generators, pumps, air conditioning, and refrigeration. Running machinery for 5 minutes and then shutting
it off generates a false sense of security. All sails should be set in a
strong breeze to try out reefing and furling systems.

Look closely at the wiring, plumbing, and machinery. If it is
cleanly done, neatly organized, and well labeled, the builder or
previous owner has exercised care and forethought. Those traits
will probably be evident elsewhere. Have a good look at structural hard spots: chainplate attachment, maststep, keel timbers,
and keel bolts. What about the rudder stock and quadrant?
Many new boats are deficient in all these areas. Be wary of any
yacht whose primary structural members are hidden. Be sure
there is good access to both the structure and the machinery.

When we build a new boat for a client, the sea trial section of
our specifications runs to 10 or more pages and includes

instructions for carrying out various tests and maneuvers. You must be thorough. Most experienced sailors demand complete sea trials.

Be careful of "deals." We live in a competitive world in which you usually get what you pay for.

And don't write off small builders. Many operate with low overhead, have much pride in their products, and can build a good-quality yacht at a competitive price. They may substitute material and labor for the higher overheads of some of the bigger manufacturers.

The more boats, new and used, you look at carefully, the better you will be able to appreciate a vessel built to high standards when you see her. A thorough, unrushed review of the market pays big rewards in the end. You may still end up being one of the percentage sailors, but if conditions deteriorate, there will be a stout vessel under your feet to bring you through.

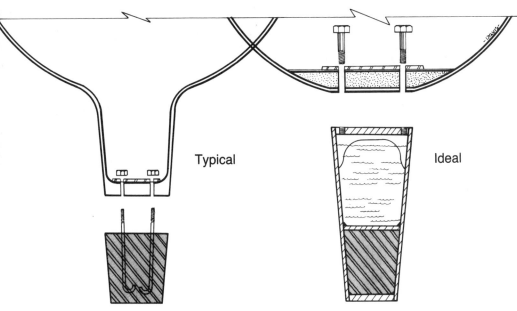

Typical   Ideal

Ideally a cruiser should be able to remove his keel without too much difficulty if it is necessary to do so in order to save his boat. With a steel plate cast or fabricated into the top of the keel, the keel bolts can be run from the hull down into the keel. With this approach the bolts can be backed off a few turns and the keel is free—and so is the hull.

Stanley Dashew photo

EPILOGUE

Throughout this book the emphasis has been on the need to think ahead, stay alert, and never let your guard down when dealing with the elements.

Some might say that this overly cautious approach to the sea would take away from the glamour and joy of cruising. Others may feel that many potential voyagers would choose to stay in port rather than risk the perils of cruising that we portray. But conservative seamanship properly exercised leads to rewards of its own, above and beyond a safe passage.

Cruising offers one of the few opportunities in our modern existence to take on a challenge at the elemental level, where the outcome is easily defined and the results are within our hands to control...if we do our part sucessfully.

Some of the grimmer photographs and stories we have used are intended as forceful reminders of the risks of a lapse. But don't let these detract from the joy of voyaging. The actual incidence of disaster in our fraternity is small. The risk level is just high enough to keep us on our toes, adding a little spice to the cruising life as a result.

With the sea the challenge exists on two levels. The first is intellectual. Defining risks, analyzing options, and making decisions is a continuing process.

Then there is the physical execution of the intellectual process. Whether you have just sailed your way into a tricky anchorage, dropped your hook neatly, and settled back to the admiring glances of new neighbors or are battling through a severe gale, in the end knowing that you have done the job well, completely on your own, brings a satisfaction almost unobtainable at other levels of our society.

We would be remiss in closing if we failed to mention the wonderful growth that sailing has brought to our family. Spending years together in a small yacht has created relationships much closer than would have been the case otherwise. Linda, Elyse, Sarah, and I have had a chance to explore feelings and interpersonal experiences denied our shorebound cousins caught up in the hustle of everyday life. The girls have learned to fend for themselves on many levels. Their return to the shore-side world brought with it the ability to earn straight A's in school, as well as to participate fully in the social aspect of school life. We feel the sea and its immediate environment has contributed greatly to their success as young adults in a conventional setting.

For Linda and me our return to the land has been a bit more sanguine. True, it was time for a change. But the horizon still beckons, and when Sarah and Elyse graduate we'll take that as our signal to head offshore once again.

Daysailing, cruising for a weekend, or taking off around the world offers many rewards: the pleasure of being away from the crowds, the solitude of a night watch with only an occasional porpoise breaking the surface to keep you company. New people and places beckon. There is no recreational activity to match this wonderful sport of ours. Maintaining a conservative approach to your seamanship will increase the pleasure you derive from it.

ACKNOWLEDGMENTS

Most of the reading public and many writers (ourselves included) have a number of mistaken ideas about the book publishing business. A writer toils over a manuscript, perhaps for years, and then expects, presto, for the book to appear in print.

Twenty, twenty-five, and even thirty dollars for a book? Those publishers must be making a killing! And why are my royalty checks always so slow in coming?

And so it goes. Well, having finally been involved in a book project from beginning to end; from writing through editing, typesetting, paste-up, and printing to marketing, we now have a better appreciation for what a publisher and those individuals who make up the publishing world go through.

The marine publishing business is a specialized field. In spite of the growing numbers of sailors and ever-more crowded anchorages, few marine books are actually sold. A bestseller in this field will run to 5,000 copies in the bookstores. As a result, the rewards are small for all concerned. Most publishers of marine books are motivated by a love of sailing rather than profit. This is doubly true for those individuals associated with putting a marine book together. For the writers, artists, and editors, the chief remuneration is the pleasure of work done well and the joy of passing on knowledge to others.

We were having just this discussion some weeks ago with the owner of a marine store in Marina del Rey, California. He was amazed at the small numbers of books actually sold and the efforts (and costs) involved in putting 'ogether a major book. He found the description of what goes into putting a book together fascinating: the same reaction we had when we started to learn the mechanics of the publishing business.

Driving home that evening, we felt that while it might be a bit unusual, perhaps our readers would be interested in a little background on how a book such as this one comes to be.

We began to outline our ideas for this book at the same time we were proofreading the typeset manuscript for our *Circumnavigators' Handbook*. That was in late 1981. In the summer of 1982, we decided to sail back to California from Florida, but before doing so we spent the summer and early fall cruising the eastern seaboard of the United States. Every morning we would sit down and bang out a few more words. By the time we had retraced our route to Florida and were ready to leave for Panama, the manuscript, we thought, was in pretty good shape. A lovely trip south through the Bahamas and a transit of the canal soon had us in one of our favorite cruising spots, Mexico. Here, we first started to pick up rumors of a disaster at Cabo San Lucas. As we have mentioned already, what we found changed our concept about what this work should be. Into the "future" file went most of the manuscript to be replaced, in time, by what you have now read. The basic, revised work, was completed in the fall of 1983, after two years of pretty steady work.

At this point the manuscript was badly in need of an editor. Catherine Baker, the first outside member of our *team* came aboard to help us out. Catherine's background is typical of most of the professionals in this business. It is suffused with the love for sailing...why else fool around with books such as this one?

Catherine learned to sail on her grandfather's 30-foot sloop and then switched to the family's Ensign at the age of 13. She taught sailing at the Harraseeket Yacht Club in South Freeport, Maine, and worked in the chandlery of the family boatyard. She has sailed, raced, won the State of Maine Adams Cup in 1971, and chartered a variety of boats since.

Catherine spent her school years at Smith, Stanford, and the University of Michigan, taking up editing while at Michigan. She has worked in a variety of editing jobs before settling down as copy and production editor at *Sail* magazine. Having lived in various parts of the U.S., Catherine now makes her home in Portsmouth, New Hampshire.

An editor has the delicate task of trying to make sense of a writer's efforts without changing the meaning or flavor; or damaging egos. The editor must also take a look at the organization of the work: all in all, a demanding set of tasks. After doing a first edit, with numerous suggestions for us to debate and/or implement, Catherine than took on the copyediting job. In this instance she reread the manuscript looking for typographical errors, checking punctuation and spelling, and ensuring that it all tied together. The manuscript then came back to us once again, and we input her final changes into our word processor.

In the midst of this process we felt we had organizational and direction problems. Unable to get comfortable with where we were heading, we gave our longtime friend and dean of yachting writers John Rousmaniere, a call. Would he be able to scan our work and give us his comments? Ever willing to help out struggling writers, John said he would be happy to.

Most of you will be familiar with John's work. He was an editor of *Yachting* magazine for five years, has written hundreds of articles about the sea, and is the author of eight books, including *Fastnet, Force Ten* (the definitive work on this infamous storm) and *The Annapolis Book of Seamanship* (the best all-around basic guide to sailboat handling ever written).

John started sailing as an infant. Along the years he has tried every aspect of the sport, from helping to win numerous dinghy championships, competing in five Bermuda races, a transatlantic race, numerous coastal races, making a couple of long-distance deliveries, and owning two of his own cruisers. He has even experienced the thrill of high-speed cats with us aboard *Beowulf V* and *Beowulf VI*.

John holds a master's degree from Columbia and taught history and writing at two colleges, although he considers writing and editing his profession. John lives with his two sons, Will and Dana, in Stamford, Connecticut.

After perusing our work John wrote a two-page letter in which he succinctly summed up our problems and gave his suggestions for corrections. His comments were, as usual, very perceptive and cut to the heart of our difficulties. John advised changing the order of chapters and combining some of the shorter pieces into longer chapters. We had some re-writing (again) to do, but that is part of the game.

Marine artwork is a specialized field requiring artistic talent, technical know-how, and seagoing experience. Steve Davis combines all three attributes into beautifully drawn, technical correct works of art that grace the pages of *Sail* magazine and form the basis for numerous boatbuilders' advertisements and brochures.

We first met Steve when he was commissioned by *Sail* magazine to paint some detailed perspectives of *Intermezzo II* for an article. He is a "country boy," having been raised in Idaho. He received a degree in architecture from the University of Idaho and got his first taste for boats working as a fish and game aide in southeastern Alaska. He decided then that when he grew up (he was 20) he would live and cruise on a boat!

After graduation he found himself in New Haven, Connecticut, working as a designer. It wasn't long before he was exploring Martha's Vineyard, Block Island, and the shores of Long Island Sound aboard his Cal 25.

Along the way Steve met Jan, a member of the local racing fraternity, and before long marriage plans had them heading off on a larger, heavy-displacement Atkins-designed doubler-ender. They spent a year heading south, enjoying the islands before tiring of warm beer, warm rum, and warm weather, and then sailing back to Annapolis, Maryland. The arrival of daughter Melissa made a move ashore necessary. The double-ender was sold, and they decided to try their hand at building a pilothouse motorsailor designed at their request by Jay Benford. Somehow they ended up in the Pacific Northwest, where at this writing, they are just about to launch their new boat.

Steve had the unenviable task of trying to interpret our sketches of what we felt the book should have in the way of illustrations. He then read the rough manuscript and came up with his own ideas (much better than ours).

As you can probably imagine, there are hundreds and hundreds of hours involved in his work. Every couple of weeks we would wait excitedly for the mailman to bring Steve's latest offerings. Then peruse these quickly getting back with our comments, usually pretty minor in content. After all the work was completed, Steve then had to size and photograph the art for "paste-ups" of the book.

Spencer Smith, the editor and director of the Dolphin Book Club, probably knows more about putting together succcessful marine books than anyone else in the business. Although the Dolphin Book Club is not a publisher, it is the world's largest seller of nautical titles. Spencer works closely with authors and publishers, frequently from the time when a book is only an idea in the author's mind.

As a sounding board for abstract ideas or down to earth details, Spencer has always been ready to pick up the phone and answer our questions. Before working with the book club, he was with David McKay, another publisher of marine titles.

Spencer and his wife own a 35-foot ketch, which they keep at City Island, New York, and regularly cruise the Long Island Sound and eastern Maine. They have cruised as far north as Halifax, Nova Scotia, south to Annapolis, been on three passages to Bermuda, and even done some cruising on the west coast of the United States. Spencer says if he had to pick one place to be sailing "it would be off Schoodic Point in Maine, with a southwester at my back."

The success of the Dolphin Book Club is an important facet of the marine publishing business. Its book orders, when combined with those of the publisher, keep the business economic and the cost of the book within reach, and its royalties help defray the high costs of putting these books together.

The other side of the publishing business deals with getting space on bookstore shelves, a difficult task as you will know if you spend much time in conventional bookstores. One of the best at doing so is the Hearst Marine Book Company, now a part of the William Morrow organization.

Paul Larson is the editor at Hearst and the man responsible for seeing that the nautical titles are both readable and saleable. Paul has been involved in marine publishing for more than a decade, having held previous positions at the U.S.

Naval Press in Annapolis, and Sail Books in Boston. Before entering the publishing business he worked as a diver for a marine archeology firm recovering Spanish galleons in the Caribbean. He is, as you would expect, an avid sailor, having participated in a bundle of offshore races and long cruises.

Paul has been the recipient of numerous of our calls with questions on content, organization, format, pricing , and titles, just to mention a few of the topics. He has the unenviable job of trying to "guestimate" how many books to print after analyzing his own reaction and those of his sales people to the rough manuscript.

When the editing chores are completed and the artwork and photos are ready to go, someone has to put all of this material into a coordinated, eye-pleasing package. Coordinating over 200 photos and drawings with 500-plus pages of manuscript has been the job of Anne McAuliffe, our parttime art director.

We first met Anne when she was art director for *Sail* magazine. She had started working with *Sail* as assistant designer working her way up to the top job. Anne began sailing in an ODay daysailor and during her years at *Sail* cruised and raced on a variety of boats ranging from 24 feet to 56 feet. Her own boat is a very practical sailboard.

When we learned that Anne was working for the 1984 Olympic committee's design department in Los Angeles, we called to see if she would have some spare time to help us out. Her job for us involved fitting the pieces together like a jigsaw puzzle, calculating how many pages there would be, which photos went where and how they should be cropped and sized, and finally specifying the type styles to be used. She also designed the book jacket and worked a somewhat unorthodox cover photo into a very eye-catching concept.

Anne's stint with the Olympics is now over, and she will be heading south to French Polynesia to join friends for an extended cruise of the South Pacific.

We have been fortunate in working with and learning from other professionals in the yachting press. Keith Taylor and Freeman Pittman at *Sail*; Peter Janssen and Shane Mitchell at *Motorboating and Sailing*; Marcia Wiley, Dick Rath, Dick

Somers, and Debbie Moiselle at *Yachting*; Joe Brown and Phil Thurman at *Sea and Pacific Skipper*-all have had an influence upon our work.

Special thanks are owed to Patience Wales for teaching us the use of the continuous present form and for helping pick our title. Karl Kirkman was kind enough to share some of his research material on capsizes. Rod Stephens took time from his ever-busy schedule to read and comment on the downwind section of the Tactics chapter.

Knowles Pittman gave us sound advice on the publishing end of the business, and Ralph Naranjo took time out from the tumult of getting ready to go to sea to help us with photos. Vicki Carkhuff, a fellow world traveler and now a yacht broker with the Fraser organization in Fort Lauderdale dug into her treasure chest of slides for a few choice shots. My dad contributed from his black and white collection. Lyn and Larry Pardee were also kind enough to lend us some of their photos.

Elyse Dashew at age thirteen helped with spelling and frequently put into the computer what her parents had changed in the manuscript form. Sarah Dashew at the impatient age of ten allowed numerous meals to be served late, because of editing or writing chores, with only minimum complaint.

There are, of course, many other members of the team that put a book like this together. There are production people at the book club, the printers, the typesetters, and layout craftsmen. All told, there are dozens of individuals and thousands of man-hours involved.

It's enough work to make you feel like going for a sail...